RAILROAD SIRENS

Railroad Sirens

by

Allan N. Campbell

VANTAGE PRESS

New York   Washington   Atlanta   Hollywood

FIRST EDITION

Published by Vantage Press, Inc.
516 West 34th Street, New York, New York 10001

Manufactured in the United States of America
Standard Book Number 533-03906-1

This is not an autobiography.

While the atmosphere is one in which the author lived and worked for several years, and most incidents actually happened, episodes have been combined and distorted for the purposes of this narrative.

All characters are composite people, made up out of various bits and pieces of real men and women, speaking the language used by these types in real life.

While the character Alton Burns may, in some cases, resemble the author, here again, he is, at times and in many situations, a composite of several real people encountered in the same kind of activities.

Although readers may think that they recognize national corporations and actual people, there is no intended similarity to any one corporation or any one person.

RAILROAD SIRENS

Chapter 1

The portly, ruddy faced man entered the president's office on the penthouse floor of the tallest building in Montreal's financial district. Before removing his blue homburg, he opened his heavy overcoat and unbuttoned the jacket of his dark blue suit. From the right hand vest pocket, he withdrew a large, gold Hamilton railroad watch. It was attached to a heavy gold chain that stretched across his belly. In the center, a large masonic emblem dangled.

It was exactly ten-twelve A.M. The commuter train had been on time. Henry Hopkins selected a key from a ring dangling at the side of his trouser waistband. He unlocked the plain-panelled door to his private toilet and cloak room. Hopkins had made it a rule that no one was allowed to disturb him for exactly one half hour after he entered his office in the morning. He wound up his morning ritual in his private toilet with a generous slug of Irish whiskey, which he kept there to ward off colds. When he emerged, he consulted his railroad watch, again. He had exactly eight minutes and ten seconds to settle himself in the high swivel chair behind the big custom-built desk on the far side of the room.

He switched spectacles, donning his reading glasses with the half lenses, over which he could peer belligerently when he did not fully understand what was going on.

From an old-fashioned, belted and buckled portfolio, he took out two worn, black leather notebooks and a copy of the *Montreal Gazette*. He laid out the two notebooks before him on the desk.

He read the front page of the paper, until his secretary came in with the morning mail.

"G'mornin', Maggie. Have y'got those guys ready for the director's meetin', or whatever it is that we're supposed to hold once a year? It's not that it matters a God-damn. We'll write the God-damn minutes same as we always do."

She nodded, about to speak, but he gave her no chance to reply.

"Well, send 'em in. Let's get it over with. It doesn't matter what they say. You write up the same minutes as last year, with this year's date."

"I'll bring them in *right away*, Mr. Hopkins. They are waiting outside."

She held the door open for three men, who entered quietly, in single file. The senior vice-president led. The junior vice-president followed him, with the young accountant behind.

As Hopkins greeted each loudly by his first name, the vice-presidents moved heavy chairs from along the wall of the office to the front of the big desk, facing Hopkins. The young accountant, timidly, placed some statements on the president's blotter.

"I thought that you might like to have my preliminary estimates for the current year. We worked late last night to have them ready for your meeting."

"I don't need 'em, Richard. Don't need a God-damn accountant to tell me how we're doin'. Got everthin' I need right here, goin' back thirty years." Hopkins patted the black notebooks on the desk before him. "Where's Muir? Decided not to come, I guess. OK, we don't need him. We don't owe the bank, so we don't need to give him information."

"Just pull up a chair, Richard, with George and Donald. I guess that makes us a quorum, eh, Richard? Let's get this annual meetin' shit over with. We never used to need one. Maggie and I will write the minutes, anyway, so you guys don't need to say nothin'."

Hopkins never expected a reply. The three men seated themselves, uncomfortably. Maggie hovered at his side, notebook in hand. With her black hair more becomingly styled, she could

have been attractive. Her dark skirt and sweater coat did nothing for her plump figure, wide hips, and matronly bosom.

The accountant was a tall, thin man, recently brought into the firm by Alton Burns, the assistant vice-president, engineering. Both had worked for the Canadian Government Railways. Burns had been successful in securing some new accounts, and, for the first time in the history of the firm, Hopkins had finally agreed to employing an accountant. Richard Jones was aware that his services were often little appreciated.

The senior vice-president, George Thurston, was a less aggressive replica of Hopkins. He wore the same type of clothes. In fact, both men bought their suits from the same tailor, Tony's Cut Rate Haberdashery, on St. Antoine Street. Thurston wore the same half-lens reading glasses. He maintained a constant expression of apology when in Hopkins' presence, but was known as a tyrant outside, in the general office. A thyroid condition, at his change of life, had led his physician to prescribe a new hormone, which had resulted in rapid enlargement of the breasts. This so distressed him that he had resorted to surgery, to reduce the appearance of femininity. He planned to retire at the end of the year.

The vice-president had been associated with the company even longer than Henry Hopkins. His age was difficult to calculate. He was tall, muscular, and bald. A physical-culture-and-health-food addict, Donald McDonald was an expert in one of the company's activities only, the manufacture and sale of the Edison nickel-iron-alaline storage battery for railway cars, locomotives, and materials handling equipment. A clue to his age could be gleaned from the fact that, as a youth, he had known and worked with the great Thomas Alva Edison himself. While he was an honest and conscientious employee, other of the firm's activities interested him little. A bachelor, he had some money, and now that the Edison battery was being replaced with cheaper lead-acid and cadmium batteries, he was contemplating retirement. McDonald was not about to "make waves."

All three men were Protestant, and, of course, Masons.

Henry Hopkins opened the meeting without formality.

"Richard, here, agrees that we got a quorum; not that it matters, when me and the wife hold all of the votin' shares. This annual meeting business is just a waste of God-damn time. Whadda we do first? Is it a director's meetin'? You wanna financial statement? Well, you're not gonna get it. That's my business. I got it all here in these here notebooks. As long as I approve it, that's all there is to that item of business. Maggie will write up the minutes. You can go over 'em, Richard, to make sure they satisfy your bloody tax friends. I'll sign 'em when they're ready."

Hopkins challenged them, peering over his glasses, then continued, "Well. Didn't last long, eh?" Hopkins forced his guffaw, which he used after a remark that he considered cutting. "Are you satisified, Richard?"

"I suppose so, Mr. Hopkins."

"While you're here, boys, I'll fill ya' in on a move that I gotta' make. Since you guys are both thinkin' of 'pullin' the pin,'* I gotta get somebody younger to do the goddamn work around here. Richard, here, is young, but he's only a glorified bookkeeper. We gotta have somebody who knows railroadin' and can entertain these buggers, to keep the orders comin' in. I was plannin' ahead, when I hired this young engineer, Alton Burns, a cuppla' years ago. He's still wet behind the ears. He has too many new ideas to suit me, but he works like hell. He's brought in some new things this year. While our old accounts are still our bread and butter, I've been a little worried, myself, about some of 'em."

Hopkins stopped talking at a light knock on the office door. A tall man entered, with a small, leather portfolio in his hand. He strode briskly across the room. Henry Hopkins greeted him loudly, as the others turned their heads in recognition.

"Waal, whaddya' know? The moneybags has turned up, at last. Our meetin's about over, Hector. No need for you to ask any question this year, anyway. We don't owe the bank nothin' "

"Good morning, Henry, gentlemen, sorry if I'm late."

* "Pull the pin" is an old railroad expression originating when railway cars, in a train, were connected by simple steel links, held together by a steel pin. When the pin was pulled out of the links between two cars, one car was separated from the train.

Hector Muir shook hands with Hopkins, who was still sitting. The others stood to greet him. He was the image of the modern Canadian banker. His dark grey suit, with vest, was well tailored for him, in the English style. His brown hair and moustache were neatly trimmed. Grey eyes, behind gold-rimmed glasses, were friendly but alert. The hands holding the portfolio were perfectly manicured. Richard Jones moved quickly to place another chair beside his for Muir, in front of the desk. Muir thanked him but did not take it right away.

"I didn't come with any questions, Henry. Acme seems to be doing a little better this year, judging from your balances with us. I accepted your invitation as a director of a very old and valued client firm of the Empire Bank. I want to be of any help I can."

"You're God-damn right we're doin' OK. We don't need no help. We just finished all there is to this God-damn annual meetin' crap, before you got here. We don't keep bankers' hours, y'know. Haw, haw, haw." Hopkins followed up his remark with his nervous guffaw.

Hector Muir knew Henry Hopkins. He smiled good-naturedly and switched his portfolio, as though he was prepared to leave. Henry Hopkins motioned to the empty chair.

"Sit down for a minute, Hector. I was just explainin' to the boys here; we was talkin' about your friend, Alton Burns. I think that I'll have to make him a vice-president, and Richard, here, says that we will need another director, to be legal. I knew that you would like that."

Muir nodded, approvingly, as Richard Jones spoke up quietly.

"Since you have decided to make Mr. Burns a director, perhaps you would like to invite him in now for the appointment of officers and approval of the budget that I have prepared for the coming year."

"Oh, to hell with that. Maggie will write up the appointment of officers as I give it to her; and I have my own budget, right here in my head. I don't need no directors to approve it. God knows where Burns is. He should be out workin' on those bloody purchasing agents, gettin' in orders for next year. He can't make sales sittin' around on his ass in some useless God-damn meetin'.

"I'll tell 'im what he's supposed to do, when I see 'im." Hopkins glared over his half-lenses, from face to face, ready to challenge any question of his judgment.

"OK, boys. God-damn meetin's over. Les' get back to gettin' some God-damn work done. I gotta get busy on my bonus list, so Richard can make out the checks for me to hand out the day before Christmas. Burns has brought in so God-damn many clerks and service people that it will take me all afternoon this year. Good job I got my own records here. Gettin' the bonus checks out the day before Christmas saves buyin' 'em Christmas presents."

Hopkins was showing his irritation, as he always did when he was faced with the necessity of paying out money.

The four men trooped out. Only Maggie remained behind, for instructions.

"Maggie, bring in Alton Burns' expense accounts, again. I've looked 'em over three times now and I can't figger out how he can spend so God-damn much money, but, on the other hand, he is bringin' in orders. What in hell does he do to get 'em, Maggie? Does he get the bastards drunk every night? Do you suppose that he is keepin' 'em supplied with women, too? Does he, Maggie?"

Maggie did not know whether to look interested or disgusted at the thought.

Chapter 2

She was tall, but it was not her height that made her stand out in the crush of commuter passengers, on the station platform, in the lightly falling snow. Her skin was the color of olive oil, tight and flawless. Smokey shading under the eyes and under her high cheekbones highlighted her beauty. It was her eyes that commanded attention. They were very large, widely spaced, slanting upward in a gentle curve at her temples. The jet black lashes were long. The large dark irises were partly covered, except when she gazed directly. Her mouth was wide, and her lips red and full. Her large teeth gleamed whitely when she smiled. Her hair was blue-black, shoulder length, and curled up at the ends. It appeared to be very thick, as she tossed it from time to time to shake off the snowflakes. The overall effect was striking and, somehow, savage.

Alton Burns studied her from a distance. He planned to ride in the same railway car, if he could force his way through the crowd of office workers. With no real conscious intent, he en-joyed watching the changing moods reflected in her expressively beautiful face. He had never spoken to her, although they had exchanged glances many times. This morning he was wondering why she was boarding the train at Mount Royal station, instead of at Portal Heights, the last stop before the train entered the mountain tunnel to downtown Montreal.

Feeling his gaze, she looked over the crowd at him. Their eyes met. Her look was casual but steady. It was, he hoped, a look of recognition, the slightest nod, the hint of a smile—or did he imagine it?

"Why is she getting on at Mount Royal this morning? Must have shacked up with someone in the town last night. Say, Alton, is your wife out of town?"

It was Larry Connors, at Burns' elbow, following his gaze. In spite of the fact that Connors was his most aggressive competitor in the railway supply business, they considered themselves the best of friends. They had known one another for years, first when Burns was a railway official and Connors vice-president of a principal supplier; and, for the past two years, as competitors for railway contracts.

They were quite different in appearance. Burns was tall, inclined to somewhat unconservative clothes. He was dark, wore a thin moustache, while Connors was clean shaven, blond, and a little shorter. He dressed conservatively and impeccably, in the latest fashion. His habitual expression was deadpan, so disarming, and his naive questions were so seemingly harmless, that he was a master at drawing out the most confidential information from friends, as well as clients.

"You mean 'the cat girl'! I've never even spoken to her."

"You are interested enough. I have noticed that when you've gotten on the train, here in the last few mornings, you've moved up through the coaches to ride in the one she boards at Portal Heights, you lecherous bastard."

Burns tried to look hurt.

"Now you know that I don't chase broads, Larry. I just find her looks intriguing. Any harm in that?" He changed the subject, without taking his attention from the girl. "I suppose you have a secretary picked out to lay this afternoon, after the office parties."

"Naw, I don't believe in shitting on my own doorstep. I'll meet you in the 'Pick' though, after the parties. We can see who else's secretary got drunk and didn't get laid, because her boss had to go home to decorate the Christmas tree."

"OK, but I'll be late. I have at least four office parties that I should attend, in addition to our own, which I must wedge in. Perhaps the 'cat girl' will be at the 'Pick,' and we can both meet her."

"What's with this 'cat girl' bit? She may be striking and dif-

ferent, but they will be a dime a dozen this afternoon, and most may be a lot safer, or are you thinking that you could use her?"

"I don't know. I just think a girl as different and as well stacked has got to be useful. I hate to see such an intriguing bit wasted on a shoe clerk or a pimp."

"Look who's talking. Since you became my competitor, you've used every angle. I know you, Burns. I suppose I'll see you at lunch at the Engineers' Club as usual, entertaining one of my prospects."

"No, Larry. You will see me at the Dominion Hotel, forcing you to introduce your guest from Pittsburgh."

"Well, God-damnit, which secretary in my office are you getting to now? In a pig's ass, I'll introduce you, you bastard."

At Montreal Central Station they parted. Instead of going directly across Lagauchetierre Street to Beaver Hall Hill, and to his office on St. James Street, Burns, with time to spare, followed the commuter crowd up Cathcart Street. He kept her in view, until she turned east on Ste. Catherine Street. He wondered what she would do in that section of the city at this time of the morning. Was she a clerk in a cheap working man's store that opened early? Did she work in a garment loft on Bluery Street? Could she be going to rehearsal at the Gaity Burlesk this early? He thought of the cat houses on DeBullion Street. It couldn't be—too early for that, he imagined.

Was it his imagination, or did she turn to flash an enigmatic smile before she was swallowed up in the hurrying throng?

Chapter 3

It was 8:10 on the wall clock as Burns let himself into the general office on the penthouse floor of the Empire Bank Building. Across the office, in an enclosure with glass partitions, a woman was working, knowing that he was first to arrive on days when he was not traveling. She had the usual bandages on her shapeless legs. As she polished the desk, her pendulous, brassiereless breasts swirled around in her loose work dress. Burns wondered how she must have looked years ago, when, as she reminded him on many mornings, she had been a young, attractive, French-Canadian girl, popular with the habitant boys in her native town of Vercherres. After working alone all night, she loved to chatter on, partly in French, partly in English, to the first arrival about those happier days.

"Bowjour, Mesue Alton," she called, with a toothless grin.

"Pas mal et vous?" he answered, and proceeded in the opposite direction, toward the president's office. He would put in a few quiet moments there until she finished cleaning his own office. He pretended that he did not hear her reply. He did not want to listen this morning to the stories about how her man chased after the young French girls in the factory where he worked, how he spent his money in the brasserie while she worked all night. According to her, he still had more than he could handle at home even after twelve *enfants.* In fact, according to her, there was always some to spare.

The president's office was as large in area as the whole outer

office, including Burns' enclosure. The rug, while thick and soft underfoot, was a somber brown. At the far side, in front of the high window overlooking Montreal harbor, there was the massive dark, oak-panelled desk. Behind it, to one side, in the corner, there was the matching roll-top, kept locked. A large, high, swivel chair of black leather, worn brown at the edges, could be swung around to either desk. Burns recalled entering that office on the day that he was hired. The big desk appeared to be about a mile from the door. It was late afternoon, in spring. The sun shining through the window almost blinded him, as he approached the president silhouetted in that high chair. Before he had taken more than a few steps, Henry Hopkins' voice had boomed out.

"You didn't turn Catholic, when you married that mick girl, did you?"

Sitting in the president's chair, Burns recalled an incident of a year before. A visitor arrived unannounced. He ignored the receptionist, brushed through the outer office and burst into the president's office, before Hopkins had finished his 12:10 "gargle."

"I'm a fighting Irish Catholic from Boston. I belong to the Knights of Columbus. They tell me that this is a bigoted organization of bloody Masons, but I also hear that you have the best God-damn railway sales connections in this God-forsaken country. We'd like you to handle our account—what do you say to that?"

After resuscitation of some kind by his secretary who bustled in at the intrusion, Hopkins was able to shake hands with Bill Fitzgerald. An agency agreement was signed, which had proven very profitable to both companies over the past year. It was the first of the new product lines that Burns had solicited and acquired for the firm.

Burns looked again at the old trophies, which adorned all four walls. There was a huge moose head, with sixteen-point antlers, on the wall opposite the desk. The mounted head of a caribou looked a little shabby. There was the head of a grizzly bear, red-lined mouth open in anger, and a mounted Canadian goose. Below the mountings were photographs. The groups included presidents and vice-presidents of railways who had, presumably,

participated in the hunt and/or the drinking bout and "French circus" which had followed it. These trophies had not been acquired by Henry Hopkins. He was not the type to indulge in such an expensive sport. They were hung there by the second president of the company, forty or more years before. Henry Hopkins was not in the habit of changing anything, so they hung there still.

The company was founded around 1910 as the W.W. Butts Company. Billie Butts was an American foundryman. Early in the century, his foundries in Hammond, Indiana, were taken over by a much larger, nation-wide, industrial complex, Eagle Steel, Incorporated. The purchase, at the time, was mainly for the purpose of acquiring control of the effective and successful, high-pressure sales organization, which Billie Butts had put together in the flamboyant days of the building of U. S. railroads in the west. Butts had needed a good team to enable him to compete with a former associate and supersalesman of the era, Diamond Jim Brady, who operated a large railway supply company in Pennsylvania. Butts learned from the spectacular successes of Diamond Jim, George M. Pullman, and Thomas A. Edison, the innovators in the railway products field in that romantic period. He observed, at first hand, how effectively Diamond Jim utilized Lillian Russell and other sirens of the chrous lines, adorned with diamonds (which Diamond Jim stripped off them at the end of the evening) to influence sales to railway executives. He observed the sales impact when Diamond Jim checked into a hotel suite or signed a tab, diamonds gleaming from every finger of his fat hands. Diamond Jim's taste for food was as gluttonous as his taste for money and women. Legend has it that he ate so much and grew so obese that, while still in his prime, he was taken to Johns Hopkins Hospital in New York City, where his stomach was replaced with that of a sheep.

Diamond Jim's rides through Central Park with Lillian Russell on a gold-plated bicycle-built-for-two, Edison's trip down Broadway in the first electric-powered, battery-operated automobile, and Pullman's spectacular crash ride in his Pullman palace railway car were sales accomplishments that inspired Billie Butts.

Wealthy already from his sale to Eagle Steel, Butts came to Canada, to organize a large railway car and foundry company, which he planned, would do for the expanding Canadian railroads of the day what Brady, Pullman, and Edison had done for U. S. railroads.

He brought with him connections with all of the successful suppliers to railroads in the U. S., including Eagle Steel. The new car and foundry company manufactured railway cars, locomotives, and all of the component parts. However, Butts was not the only shareholder in the new venture and, in order to syphon off a greater part of the profits for himself alone, he founded the W. W. Butts Company. Thus, the car and foundry company made a profit on the manufacture of rolling stock, but Billie Butts, personally, made a bigger profit on selling to the railroads. Butts' fellow shareholders held still for this only a couple of years, then demanded that he divest himself of this profitable sideline, hoping that the car and foundry company could handle both manufacturing and sales. It was too late. The supply company retained the exclusive agreements which Butts had arranged.

At first, as a front, and a little later, as a principal, Butts brought in Sir Giles Humbolt, a director of numerous Canadian corporations, including the Empire Bank. He was a society figure on two continents, a big game hunter, a bon vivant, and a spectacular salesman. The name of the company was changed to Acme Railway Power and Engineering Company, Limited. Because of Sir Giles' connection with the Empire Bank, the company was housed on the top floor of the bank's first head office building on St. Antoine Street, in old Montreal. When, as the bank expanded across Canada and overseas, a new skyscraper head office building was erected, on St. James Street, the Wall Street of Montreal, Acme went along to occupy the penthouse floor.

While Sir Giles was not a mechanical man and concerned himself little with detail, he had the aid of Billie Butts in getting together a good team, selected from the ranks of ambitious railway officers. Miles Smale, executive secretary to Lord Strathroy, chairman of the Atlantic and Pacific Railway, was hired as a reward for confidential information supplied, some of which could

be used as a form of blackmail. He also brought with him the goodwill of many railroad officials that he had been able to help as a confidant of Lord Strathroy. George Thurston had been designer and chief mechanical officer of the government railways. With the help of all of the government railways' resources and staff, he had originated many patents, which could be assigned, from time to time, to railway officials. The "royalties" were used to influence the purchase of Acme's products. To assist Smale and Thurston, Henry Hopkins, a master mechanic, was hired from the Grand Trunk Railway. Donald McDonald, an electrical engineer, was brought in from the A. &. P. Railway, to supervise the manufacture of the new Edison battery used to power railway cars, electric locomotives, and baggage trucks.

With this staff, together with a secretary and an order clerk, the company prospered. Following Sir Giles' death, in a hunting accident in Scotland, however, the loss of his imagination and flare for sales promotion became noticeable. Volume of sales continued more or less constant, but new, more sophisticated products were appearing in the hands of competitors. New companies were being formed. Reporting for tax purposes required more clerical staff. Costs were rising, and profits were shrinking, year by year. Miles Smale survived Humbolt for only a couple of years before cirrhosis took its toll. Thurston, for health reasons, waived succession. Henry Hopkins, with the help of his first wife's inheritance, purchased the majority of the shares, and became the third president.

As time passed and more of the original group dropped out, Henry Hopkins, a plodder, never a salesman, found it more and more difficult to prevent control from passing into the hands of outsiders. Finally, at the urging of his bankers, which he strongly resented, he was forced to look around for a younger man to keep the firm alive. Hopkins had followed the career of Alton Burns. The Burns family and the Hopkins family came from the same part of rural Ontario. Burns had to struggle hard, after the great depression, to complete high school. Upon graduation, he worked for a short period in a bank in a country town, still working mornings and evenings on his father's farm, to save up enough money

to attend teacher's college. This profession was selected simply because it could be acquired with the least time and expense. Hopkins did not hold against Burns his knowledge that Burns' teaching career had come to an end before it had started when he was caught in bed with a coed in the teachers' college dormitory. Hopkins realized that, in farm areas, everybody did it, except schoolteachers, who did not get caught at it.

Hopkins heard when Burns was hired by the government railways for the tough task of instructor of apprentice tradesmen in the railroad shops. It was work that Burns detested, acceptable only as a means of obtaining a mechanical engineering degree at night school over a period of several years. Burns' progress was noted, as he clawed his way up the ladder in the face of government seniority system and politics. Reaching the position of chief mechanical engineer in the railroad head office, Burns had been ruthless in condemning products with defects or weaknesses in design. It was reported that he worked fourteen hours a day, seven days a week, gathering information from every source available: in the old files, from subordinates, associates, suppliers, by any means. This made him respected by his superiors and feared by the manufacturers selling supplies and equipment to the railroads.

When Burns received the offer from Hopkins over a lunch at the Mount Stephen Club, he was not sure that it was not just an effort to delay his plans to halt purchase on some of Acme's most outdated lines. While Burns had done well on the government railways, as a farm boy with no political connections he was finding it more difficult as he ascended the ladder. Just at the time of Hopkins' offer, the next step to vice-presidency of the railroad was about to become available. Jules Lamont, a much older man with good political connections, wanted it badly. It was Lamont's last chance for promotion and the large salary which would enhance his pension. Based on experience in head office administration and education, Burns was the logical selection. However, great political pressure would be brought to bear on behalf of Lamont. He was, in addition, a French-Canadian. Burns was not. If Burns was appointed, every French-Canadian member of par-

liament would be up in arms. On the other hand, railroad top management was aware that Burns had completely researched the railroad archives and, no doubt, had much very politically damaging information. He had made no secret of it. In his position, his research could not be stopped. A decision might be delayed indefinitely on this account.

Burns studied Jules Lamont, as he had studied the old government files. He cultivated Lamont, when he was a junior, and no threat to Lamont's career. They spent nights together, carousing in Lamont's fashion, pub-crawling in the redlight district of Montreal, Lamont talking and bragging when he drank too much, Burns listening. Now, returning from lunch with Hopkins, Burns dropped into Lamont's office. The door was open. Lamont's secretary was out for coffee. Burns slouched in a chair, put his hat on the desk, and took out cigarettes.

"Busy, Jules?"

"Naw! Justa buncha fucking crap."

Lamont looked up from some papers, leaned back, sleepily rubbing his eyes under his thick glasses. He lit the cigarette that Burns offered.

"Lousy God-damn lunch in the 'greasy spoon' down at the corner with a cheap peddler from Chicago. Whatcha got on yer mind, Alton?"

"Just tired, frustrated, and bored, Jules. Think I'm going stale. I feel like going out on the town tonight. I need to get drunk."

The slits of eyes in Lamont's puffy face opened with interest. He loved a binge, so long as he could enjoy it out of sight, with someone that he trusted. It was particularly important that his wife did not know.

"I'm due, too, God-damnit. I could phone my wife and tell her that my brother from New Brunswick is passing through and that I gotta see him on family business. She hates his guts. She don't want him in the house. Mind if I go along?"

"OK! That's why I dropped in. How about six o'clock, at the Blue Heron. We'll start out from there. We'll meet in the back room."

"The back room, eh! you must have something lined up, you

bastard. Make mine a plump little blonde with lots of tits, about yea big—and no brains—no questions."

"That's the second time today that someone has called me a bastard. Must be a coincidence."

"No coincidence," Lamont called after him, as Burns left the office.

The back room of the Blue Heron Club, on Beaver Hall Hill, was small and simply furnished with only the essentials for its purpose—a table, four chairs, and a hide-a-bed. The lighting was bright, compared to the lounge in front, dimly lit by artificial blue candles in the booths along the walls. In addition to the door from the club, there was one to the kitchen, another to the alley at the back, and a fourth door leading to stairs and the small rooms upstairs reserved for lounge guests who wanted more entertainment than the "B" girls could provide at the bar or in the booths. All of the doors were covered by curtains of red velvet that had seen better days.

Lamont arrived a few minutes after Burns. On the table there was a bottle of Johnny Walker Black Label, glasses, soda, and a bowl of ice. As Lamont hung up his coat, a heavily made-up blonde opened the door from the club and looked through the slightly parted curtains. Only Burns noticed her and motioned her off. He did not want Lamont's attention distracted until he had a chance to talk seriously with him. When Burns needed her, he would press a button under the table.

They seated themselves and Lamont removed his high galoshes. Burns poured a drink and handed the bottle to Lamont, who poured a heavy shot on one small ice cube. While they carried on small talk about events on the government railway, they had several drinks, Lamont taking half a waterglassful each time, while Burns tried to give the appearance of keeping up. From time to time, Lamont glanced at the door to the lounge, anticipating the female company that he felt had been promised.

Finally, Burns casually mentioned the offer that he had received at lunch from Henry Hopkins. "By the way . . ."

Lamont was intensely interested.

"You are going to take it, of course."

"I don't know. That is what I wanted to talk to you about. You are the only man I know that I can trust in a situation like this. I wanted your advice before making the big decision. You have been around headquarters much longer than I have been. You know the politics. You know Acme. You know Henry Hopkins. Only you can help me to decide."

Burns scowled as an attractive brunette entered from the kitchen and passed by the table on her way to the lounge. Lamont's attention was diverted when she offered a plump buttock for his feel. She looked at Burns, inquiringly.

"We have girl friends arriving soon," he said, waving her away.

She pouted and left.

"The girls will be here any moment, Jules. Let's have another drink." Burns continued, "You know, Jules, I like the railroad. I think that I have a pretty good chance of being a vice-president and that would pay more than Acme is offering."

Burns was watching Lamont's face, as he poured a drink. Lamont said nothing, but his expression had soured.

"On the other hand, if I could be sure that Acme's products would always be favored, whenever the railroad was buying, I'd be able to call my own shots at Acme, in a year or so. I would be able to pick up in bonuses whatever I lose in salary—and in a supply company, as long as the business is coming in at a good profit, no one questions the expense account. The booze and women that go with a job like that are worth considering. We could really have some parties, couldn't we, Jules?"

Lamont's fat face lit up.

"Yah! Listen good, Alton," Lamont was lisping a litttle now, "With me as veep, you would never have to worry about getting an order from the government railroad. Whatever you had to sell, we would buy at your price. You see, Alton, you didn't know this, but I want that job so bad that I can taste it. I know that they will pick you if you stay. But you are young. You will have other chances, like this. This is my last chance and I'm thinking of that pension based on my last five years' salary. If you go to

Acme, Alton, with your knowledge and, pardon me, your God-damn ruthlessness, you'll be top man there in a year. Then we'll both have the world by the snatch. You will be able to sell us pigshit at platinum prices.

"You really mean that, Jules? This is very important."

"God-damn right, I mean it."

"Is this 'on the square' between us, Jules, as Mason to Mason?"

"On the square, for sure."

"And you won't forget in the morning when you are sober?"

"I won't forget. Whadya want me to do, sign a God-damn notarized statement or something? You've got my word."

"Thanks, Jules. You've made up my mind. Shake on it. I'm putting this on tape, word for word, and if you ever cross me after you get that job, so help me, I'll publish it."

"I have always known that you were a ruthless son of a bitch. You might even publish some of the dirt you've been digging for years about me out of those old files. I know you, Alton. But you won't have to. I'll keep my word. I'll have to, God-damnit. Let's drink on it, you son of a bitch."

"Come on in, Claudette, beezness toute finis. Es go, bebee."

Concluding his reverie, Burns glanced at a picture of Diamond Jim hanging under the moose head. The thought occurred to him that the "cat girl" on that gold-plated bicycle would have caused much more stir in Central Park than Lillian Russell.

It was after nine o'clock; the staff were at their desks, when Burns emerged from the president's office to go to his own. They answered his good morning without a hint of surprise. Most had been hired by Burns, from his old railroad staff. They knew how their bread was buttered.

Chapter 4

Al Lette followed Burns into his office.

"I woke up about one o'clock and saw your light on from my bedroom window on St. Antoine. I intended to come down to help you, but since it was the night before the Christmas party, I figured that you might not stay late. I woke up again at two-thirty and your light was still on. Sorry about that, Mr. Burns."

Lette was the ever-faithful office manager. He was a very short man, always in a hurry, always anxious to help. He had a short, grey crewcut, and he peered attentively through thick-lensed spectacles. As file clerk for Burns in the railroad offices, Al felt that he was letting his boss down if he was not always on hand. He liked to brag a little, after coming to Acme, about how he and the boss had been an inseparable team at least twelve hours a day, when they worked for the railroad. He knew almost as much as Burns about the dirt in those old files. He had led Burns to the most important, having worked at headquarters all his life, since office boy at the age of fifteen.

"I really don't want you to come in when I am in the office late at night, Al." And to mollify the little man, Burns added, "I can't afford to have you off with another heart attack, you know. Anyway, I just read over my mail when I came in from a trip."

"I took the tapes out of your Edison dictaphone and gave them to your secretary this morning," Lette's voice was reproaching. "I could have dug out the files for you."

At the sound of the buzzer, Burns pressed the button on his phone.

"Mr. Morton calling from New Jersey, Mr. Burns."

"Hello, Joe. How the hell are you?"

"Just wanted to be first to wish you Merry Christmas, or whatever the frogs call it up there. Is the old man in, Alton?"

"Merry Christmas to you, too, old buddy. No, the boss does not come in on the day of the office party. He figures it's too risky, with his high blood pressure, when these young French girls down a few and begin looking for a raise of one kind or another."

"I know what you mean, Alton. When you start popping cherries tonight, save the little sultry one with the short skirts and the big boobs for me on my next trip. But that's not the real reason I called. I want to ask the old man for your help."

"You know that we will do anything we can, Joe. Just name it."

"When you represented the Canadian railroads on the car construction committee of the American Railroad Association, you played around with Lou Waldorf. He was the chairman, I think."

"Yes, we worked some and played a little in every railroad town in the U.S. and Canada. Why, Joe?"

"I've been told that you did the work on new car designs and Lou, as chairman, took the credit, right? Well, he made a trip to Chicago last week, about some new locomotives that they are buying from U.S. Motors. He expects a lot of attention when a big order is awarded, right? Well, it seems that those stuffed shirts over there left him at the plant to find his own way back to his hotel in the Loop. He had to pay his own cab fare, buy his own dinner, pay his own hotel bill, get his own woman, and they did not even send down a bottle of booze. You know how that would sit with his type. They didn't care. They had the order. Now, he hates U.S. Motors, and all of its divisions, including Precision Bearings. I'm caught in the middle."

"How, Joe?"

"Well, you see, three of the largest railroads in the South are buying, together, a pool of ten thousand coal-hopper cars. They have standardized the design to save start-up costs. They are going to buy them in a block, all exactly the same. Lou, the son

of a motherfucker, as vice-president of the biggest railroad, heads the design and purchasing committee. Scuttlebutt has it that he is so mad at U.S. Motors that he is specifying all Timken bearings—not a single Precision bearing is to be used. We are blackballed by the mother. He just wants to get back at our parent, U.S. Motors. You know where that would leave me, Alton. U.S. Motors would find a new general manager of Precision Bearings Division the same day the order went out."

"But you can explain, can't you, Joe? You can't be blamed for what the fat cats in the locomotive division do."

"No excuse, pal. You know the U. S. M. motto, 'the difficult, you do today, the impossible, tomorrow.' It's this order or my head. I'm under the gun anyway for some stupid things I did this year, like leaving my briefcase, with those confidential contracts, in that whorehouse in Montreal. That didn't help. There were some other things. They are all in that black book on the group VP's desk in Detroit."

"Can't you pull in traffic, Joe? U. S. Motors is still the biggest railroad shipper in the U. S. Timken cannot compete in that department."

"No way, just now, Alton. In Canada, OK, but you may not have heard of the restraint of trade prosecutions in this country. We are already working under consent decree. Anyway, how could you promise your traffic to one railroad when all of their competitors are in on the same purchase?"

"Where is Lou Waldorf, Joe?"

"In Mobile, I'm sure. You know that he would not get off his fat ass between Christmas and New Year's except to piss out the Old Crow!

"I'll phone you back before noon, Joe. Meanwhile, you can do something for me. Ever hear of a guy named Matt Marra?"

"Sure, VP of M. A. Marra, Pittsburgh, his grandfather's company. Good guy, but not a swinger. What do you want to know about him? You know U. S. Motors has a better F. B. I. than Washington. They can tell you how many warts he has on his pecker, if you really must know."

"I am meeting him at lunch today, I hope, and I'd like to

know why he is in Montreal on the day before Christmas. Must be important."

"I'll get right on it, Alton."

Burns' finger had been on his buzzer before he hung up. His secretary was seating herself across the desk, notebook and three sharp pencils, in hand. She placed two pencils on the desk and poised herself for dictation. She was dark, petite, half French, half Scottish, favoring in appearance her French side. Her thick, dark hair was neatly coifed, her nails freshly manicured. Her eyes were large and dark with long lashes and highly arched eyebrows. She was, obviously, dressed for the Christmas party, in a black, form-fitting, princess-style dress, exposing near perfect proportions, and a little less than half of two firm breasts.

Vivian Stuart had been hired six months before, as an experienced secretary in both French and English. She claimed ten years' experience, which did not tie in with the age of twenty-four shown on her application. Like the "cat girl," there was something about her eyes, her confidence, at the first interview which interested Burns, and he had not regretted hiring her. What she lacked in experience, she made up in willingness to work at any hour, without complaint. She showed determination to help in any way, and there was always a suggestion of impropriety that appealed to both Burns and his customers. Perhaps most helpful was her keen perception of what was required of her in any office situation. She already knew which of Burns' clients and associates were must important and which were simply tolerated with courtesy. She was developing into an indispensable girl Friday, which is what she seemed to want most to be.

Her predecessor had come from the railroad with Burns. A war widow, with only two nights in bed she claimed, she had been the clinging-vine type of a secretary, who used her limited intelligence to concentrate more on her own desires than on understanding what her boss required of her during the day. When the position of secretary to the president became vacant, with the retirement of Hopkins' sixty-year-old secretary, more because Hopkins married a second time rather than age or requirements of the job, Burns convinced Maggie to take that position. The

slightly higher pay and the prestige that went with being secretary to the president appealed to her. Burns wanted a pipeline to the president's office, anyway. Maggie would be around at the office party, when she could corner him, out of sight, with a wet kiss. She would ruefully refer to Vivian Stuart's high-handedness, a little presumptuous, she would suggest, as a new employee, and only the secretary to the assistant vice-president.

"You look good enough to eat, today, Miss Stuart."

"If you haven't tried it, don't knock it, Mr Burns." She had a way of looking very innocent about such remarks.

"The government railroad party—is it looked after?"

"I sent a case of Dewar's and three bottles of Bacardi. Oh yes, and a small bottle of Spanish fly that Mr. Lette suggested!"

"You're kidding, of course."

"Yes, I was sure that those railroad stenos wouldn't need it."

"You kept it for yourself?"

"Are you suggesting that I need it? I sent a couple of cases of Coke, a couple of boxes of sodas, and a wheel of cheese to the A & P. There are six bottles of champagne wrapped and packed in your old briefcase. Anything else, Mr. Burns?"

"Yes, have the switchboard get me Mr. Lou Waldorf of the Gulf and Ohio Railroad, in Mobile, Alabama, person-to-person, and bring in the airline guide."

While waiting for the call to go through, they selected a flight.

"Hello, Lou. Merry Christmas."

"Thanks. Nice to hear from you, Alton. Now that you are a peddler with a big expense account, you got telephonitis or something? You did not call me long distance just to wish me a Merry Christmas."

"You're right, Lou. I need a favor. Very simple. Nothing to do with the Gulf and Ohio, and it won't cost you anything. This is strictly personal, but very important to me. It is so important that I have reservations on Delta, arriving Mobile at four P.M. next Tuesday, if you will be there. I have to talk to you, personally."

"I'll be here; but why in hell would you want to come to this lousy town between Christmas and New Year's Day? Want to

change your luck or something? I've got some addresses in Detroit. It's closer."

"Simpler still, Lou, but you always have some good ideas. See you Tuesday."

"OK, OK, a Gulf car will meet you. Bring a couple of bottles of that Chivas Regal, that good Scotch you fed me up there—and some of that English mustard—Keene's, is it?—and some of that Black Gold or Black Diamond cheese—that cheddar stuff. Wait a minute. Listen! My driver will hand you an envelope with the key to my little hideaway here in the Mobile Arms, in case I am not here when you arrive."

"Mr. Buckley calling from Chicago, Mr. Burns." It was the switchboard on the intercom.

"Hello, Buck. It's the president of Eagle Steel, I hope. I've been waiting for word all morning. I thought that you would be back from St. Louis, if everything worked out right."

"Yes, Old Charlie resigned before the meeting and I was elected, without a dissension. Not a murmur from Seaway Steel or Commonwealth. It all worked out beautifully. The old man will be better off, considering his health, and I have *carte blanche.*"

"Congratulations, Buck."

"Remember, Alton, our Christmas party was postponed because of the change. Now, we've decided to hold it next Friday, when I can greet all the staff for ths first time as president. It will include Wrigley Building staff only, and you are the only outsider invited. You'll have to make it."

"Wouldn't miss it, Buck, but it's going to be tight for me. I may have to fly in from the South. Please have Marcy Smith reserve a suite for me at the old Medina Shriners Club, across the street. We can get together there before your bash. Meanwhile, Buck, you can do me a favor. Get a rundown on what big interest M. A. Marra of Pittsburgh might have in Canada just now."

"That should be no problem. We have an interlocking director, you know. They've done some turnkey contracts on new mills for us, but they are mainly into operating mines and building mining railroads in foreign countries.

Vivian Stuart was standing, silently waiting for him to cradle the phone.

"What time will I put on the notice for the office party.?"

"Three thirty."

"Pretty late. The boys will have sneaked a few by then."

"Some may have started already. It doesn't matter today. I can't see how I can get back here earlier to start it off officially. By the way, I want to have lunch with Jules Lamont."

The scent of Fleurs de Rochielle remained when she left.

"Mr. Morton is on line one."

"Hello, Joe. I talked to Lou. I'm meeting him Tuesday in Mobile. Have a happy Christmas, and don't worry. We'll get something."

"Did you change his mind? Do you want me there?"

"The answer is no to both questions, Joe. It is important that I see him alone. I don't want him to know that we have been in touch at all. I know Lou. He's suspicious and stubborn, but he will change his mind himself, unless he feels that someone is trying to change it for him. I'll guarantee half of the order, at least, so don't worry, Joe."

"I don't know what you have on the fat old fart. Whatever it is, I hope it works. At any rate, Alton, all of your expenses are on U. S. Motors, and the sky is the limit. We gotta get part of this order, profit regardless. Do you realize what the commission would be if we had to pay an agent on an eight million dollar order. I'm going to see that you get some of it, one way or another, even if it comes out of my bonus."

"You may be able to repay me some other way, Joe, and sooner than you think. Anyway, you think positively. Happy Christmas."

"My life is in your hands, old Buddy. Call me from Mobile, collect."

"Merry Christmas, Joe."

Again Vivian Stuart was trying to get his attention without interupting his call. "Mr. Lamont is on line two. He is furious. He had left his office to meet his wife. I had Florence Ridout and most of his staff out heading him off. He's on the office lobby

phone, now. He just chewed me out good, so look out."

Lamont was on the line.

"Sorry, Jules. I need your help, today, now, in fact."

"So what's different? What the hell is new about that? I'm going to need the help of God Almighty for keeping my wife waiting. What in hell can be so God-damned important on the day before Christmas."

"Lunch, Jules. I want you to have lunch with me."

"You better get your God-damn ears examined, Burns. You don't hear so good. I told you, I'm meeting my wife for lunch. She is at Morgan's Department Store waiting for me right now. I'm late already, thanks to you, God-damnit. Now good-bye!!"

"Just a moment, Jules. Vivian Stuart will meet your wife. She'll buy her something, with my compliments, and your apology, then take her to lunch at Morgan's."

"Alton, for Christ's sake! You know that we should not be seen together. I can't even have a drink with you in public. We've got a good thing going. Why bugger it up?"

"It would look rather queer if we were not seen together once a year. After all, you are our biggest customer. You won't need a drink at lunch. We will meet at room 15 first and have a couple of real good smashes there. I'm sorry to insist, Jules, but I must meet you at lunch, today, for a reason that I will explain later. What department at Morgan's is you wife working over today, so I can tell Miss Stuart where to find her."

"Baby clothes."

"Congratulations!"

"Shit!"

Putting on his coat as he hurried out, he glanced toward Vivian Stuart's desk and noted that she was already heading toward the elevators.

"Your habit of listening in on my phone calls saves time, Miss S. I don't have to repeat instructions. You're going to Morgan's, I presume."

"Shit!" she replied, in a very dignified way.

Chapter 5

Snowflakes floated down between the tall buildings on St. James Street, melting on the tops of the cars parked tightly along the curbs. The wet surfaces glistened with tints reflecting the neon signs and lighted show windows, even though it was noon time. On the sidewalks, the snow changed to slush. Office workers rushed from the buildings and returned to them with parcels purchased in the lunch hour. Last minute shoppers were hurrying along, weaving in and out through the throngs before the storefronts. There was a long queue blocking the sidewalk in front of the Quebec Liquor Commission outlet across the street. It inched forward, as people who rarely bought all year joined the regulars to buy their Christmas supplies of *alcool*, screetch, and wine. There were Salvation Army Santa Clauses tending their pots on each side of the street, forcing the crowd to press around them to get by. Gaily wrapped parcels added another bit of color to a dull winter day in the north.

A black limousine stood before the steps of the Empire Bank Building, its motor running to keep its interior warm. White vapor showed at its twin exhausts. The uniformed driver of the unmarked Murray Hill Cadillac stood on the sidewalk, his hand on the rear door handle ready to open it for his patron. Pete Bouchard was a small, wiry man of about sixty. White hair showed at the sides below his uniform cap, but his thin, straight moustache was jet black, obviously pencilled. Burns did not own an automobile. He told his clients that he could not afford one, which was partly true. However, there were other reasons for hir-

ing a chauffeured limousine almost every day that he was in Montreal. With a driver, the car could be parked in "No Parking" zones, right outside an office, a restaurant, or a hotel. It gave him a chance to relax between calls, or give all of his attention to a guest. When entertaining with a lot of drinking, it was safer. At parties, the car stood by to send someone home when they had too much, or to deliver a girl, or take one home, when she had served her purpose.

Pete Bouchard worked regularly for Burns and considered himself a sort of bodyguard, as well as attendant. He knew the police and the doormen. He spoke their language, and gathered information from them that he thought useful to Burns. Another good reason for employing Murray Hill was that the company was billed monthly, including overgenerous tips for Pete. The cost did not appear on Burns' personal expense account and was not subject to tax inspectors' scrutiny.

Seating Burns in the rear with a salute of his black gloved hand, Pete ran around the car and slid into the driver's seat.

"Dominion Hotel, Pete, the back door, off Stanley. You can wait there. I'll be out about two. You can have a rest. You must be tired today. We were late last night. It may be later, tonight."

"I'll be OK, Mr. Burns, but tell me if you're going to be out as late as last year, so I can tell my woman. She was about crazy last year when I phoned her from Ahunsic at six in the morning and told her that I had lost you."

Burns laughed. "It's the end of the week, Pete. Did you get a chance to go over the driver's log in the garage?"

The Cadillac threaded its way through heavy traffic, slowed by the snow. They were turning up Windsor Street now and Pete consulted some notes when the traffic light caught them. He gave Burns a rundown of drivers' assignments for limousine service to businessmen which, from experience, he thought might interest Burns. By the time he had finished and elaborated as much as he could on where from, where to, who was with who, they had been parked for several minutes behind the hotel. Burns thanked Pete, got out quickly, and hurried up the back stairs to room 15, second floor, front.

It was a combined office and convertible sitting room in the old opulent style. Panelling was highly polished walnut with birdseye maple inlays. Gold-brocade drapes, ceiling to floor and the length of the wall, were held back from the one two-story window with tasselled silk ropes. The ceiling was twenty-two feet above the Persian rug laid on polished parquetry floor. The window looked out across Windsor Street to Dominion Square. A massive door to a large, Italian white marble bathroom stood ajar. In it was a huge, black marble circular sunken tub. Eight white tubes with shower heads were hung from the three walls around the tub and positioned to give a needle spray to all parts of the anatomy, adjustable for short or tall, thin or fat.

The room was entered through a small foyer formed between the outside corridor door and an inner door six feet beyond. This arrangement was designed to prevent any eavesdropping from the corridor on activities in the room when both doors were closed. Also, it allowed a visitor to be received without being able to see anything that might be going on inside. It made room service possible without interrupting the activities or exposing the participants. The remainder of the corridor wall was composed of narrow panels of polished oak joined by piano hinges. When folded back, they exposed a complete wet bar, with refrigerator and icemaker.

The inner wall, to the left, was most interesting. It held the framing of a door which had been sealed up, the locks removed. At the building of the hotel, this door had connected room 15 with the royal suite of six rooms, which extended across the front of the building, at the second floor. Behind the blocked up door was the main reception room. This was located above the main entrance. The roof of the portico provided a large balcony above the Windsor Street sidewalk. Flagpoles extended out at a forty-five degree angle over Windsor Street. In the center of the waist-high, limestone railing, there was a mast for the royal standard. King Edward the Seventh of England and its dominions beyond the seas had been the first tenant, as guest, of course, of the government of the new Dominion of Canada. The hotel had been rushed to completion to accommodate him on his first offi-

cial visit. His statue stood in the square directly in front. It was on this balcony that British monarchs, right up to the present Queen Elizabeth the Second, on their official visits, accepted the homage of their Canadian subjects from the street and square below.

Room 15, out of respect for the mortal tastes of King Edward, was provided as a discreet retreat, in which his majesty could entertain guests less than generally accepted in royal circles. However, its use was so frequent and so obvious to the Montreal social climbers missing out on his attentions, while he preferred its privacy, the External Affairs Department ordered the door closed up. King Edward did not return. Sir Giles Humbolt, an ardent admirer of the royalty that had bestowed his title, and sympathizing with the lovers of the good life, wished to preserve the facility for the purpose intended. The hotel was glad to receive compensation in the form of ten years' rent in advance with the stipulation that, should the hotel be required to place it at the disposal of Edward, it would revert to that during a royal visit. It was required only once afterward, and that was on the occasion of the one and only visit of King Edward's grandson, the Prince of Wales, later, briefly, King Edward the Eighth. Sir Giles was happy to oblige, and may have participated in its use on that occasion. Acme sent a check at the beginning of each year after the tenth. While Henry Hopkins may never have visited the room, and, while he was most penurious concerning other matters of business expense, his reluctance to change anything after he became chief executive made him reluctant to abandon this facility. He simply turned all of the keys over to Burns, as head of sales, and, thereafter, ignored its existence.

Burns unlocked both entrance doors, then unlocked the folding doors to the bar. He was hanging his coat when he heard his guest loudly stamping the snow from his feet in the entry. Lamont lumbered into the room. He threw his tweed overcoat into a chair. Keeping on his small-brimmed, blue-black homburg, he dropped into another chair.

Lamont's face was full, with fat jowls, a small mouth, and tiny, blue, watery eyes, squeezed apart by very large, blue-

veined nose. Beneath the hat, which appeared too small for him, he had a dome-shaped head, with thin, reddish, uncombed hair. He wore a grey-plaid suit, wrinkled from his attempts to button three buttons over a grossly protruding belly. He was in a very bad mood, and his greeting was in the form of an ill-natured growl.

"Make mine a double after all the God-damn trouble that you are causing me with Lena. Who's the fucking customer, you or me, Burns? What's so God-damn urgent?"

He accepted a strong drink from Burns, and, after examining its color to assess its strength, downed it in two closely spaced gulps, between which he glared at Burns.

"Well, what is so God-damned important?"

Burns waited out the storm. He took Lamont's glass and poured him a second drink, before sipping his own.

"Larry Connors has a special guest staying in this hotel. They have reservations for lunch at the club downstairs. His name is. . ."

"So what, you bastard. Why should that prevent me from meeting my wife? I don't give a good God-damn who Connors has lunch with."

"Neither do I, ordinarily, Jules. Today, I just want to know what Mr. Matthew Marra—that's the guy's name—finds so important here to make him travel up from Pittsburgh on the day before Christmas, and why Larry wants to be so secretive about it? It's got to be important."

"Important to who? So what? I don't know who the motherfucker is and I don't give a fiddler's fart. Who is he?"

"He is a vice-president of M.A. Marra and Company, Pittsburgh. They are consultants for mining companies and turnkey contractors for mining railroads, often taking a participating interest. They have had, now have, in fact, contracts in Brazil, Venezuela, Argentina, and have been involved with all of the iron ore developments on the Mesabi Iron Range. They have never been involved in Canada, until now, so there must be something big in the wind."

"So, he doesn't need me, and I sure as hell don't need him,

so gimme another drink and I'll go meet Lena. Fuck him, whoever he is!"

"No, you don't need him, Jules, but I need you today. We
are going downstairs to a once-a-year lunch together. Larry would
not and could not ignore you. He could ignore me, alone. As one
of his biggest customers, you can insist on speaking to him and
his guest. He does not even have to introduce me to the guy, but
he can't turn me away if I am with you. So as soon as you finish
your drink, we'll go down to lunch. Take your coat with you, and
check it at the door, as though you came in with me from the
street, OK?"

"OK! Jesus Christ, lemme finish this."

Inside ths club, Burns scanned the faces at the long bar,
then he looked around the tables. "There they are!" He nodded
toward a small table for two in a corner. Larry Connors had anticipated his arrival.

The guest was a well dressed man of about thirty-five. He
had a clean-shaven, chubby, boyish face, with the rosy cheeks of
an all-American boy. Marra was smiling at some comment from
Larry.

"Let's go over, Jules. You first."

"Why in hell should I? What's in it for me? Just a God-damn
pain in the ass. Jesus Christ!"

Jules kept mumbling as they worked their way across the
room. The head waiter tried to distract them, but Burns continued to guide Lamont forward. As they reached his table, Connors frowned, but looked up. He ignored Burns, but was forced
to greet Lamont. He rather reluctantly extended his hand.

"Merry Christmas, Jules. Intended to get down to see you
today but got tied up. We'd invite you to join us but this table is
too small."

When Lamont did not move away at once, with Burns standing at his side holding his arm, Connors' guest looked inquiringly,
so Connors was forced into an introduction.

"Oh, Matt Marra, this is Jules Lamont, vice-president of the
government railways, and this other guy. . . ," Connor's voice

trailed off, as Marra, standing, took an immediate interest in Lamont.

"This is really fortunate for me, Mr. Lamont." He shook hands with Burns, too, but all of his attention was on Jules. "You were on my list of people to see first, on my sort of crash trip up here today. This can save me a call. Can we have a larger table, Larry? I'd like these fellows to join us for lunch. It will be my pleasure. This is fortunate, indeed."

Larry reluctantly signaled to the waiter, and while Marra guided Lamont to another table, Larry and Alton followed, Larry muttering, "You son of a bitch!"

As soon as they were seated, Lamont reached for the menu. The waiter took his and Burns' orders, at once, as Connors and Marra had already ordered. Lamont was still in a petulant mood, although somewhat mollified by the attention from Marra.

"I don't have time for a drink, so I'll just have a beef sandwich. I missed lunching with my wife, so I gotta get back to my office early."

"That's too bad. Be glad to get you one if you had the time." Mara placed his hand on Lamont's arm. "You've heard of Char Lake, Mr. Lamont?"

"Yah," Lamont was more interested in the waiter placing the extra settings. "Supposed to be iron ore there. It's not on our lines, thank God. We have enough trouble with Steep Rock."

So that was it, thought Burns. Char Lake had been described in the *Northern Miner* sheet as the largest iron ore body—or was it the highest grade of ore body?—he was not sure which—but it was said to be important.

"You are right, Mr. Lamont. High grade ore and plenty of it, and while we are not on your lines, now, we are going to be your biggest shipper from Churchill to Lake Head."

"Yah! When? In the twenty-first century, I hope. I am retiring in five years. It won't concern me, hopefully." Lamont was already attacking his sandwich.

"Much sooner than that. You will be moving our trains before the end of Great Lakes navigation next year, Mr. Lamont. Day before yesterday there was a board meeting of our partners,

who, by the way, include Seaway Steel, Detroit Steel, and Eagle Steel, along with a large national insurance company. It was decided to go ahead full speed, assuming that we can depend upon the cooperation of the government railways. We know, of course, that as a common carrier, you could not refuse our traffic, but we would like it to be by a friendly, mutually profitable arrangement. You see, Mr. Lamont, Mesabi and Steep Rock ores are running out faster than anticipated, before a recent survey of reserves was completed, so much faster, in fact, that we were shocked to a state of near panic. Newfie and Shefferville quality is going down. More beneficiating is too costly to consider, when we have the highest grade ore in the world at Char Lake. All that stands between us and this abundant supply is transportation to Lake Head. As I said, we must move ore by next summer. M. A. Marra, my company, is a minority partner, but we will be the operators.

"We already have a start, as you probably know. We have completed surveying and clearing of right-of-way to connect with your lines at Churchill. We have been moving ahead slowly and quietly for over a year. Now, all stops are out. We must finish the seven hundred miles of track next spring. We must place orders at once for about ten thousand ore cars, depending upon the capacity selected, you understand. We will need about one hundred and fifty locomotives; U.S. Motors have confirmed that this presents no problem. We will be buying cranes, shovels, and other equipment, wherever we can lay hands on them. This is only for the first phase, of course. We worked out a critical path schedule yesterday. I am here today to begin the process of locating and selecting Canadian design and management personnel."

Marra talked fast. Burns was intent on every word. Connors was toying with his food. Lamont scowled as he ate.

"Hundred-and-twenty-five-ton cars, too, I suppose. Knock our roadbed all to hell, like Steep Rock does. Hope your tracks sink into the God-damn permafrost till after I retire."

Lamont wolfed the last of his sandwich.

"C'm on, Burns, drop me off at my office. Glad to meecha, Marra. Seeya, Connors. Let's go, Burns."

Burns left one half of his sandwich, and standing, fished a business card from his pocket. Marra studied it as they shook hands. He looked at Burns as though seeing him for the first time.

"Sure! Sure, Mr. Burns. Now, I know you. I thought that you looked familiar when Larry introduced us, but I didn't get the name." He looked down at Connors who was chewing, trying to look unconcerned.

Marra continued,"You were on the car construction committee of the Railroad Association with Lou Waldorf. I heard you give a talk on car design to the Allied Railway Suppliers' convention in Chicago a couple of years ago. Damn good! It made sense, even if it did not please everybody. I had made a note to look you up here. One of the first things on my list. Do you have all designs and details of ore cars prepared for the Railway Association's approval? I understand that many of the designs that your committee developed were never published, for reasons of politics, or whatever. We want to consider all of them."

"Yes, I have complete files, Mr. Marra. I have the general arrangement drawings and detail drawings. As you say, there were good designs which were never published. I have the stress analyses, test date, including squeeze tests, in some cases, which prove it. Whenever you have the time, we can go over them and select what you need. You may be interested to know that I am meeting Lou Waldorf in Mobile next Tuesday, on the matter of designs of equipment for his pool."

"You will have just what I need, Mr. Burns. We'll make it worth your while to sort out some appropriate designs for us, and, while you are at it, please give some thought to competent Canadian engineers who may be available. You will know them, since you employed many when you were with the government railways. Perhaps your friend, Mr. Lamont, will help."

Marra winked, as they shook hands again.

"Please call me Alton. I can come to Pittsburgh on short notice."

"I'll be here on January second and I will set up an appointment with you on arrival, Alton. Mine's Matt."

Lamont was impatient at the door.

"Thanks for the lunch, Matt. See you January the second. So long, Larry."

In the limousine Burns turned to Lamont.

"What are you in such a bloody hurry for? That was important."

"Not to me. My wife. . . "

"For Christ's sake, quit worrying. Vivian Stuart is looking after her, and you can't do much in the office this afternoon. Most of your staff will be half lit already in the shop method's office. I suppose that you are in a hurry to join them?"

"Naw, I'm not going to no God-damn office party. I'm not foolin' around with those amateurs. No dry fucking for me. A whore knows what she's supposed to do, and gets right to it. No silly conversation, no jokes. When it's up, I want it there and then. No God-damn fooling around, and no gossip after."

Lamont continued to grumble all the way down the hill to the government railways' offices, where he left the car with a surly grunt.

Chapter 6

The limousine made a "U" turn and parked across the street. Burns got out, instructing Pete to wait, but to come inside for him if he was not back in three quarters of an hour.

The office on the fifth floor was abuzz. The party was in full swing. He was greeted by his first name from all sides. The men shook his hand. The women puckered for kisses. The popularity which had developed, with his modest success, never ceased to surprise him. It was hard to believe that it was not genuine as it may have been, in a fashion. He had to remind himself that when he was only a junior engineer, much more attractive, no doubt, certainly less shop worn, he would have been delighted by these attentions. His popularity had developed as they recognized that he had some influence on salaries and privileges. Now no doubt, they had heard about some gifts given for those they considered to be high officials. They knew that it was he who supplied the booze for the binge last year, and again this year. In return, he was the only railroad supplier invited to their parties. While this was gratifying, Burns had another motive for wishing to be with them. Many of these people were in a position to give him confidential information, the full value to him unrecognized. Any failure by Lamont to honor their pact would be reported to Burns. Lamont knew it. It kept him honest.

A very attractive raven-haired beauty, with flashing black eyes, full red lips, and the figure of a nineteen-year-old Greek goddess, hurried to him. To derisive remarks and groans from some male revelers, she grasped Burns by the wrist and tugged

him around behind some filing cabinets. Out of sight, more or less, she put both hands to the back of his neck, to pull his lips down to her sensuous mouth. She wriggled her pelvis against him. Not feeling the right spot, she reached down with one hand to unbutton his top coat, which he had not had time to lay aside. Still holding the kiss, he could feel her pubic mound through her thin dress, as she drove it against him. He gently took her arms from around him. Her body continued to press against his.

"Look, Des, you know that there has to be blood on the sheets on your first night with that Greek boy that your father has picked out for you. So please don't spin your wheels and mine."

She flounced away to corner some other man that she considered important at the moment. She was of no particular use to Burns. She was only a junior in a pool of stenos used by the draughtsmen. She would not understand a valuable bit of information if she saw it. She had no information that would help him to get an order, and no influence at this time, with anyone that mattered. With her beauty she was unlikely to be employed long enough to form a useful association. There was one in every office. *A waste of sex*, he thought.

Across the long, narrow room, past a group of younger people, Burns picked out the opposite type of woman. Florence Ridout was half sitting on a drawing board near the makeshift bar. She was alone. Florence had been an attractive woman in her day. She had the scrubbed, well-groomed, but prim, look of a businesswoman over fifty. Today, she looked on as someone who had seen it all before.

She came from New Brunswick Province. Fresh from high school, she had taken a position as typist in the offices of the Intercolonial Railway in Moncton. Popular with the men in the office, she had taken her fun where she found it. Soon, she was selected as a head office assistant secretary. Her boss, much older, was attracted. At that age, he appeared dashing to her. He knew important people and attended important affairs. He was married, but when he found that he had too much work for the male secretary who accompanied him on business trips in his private railway car, and began taking her along, propinquity had its effect.

The Intercolonial Railway was consolidated with other government rail systems and he moved to the head offices of the government railways in Montreal. She requested transfer, and took an inferior position in another department to be near him. She loved him faithfully, until his sudden death. When Alton Burns was promoted, Florence was secretary to the chief mechanical engineer, and she stayed on. She took an interest in the younger man, possibly because, in some way, he reminded her of her dead lover when that man was younger. They became fast friends, with a bond of sincere respect for each other.

In a macabre gesture, during his short, terminal illness, Florence's lover had willed that a bouquet of roses should be sent to her on every Christmas Eve. Burns was thinking of this as he worked his way to her side, shaking hands and kissing a cheek here and there.

"You never change, Alton. Causing an uproar in the office on the day before Christmas by ordering my boss out to lunch, when he did not want to go. Everybody in the office suffers when he's upset. Why don't you let me arrange things like that for you?"

"I *wish* I could, Florence, but you know that he won't even take a call from me, except on his private line. You know why, of course. I always knew that I could trust you implicitly, Florence, but he does not trust anyone."

"He is such a stupid tyrant, Alton. I don't talk to anyone but you this way, you understand. I try to be the loyal secretary. I know that I could not get the money anywhere else, at my age. My job, with my seniority, is secure, until I retire on a good pension in a couple of years, but sometimes I wonder if it's worth it. I have a little money, you know, and there is an annuity provided by such a different type of man."

There was a misty look in her eyes.

"Working for you was different, Alton. You were more like Humphrey. You were going somewhere. You let me know what was going on and it was fun trying to help. You showed some apreciation. Lamont just grunts."

"I'll drop by tonight for our little toast."

"If you did not come, Alton, I don't know what I'd do. I know that you are very busy, but you have not missed dropping

in for six years, and it is so much appreciated, believe me."

"See you a little after six, Florence. Oh, I forgot. Here's a little yule card!

"A Ruby Foo's credit card? Do you realize that this could cost you a hundred dollars if I took my sister and her kids?"

"Your friendship is worth a million, Florence." He leaned and whispered in her ear, "Thanks again for those carbon copies of Lamont's letters. He often looks at me as though he thinks that I am reading his mind. He's afraid to double-cross me."

Tonight, in front of her old lover's roses, he would embrace her, while she closed her eyes and thought of that other railroad man of long ago.

A man was making his way toward them. He was of medium height, medium weight, medium complexion, dressed conservatively in a blue suit, light blue shirt, and black tie. He held an unlit pipe in his left hand, as he shyly shook hands with some of the older staff members who recognized him.

"It is facetious to say Merry Christmas, Hal, but I'm glad that you got away for Christmas."

"I just had to get away from Edmonton, Alton. At least I have a few old friends, like yourself and some relatives, here."

Hal Ives was four years younger than Burns. He, too, had left a farm home to seek work in the railway shops. He started as an apprentice. Burns was his instructor in kinetics, as part of the railway training program. Neither of them was at home in the big city. Both were hard working and ambitious. It was natural that they should spend much time together, including the occasional shop crafts social, at which both stood out most of dances. Burns, the more outgoing, meeting people more easily, became involved in some social life in the city. Ives shyly accepted, gratefully, when Burns invited him along.

It followed that Hal became interested in the same career. When he decided upon mechanical engineering, he was able to take advantage of a railway scholarship, when Burns recommended him for it. With help from his family, which Burns did not have, Ives was able to take his degree at Toronto University, attending seven months, and returning to work for the railway for the rest of the year. In this way, he was able to graduate only a

year after Burns had completed his credits at night school. But in that time, Burns had established himself in the regional engineering offices of the railway in Toronto. Burns was able to have Ives posted to his department. For several years, they worked as a team, originating several new concepts in the design of railroad equipment. Hal Ives was the originator and designer. Burns acted as mentor, and sold the ideas to management. It was a satisfying association for both of them. Burns married first, then Ives married a school teacher, a former classmate, introduced to him by Burns. Shortly after, their careers branched apart. Burns was promoted to several successive executive positions at the railway headquarters in Montreal. Ives was transferred to regional offices in Edmonton, Alberta. There, his wife, Enid, died of cancer of the breast. Operations and treatment held hope, until just before her death, suddenly, two weeks before Christmas. Ives phoned, heartbroken. Burns flew to Edmonton for the funeral. Burns considered Ives one of the most able railway equipment designers.

"This is a bitch of a day for me, Hal, and next week will be worse. We must have some time together, though. Look! I have to go to the Atlantic and Pacific party but, within an hour, I must be back for our own Acme office party. Why don't you join me there. I know that you don't feel like any frivolity, but it may help to take your mind from other things.

"I'd like to go along. I do need the diversion. Sure, I'll be there, at, say, four o'clock."

Burns nodded to Pete Bouchard, who had appeared at the door, cap in hand. He said hasty good-byes as he recrossed the room to leave. In the limousine, Pete produced a small paper carton of milk. Burns drank it, as they moved up McGill Street. At the entrance to the bank building, it was 3:30, perfect timing for the official start of the Acme office party.

Vivian Stuart had arranged for the desks in the general office to be set to one side, to provide a small dance floor. A bar had been set up. Some glasses seemed to have been used already, but the men standing around the bar were empty-handed, awaiting Burns' arrival. Most of the girls were missing. They were in the ladies lounge doing some last minute primping. Mistletoe had

been hung with red ribbon over the dance floor.

Burns handed his coat and briefcase to Vivian Stuart and went straight to the bar. He officially opened it by downing a shot of Scotch one of the men had ready for him. When the staff had collected, he thanked them briefly for their help to him during the past year. He led a toast to a happy New Year for all, then excused his need to leave, explaining that he had to attend the A. & P. party in the interest of more business and bigger bonuses next year. Several patted him on the back, assuring him that they understood. Secretly, he suspected, they would be glad to see him go. This would leave some of the men free to arrange some stiff drinks for the girls and the chance to set up some secret trysts in a hotel later.

In Burns' office Vivian Stuart and Al Lette were waiting. Al had repacked the briefcase with small labelled gifts and sealed, addressed envelopes. Vivian Stuart reported on calls received while he was out.

"Tom Cable called. He seemed to be feeling no pain but said he was lonesome. I asked him if he wanted you to call him back and he said that I would do. He asked for a date with me, tonight. Said he would fly in from Chicago. He said that his wife is taping a TV show in New York, and his second wife is with her parents in California. According to him, they hate his guts, so he asked me to tell you that he would be at the Barefoot Mailman in Pompano until Tuesday, and if he did not come across anything interesting there, he would go on down to Roxy's Green Turtle in Islamarada, wherever that is. He said that you would know. He said that this was all providing that I would not spend the night with him or find someone in Montreal who would. He said that he wasn't fussy, just horny, whatever that means."

"And what did you say, Miss S.?"

"I told him that I was going to the mountains, skiing with my boy friend."

"You won't be in Monday then."

"Not unless you need me."

"I'll keep you advised as to where I may be reached next week."

Out of the corner of his eye he could see Maggie hovering

outside the door to his office, waiting for Vivian and Al to leave. Lette was waiting patiently on the other side of the desk, no doubt thinking of the drinks that he was missing outside. Vivian Stuart put a small hand on his arm and stood on tiptoe to give him a quick peck on the cheek. She was still uncertain of herself at close quarters, in spite of her bravado.

"Have a happy Christmas, Mr. Burns. I may have to leave before you get back. Please have fun, but save some for next year. Men have been known to hire new secretaries at Christmas parties, but please don't. I promise that I'll get better as I know you better." She reached up to whisper, "My horoscope tells me that you will have a new office next year. Good luck!"

"Thanks, Miss S. You will be OK. If you can't be good with the boy friend in the mountains, be careful of those bearskin rugs in front of the fireplaces. They can be dangerous after eggnogs and rum. I really wouldn't like to lose you. You're starting to grow on me."

When she left, Al Lette brought out the large manila envelope that he had been waiting to give to his boss. He placed it in the top drawer of Burn's desk and locked it with his key.

"The old man keeps all the figures to himself. That's what he thinks. He spent two days alone in his office last week. He was working on those black books of his. He was totaling sales volume and profit. He asked me to bring in an adding machine. I could see that he was working out the bonuses for the staff by himself. No one knows how he figures them out, but all of the tapes and notes from his waste basket are in this envelope for you to look over when you have time. He totals all of the bonuses on the adding machine, and since he takes them in order off the payroll list, I have written in the names opposite each bonus on the tapes."

"Thanks, Al. You're something else. I gotta go now. I'll talk to you later. Please take care of Ives when he arrives. Don't let him get away until I get back."

Burns grabbed his hat, coat, and briefcase, waving to the staff as he hurried out.

Chapter 7

Edger Hays, vice-president of the A. & P. Railway, was a tall, slightly stooped, greying man. He gave every appearance of the confident, well qualified, well respected, and successful executive which he was.

Born in a railroad town on the prairies, of the third generation employed by the A. & P., he had worked up through the ranks to obtain his position at headquarters on ability. While politics did not help or hinder a man on the A. & P., origin might. The president, and most of the directors, came from western Canada. They were sometimes referred to as the "western Canada clique." That most officers should come out of the west was not unreasonable, since much of the railway's route lines, many of its subsidiaries, even most of its hotels, were located in the west. At any rate, the espirit de corps in management of the A. & P. was at contrast with the petty jealousies and intrigues noticeable among the less qualified political appointees at the government railways headquarters. The officers were intensely loyal to their company, and, while they were no less human, they enjoyed favors discreetly given, but only when such favors could be reconciled with what was felt to be the interests of the company. Of course, this was often a matter of individual judgment.

Hays had traveled extensively on railway committees with Burns, when the latter was employed by the government railways. Now, they met often, but any conversations or meetings which might, by timing or otherwise, be construed as improper

were limited to room 15. There it was assured that no more than one official of any railroad would be present at any one time. Most railroad officers knew about the room's existence and suspected that fellow executives had been there, but it was never mentioned. As long as no discredit was brought upon the company and the company's interests were not obviously sacrificed, no stigma was implied. Burns enjoyed their confidence. He had built it up deliberately and was careful to maintain it, even at the expense of a small order now and then.

When he entered the general office, Hays had just completed a friendly review of accomplishments during the past year. He was outlining some objectives for the year to come. Burns quietly joined the group of executives at the rear, while Hays finished speaking. The formalities over, greetings were exchanged all around. The staff dispersed to help themselves to coffee, Cokes, cheese, crackers, and cake, spread out on three desks placed together. The officers and Burns chatted briefly. The executive group began moving, one by one, to their offices, to gather up coats and parcels. Each wished Burns a formal Merry Christmas, as though they would not see him again that evening.

When the bosses left, there was a change in the level of conversation. Lively groups formed. Some mickies of liquor appeared, handled furtively, mindful of railroad general rule "G," to spike some Cokes. The stenos and secretaries took a little gentle kidding, some, the boldest, offered friendly kisses. Most were soon closing up their desks preparing to leave. Burns followed a middle-aged woman into the little private office adjoining the vice-president's.

"Off to North Bay tonight, Pam?"

"No, my sister, Joan, is here. Remember her? She insists on having that twerp that she used to work with for dinner tonight. It will be early, of course, so he can be home with his wife on Christmas Eve."

"And what are you going to do, Pam?"

"I'm no better off than she is. Jack will drop in about six with some flowers and a little present. Then he will go home, too. Joan and I will be consoling each other alone by eight o'clock, as

usual. We'll leave for North Bay on the nine-ten train tomorrow. We'll be there in time for a late Christmas dinner with the kids. I dread Christmas, actually, but I owe it to them."

She was quite ordinary, never beautiful, but she still had a good figure for her age. After some ten years of service with the railroad, she had been able to command the position of secretary to an assistant in the public relations department. He was the ne'er-do-well son of one of the largest stockholders, who was destined to become president of the company. He had already disgraced his father in some public indiscretions with women. Anyway, Pam fell in love with him, or with his position, or because his father would be president. She could not say why. She found herself pregnant by him, at the same time giving his wife the grounds that she needed for divorce. Pam took a leave of absence from her job to have his baby, with her family in North Bay. By the time his divorce became final, she was pregnant again. But, again, he embarrassed her and his father, now elected president of the far flung empire of the A. & P., by running off to Mexico with another secretary. No one seemed to know or care what had become of him, or, for that matter, whether he and Pam finally, married or not. She bore his name anyway. Pam placed her children with her mother. For the past twelve years or more she had held the very secure position of secretary to the vice-president. No one in the office referred to her past, and she avoided the subject with most people.

Pam was the type of woman who liked to have a man around her, as much to lean on as for affection. She gladly gave the latter to obtain the former. She began confiding in Burns when he sat in her office awaiting an appointment with her busy boss. Then, one hot, summer Saturday afternoon, they had met on Windsor Street. They were leaving their respective offices for the day. Pam's half-sister, Joan, was with her. Jack Wright, an electrical engineer for the government railways, was with Burns. After a couple of drinks in the cool bar at the old Drury's, Pam invited them to her apartment for a sandwich. The apartment was not air-conditioned. They sweltered over several rum and Cokes. The men asked permission to take off their shirts. The girls envied

their comfort, and with the enthusiastic permission of the men, finally did likewise. Dancing to the hi-fi, other items of clothing were discarded in the heat. Bets were placed as to which couple could longest resist the lure of the bedroom. Pam led Jack, to lose. They had been seeing one another ever since. However, Jack was married and had one child that he adored. The oft-discussed day of reckoning with Jack's wife continued to be postponed. Pam was forced to face the fact, now, that it would never come. She resigned herself to the situation, went on the pill, and made the best of it.

"You will have a lot of parcels for the kids and all. I'll pick you up with Pete and drive you to the station."

"On Christmas morning! That's too much, Alton! But I do have a copy of Mr. Hays' forecast at the apartment that I could go over with you—but—not here, of course. He is recommending a large program of replacing journal bearings next year, about four million dollars' worth. He is recommending that only half be purchased from Acme, the rest from S. K. F. Has he told you?"

"No, he hasn't told me, but it is the usual policy to split the business. Nevertheless, I would like to see his wording. I would like to get more than half. Anyway, Pam, I have a little gift for you that I would like to present somewhere else. I'll see you about seven A.M."

"We won't even be up at seven. It's only fifteen minutes to the station and we have to bathe and . . ."

"Leave your key behind the mail box when you go to bed. I'll wash your backs."

"OK. Joan won't mind. But remember, you won the bet once. You may lose this time with the two of us."

Only stragglers were left in the office. Pete was dozing in the warm car. It was getting colder now and the snow had stopped falling; lighter with the cold, it eddied around the corners of the buildings.

Back at the Acme offices, three couples were dancing cheek-to-cheek to a portable radio. Four younger ones were cuddling and giggling on some chairs bunched in a corner. A small group of older men, including Al Lette and Hal Ives, were having "one

for the road" at the bar. Maggie Smith, an empty glass in her hand, was at the door to take his coat.

"I guess that our party was not interesting enough for Miss Stuart. She left right after you did."

Maggie had the look of a little girl telling on someone. Burns knew that she wanted to get him alone, to explain over again, as she had last year after a few drinks, how she never wanted to leave him to be secretary to the president. She was very much afraid that Henry Hopkins would decide to retire, and who knows? While Burns would be still second in line, it was just possible, the way Donald McDonald was acting, that Burns might wind up being the president. Would he follow the practice in some firms and take his secretary with him? Where would that leave Maggie? This might be the chance to show him that she was capable of any service that he might need, now, or as president. After all, a little insurance would not really cost her anything, and this might be the right time to offer something that no one else was offering at the moment. He avoided the situation by quickly joining the group at the bar.

"Did they find you a glass of wine, Hal?" Ives had no glass in his hand; he drank very little. "Did you have a snack, a sandwich, some cheese? Is there any left?"

At the suggestion, Al Lette scurried around with two paper plates, gathering up a few pieces of cheese, crackers, and some olives. It was about all that was left.

"Better have some, Hal. If you can spare the time, I'd like you to make the rounds with me. We will have a chance to talk but we won't get dinner until very late, I'm afraid."

They nibbled on the food while saying good night to the last at the bar. Lette put out the lights and locked the door behind them. He accompanied them and the last of the young couples to the street.

In the limousine, Pete awoke with a start when they opened the rear door. Burns gave him a list of calls, then, with Ives, he settled back for quiet conversation, interrupted from time to time as he made a brief call at the home of a railway official.

At each call, Burns' pitch was the same. "I could not let

Christmas go by without thanking you, especially you, for your help in so many ways this year. I really needed that order for. . . " And he would refer to a large order received by Acme, whether the particular official had anything to do with awarding the contract or not. In fact, in a few cases, Burns knew, from information supplied by secretaries and juniors, that the official may have opposed placing the order with Acme. None refused credit now. Burns would go on to say, "That order will make a big difference in my bonus for this year and I must share a little of it. It looks like it may be even better next year."

The first Christmas that he had headed sales for Acme, Hopkins had insisted on adherence to custom by sending packages of tea or small wheels of Black Diamond cheese to officials at their offices. As an official of a railroad, himself, Burns had been embarrassed when the gifts piled up in his office on the day before Christmas, so much so that he had felt obliged to pass on most of the cheese and tea, gifts, favored by so many suppliers, to the staff. He had noted that year, the happier expressions of those to whom he had dared to offer a gift certificate from a department store, that being the equivalent of cash. A sum of money in an envelope, he found, most acceptable of all. Of course, these "gifts" were never inferred as bribes. However, Burns, while emphasizing that it was simply a token of friendship, made it a point, in the same breath, to mention some order for a product which he particularly wanted repeated in the next year. It was not uncommon for some railway officials to mention, just before Christmas, some order that Acme had received and for which, they felt, some credit was due.

Hal was content to sit in the car during these visits, resuming their conversation, when Burns returned, without comment or question.

At six-thirty exactly, Pete was directed to take them to a small second-story flat on McKay Street. It was occupied by a life-long friend of Florence Ridout. The two aging women had spent every Christmas Eve together for years. Burns invited Ives to come in with him. Florence was waiting at the door at the top of the stairs. She led them into a cluttered little room. Her friend,

about the same age, but not so well preserved, took their coats and showed them to a love seat, while Florence busied herself with sherry and cakes in the tiny kitchen. Together they looked at some old portraits and snapshots, bringing to mind gossip about former fellow-employees of the railway, dead or retired.

At seven, Florence was near the door again waiting for the knock. When it came, the rest ignored it, continuing their conversation in muted voices. She accepted the roses from the delivery boy with her back turned. She stood at the door after it closed, looking at them silently. The conversation faltered when she took them to the kitchen, arranged them in a vase, and placed it on a small table near the door. No one mentioned the roses or looked that way. The women talked of getting dressed to go to hear the singing at mass in the cathedral. Burns put out his cigarette. They put on their coats, shook hands with the women, and wished them compliments of the season. Burns fell behind and took Florence in his arms before the roses. He kissed her gently on her moist eyelids, stroking her hair, which was streaked with grey. She took a sealed envelope containing a draft of the railway budget from under the table and handed it to him without speaking. Both women stood in the door and wistfully watched the two men go down the stairs to the wintry street.

Resuming his calls, in the suburbs now, there was time to talk more. Ives confided that he was seriously considering resigning from his railway position. At any rate, he felt that he had to leave Edmonton, with its frigid winters, and its memories of his wife's illness and death. His work no longer interested him. The challenge was gone out of it. Although it was not his nature to be disloyal, it was obvious that he considered his immediate superior to be somewhat incompetent. He recalled, several times, the happier days, when the two of them worked as a team. He felt that together they had made meaningful contributions, if not to the operations of the government railways, to the state of the railway engineering art, through Burns' activities in the Railroad Association.

They discussed Ives' salary. While his tastes, like Burns', had always been modest, there were things that he would like to be

able to do someday. He would like, he admitted, to be a gentle-man farmer and operate the farm inherited from his father. Above all, he would like to have a string of good horses, breed them, train them, and race them, when he found good ones. He loved horses.

It was nine-fifteen by the time all of the deliveries had been made. With the frustrations of months pent up inside him, Hal had talked more frankly than at any time in his whole life. Each time that Burns left him to make a call, he had time to think of some irritation or obstruction that had bothered him in Edmonton. When they alighted from the limousine at the Mount Royal Hotel, the die was cast. Ives was the man for Marra and Char Lake. In the lobby of the Hotel, before the two-story Christmas tree, ablaze with colored lights, Burns paused and turned to Ives.

"Look, Hal, we are going into the Pick bar for a little while. We may be separated. You will be with your relatives here over the holidays. I will be out of town all of next week. Can you arrange to stay around Montreal until I get back and contact you? I may have something very, very interesting for you then."

"No reason why I can't. I have leave of absence. I certainly don't feel like going back to Edmonton next week, or ever for that matter."

Chapter 8

The Pickadilly Club was jammed. The booths along the walls bulged with double design capacity. Waiters were serving with difficulty, trays held high. There was a standing crowd, six or seven deep, around the circular bar in the center of the room. Burns shouldered his way in, looking for Larry Connors. Ives squeezed along behind him. Connors was located in a booth. He was sitting next to the wall, hemmed in by several animated couples. He had arrived before the crowds from the office parties. He was enjoying himself. As usual, he held no rancor about the events at lunch time with Marra. He shouted over the babble when he caught sight of Burns.

"Hello there. Sit down. Be my guest, if you can find a seat. I can't even get out of here to go to the can. I've been suffering here with my bad prostate for a couple of hours. They won't let me out."

A couple got up and apologized to Larry.

"That's OK! It's numb now. Another half hour and it will be pickled like the rest of me."

Reference to the prostate brought a laugh from Burns. He explained to Ives and several strangers around them, as they waited to be served. The incident occurred some ten years before. Connors was with Burns in Atlantic City for a railroad convention. They were hurrying along the Boardwalk from one cocktail party, going to another. Each had an urgent call of nature. They found a men's room in the lobby of the Shelbourne Hotel. Both stood up to the urinals with a sigh of relief. Burns finished first

and walked out. Connors stayed behind. After waiting outside for several minutes, Burns reentered the men's room to find Connors still standing at the urinal.

"Christ, Larry. You must have something wrong with your prostate when it takes you so long to have a piss."

"You think so, eh? Just because I don't piss like a horse, with a one-inch stream?"

The incident was forgotten until one morning, months later, Connors burst into Burns' office and demanded a key to the washroom, urgently. Returning from the men's room he explained. His yearly medical, in connection with an insurance policy, came due. He made an appointment with the insurance company doctor in the clinic near Burns' office. Anticipating that a urine sample would be required, and recalling that when he had been asked for a sample once before he could not come up with it, he had refrained from going to the toilet since the evening before, so as to have it available. At the clinic, Larry's blood pressure was taken first.

"Can I give a sample now?"

"What sample?"

"My urine sample. Can I give it now?" Connors was holding his crotch.

"You look OK to me. I'll just write you a certificate."

"But, doc, aren't you going to check anything else?"

"Why should I? Is anything bothering you?"

"No, I feel OK, but one of my friends says that I have prostate trouble. You will need a sample for that, won't you, doc."

"Prostate trouble, eh? Well, we'll soon find out. Take down your pants and lean over the table."

"But you will need a sample, won't you, doc? I can give it."

The doctor was glaring ominously as he pulled a long rubber glove on his right hand, unrolling the cuff up to the elbow. Greasing a long finger with Vaseline, he roughly shoved Larry forward over the table.

"This friend who says you have prostate trouble, is he a physician? If he isn't, what does he know about it?" The doctor jabbed a long finger and part of his fist up Larry's rectum. "This

will teach you"—he jabbed hard, to emphasize the point—
"to" . . .—another hard jab—"avoid advice" . . .—jab— "from un-
qualified quacks"—the final jab almost ruptured Connors' swollen
bladder.

"And you don't need a sample?"

"Certainly not. You've taken up too much of my time already, taking advice from someone who dosn't know a God-damn
thing about medicine. Now pull up your pants and get the hell
out of here, I'm busy."

The doctor pulled off his glove and threw it in the trash con-
tainer. Larry just made it to Burns' office.

Both laughed at the recollection, as Burns looked around for
a waiter.

"Guess I'll have to get our drinks at the bar."

Burns worked his way through the crowd to the bar, timing
his arrival to coincide with the departure of a man with drinks in
both hands. He wedged himself into the narrow space next to the
girl seated on a bar stool. He called to a bartender that he knew
by name.

"Two Scotches with water, Mike, and one sherry, for my
table over there."

As she heard his voice, she turned her head slowly toward
him, with her dazzling smile, as though she was expecting him.
He had never seen her smile from this close up on the commuter
train. The mouth was full and sensuous, but what he had not
noticed before were the long incisors in her otherwise perfect,
white teeth. With her large, slanting, black velvet eyes, they contributed to the cat look.

She was with another girl. They had no coats, and since
there were no purses in sight, he assumed that they either
worked nearby or had access to a room in the hotel. She had
been carrying a large purse that morning. He was sure that she
would not have left it in a check room. He spoke to her for the
first time.

"How are you doing in this mob?"

"Well, and you?"

Her voice was throaty. It was friendly. There was no trace of

an accent, but the construction of her reply suggested a French-Canadian influence.

"Would you like to join us?" He nodded toward Hal and Larry, who, he noted, were watching. "It may be crowded, but we can make room."

"Thank you, but we are expecting company. We are staying with friends in the hotel tonight." She seemed to invite a question.

"Male or female?"

"Male, of course," She studied him for his reaction. "But I'll take a rain check."

"When and where can I call you?"

"You can't call me. I will call you, if you will say when."

The bartender brought Burns' drinks.

"My number at the office is. . . "

"I have it," she interrupted. "Just say when."

He searched his mind for some reason for her to know his office number.

"Monday afternoon? I'll be in the office alone, I expect."

"Monday afternoon, about four?"

"Monday afternoon at four. I'll wait for your call. Meanwhile, Merry Christmas." On impulse, he moved to kiss her cheek, but with a quick toss of her head, she offered soft lips instead. *Amazingly exciting woman*, he thought, as he carefully made his way with the three drinks in hand to the table. Connors had a crack ready.

"Turned you down, eh? You've got eyes like a ragpicker, Burns. I didn't see her there. I wondered why you wanted to buy a drink."

"I didn't. I added it to your tab."

As they exchanged small talk among themselves and others around them, thinning out now, Burns kept an eye on the bar. Three well-dressed young men without coats came in. One he recognized as a customer's man in the stock broker's office across the street. They joined the two girls at the bar. There were introductions, then, all five went to the door. As she left, the girl turned and flashed the same half smile that he had glimpsed that

morning as he lost sight of her turning on East Ste. Catherine Street. Hal Ives was watching, too.

So she worked in a stock broker's office. She must be a secretary. But the hour at which she went to work each day on the train didn't fit. And she turned east on Ste. Catherine. Burns could not get that out of his mind. There were no brokerage offices in that direction. In fact, there were few offices where a girl with perfect English would be employed in the east end. Ste. Catherine Street East led to a predominately French section, the garment district, St. Lawrence, "The Main," to the docks.

The standing crowd had left now. Only a few groups were huddled around the booths. Burns was first to make a suggestion. "It's almost ten-thirty. I, for one, have had nothing but snacks all day. Let's get something to eat and go home. I'm getting too old to bang around all night with guys who are not buying."

"Speak for yourself, but, come to think of it, I'm hungry, too. Where will we go? You could have asked your oriental girl friend to take us home for chop suey, but you didn't make out so good, eh, Burns? She left with some other guys. Did you notice?" Connors was rubbing it in again.

"I get the needle, Connors, but it gives me an idea. I've got to call in at Cafe Este to deliver a gift to my faithful dinner wait-ress. I think that the kitchen closes about ten-thirty. Shall I phone?"

The conversation had been between Burns and Connors, but now Ives showed interest. "Suits me," he said.

Burns used the phone at the bar, and returning to the table, he did not sit down. "I got Jeanine. The kitchen is closed. She is about ready to leave. She says that there is some lovely chateau-briand still hot. She will wrap some for us to take out on her terms."

"Yeh, what's the terms?"

"We have to drive her home, eat there while she changes, then drop her and her sister at the church for midnight mass."

"Nothing wrong with that, as long as we don't have to go to mass with her. Let's go. Do you suppose that she would wrap a sandwich for Greta. She always likes to eat a snack in bed when I

come home late. I fill her in on everything that I have done all evening while she eats."

"Buull-she-it. Every word a lie. Let's go."

Pete Bouchard did not need directions to either the Cafe Este or to Jeanine's apartment on Sherbrooke Street East. He had been to both addresses many times. Often when Burns intended to be with clients until late at room 15 or at a nightclub, Pete was instructed to pick up Jeanine at the end of her shift to take her home. Otherwise, he would simply sleep in the car, waiting.

Jeanine Surgeon was a typical French-Canadian woman in her early thirties. She was quite attractive in her sheer white uniform, a red handkerchief protruding from a breast pocket and a small red kerchief around her neck. Her hair was dark brown, worn shoulder length. Her brown eyes twinkled with mischief. Her lips were carefully pencilled to make her mouth look fullest over a slightly receding chin. Her breasts were large and held high. Her figure was trim, and her legs, below her short uniform, were muscular from years of working on her feet. What she lacked in beauty, she made up for in energy, good nature, and love of good food, wine, and men.

Born on a small, narrow tract of land on the Richelieu River, granted to original French colonists when the river was the only mode of travel, she had twelve living brothers and sisters. Three of the boys had entered seminaries to become priests. All of the girls, except two, had followed the French-Canadian tradition, married young and had large families living among friends and relatives on the river. There was a reason for Jeanine and her youngest sister to be different. In Jeanine's case, separation from the little community was necessary when she was seduced by an uncle and was pregnant at the age of thirteen. It was not a case of rape per se. She had welcomed and enjoyed it. She was so innocent, however, that it had never occurred to her that, while doing something that came naturally, she could have a baby without a priest performing a marriage ceremony. While it was not such a disgrace to become pregnant at an early age, the priests did frown on incest. Her mother sent Jeanine to Montreal to have

her baby with relatives there. The child was placed in an orphanage. Jeanine went to work as a waitress at fourteen. Her first job was in the canteen at the nearby shops of the A. & P. Railroad, where she worked a few hours each day at lunchtime. The rest of the day, she cared for the children in her relative's large family.

Getting to know the railwaymen, she eventually moved to a full time job at a restaurant and bar that catered to them. She had an excellent memory for names and faces. Her warm, friendly disposition endeared her to her clientele. She made a game of her work. She enjoyed being of service, sometimes even after hours.

As the French owner of the restaurant prospered, he moved further uptown to a larger establishment, where Jeanine added to the patrons who followed her. At Cafe Este, her regular clientele included railroad executives and officers of manufacturing, supply, and financial concerns who dealt with railroad officers. With small salary and the generous tips which she earned by the way she applied herself, she was one of the best paid waitresses in Montreal, largely tax-free. She lived better than she ever dreamed possible as a farm girl in rural Quebec, much better than any of her hundreds of relatives. She no longer could be content to marry in her class and raise a large family, as a devout French-Canadian Catholic should. Her many nieces and nephews seemed to satisfy her instinct for motherhood.

For years she enjoyed a relationship with a handsome head waiter. He was married and had children but he satisfied some of her sex needs. Since she did not ask that he give up his wife and family, Rosaire did not object to her indulgences with other men when she felt like it. If there was anything missing from such a life, Jeanine gave no indication of it. Now, she lived comfortably with her younger sister, who also worked in a good cafe, as a hostess.

Their basement apartment included a large combined kitchen and dining room. There were bedrooms at either end of a rather crowded and overdecorated parlor. The furniture was of red velvet, as were several hassocks and floor cushions. All of the rooms,

including the entrance foyer, opened into the parlor. Aside from the entrance and the bathroom, there were no doors. Openings were filled with heavy curtains. Family and religious prints covered the walls. A crucifix hung over every doorway.

Jeanine's sister, who had worked an earlier shift, opened the door for them. The relationship was, at once, noticeable, the pert appearance, the same coloring and features. The difference was in the figure of the younger girl. She was dressed in soft, one-piece lounging pyjamas, to reveal what she considered to be her most attractive attribute. Jeanine often introduced her as *"La Juene fille avec le plus beaux derrière de Montreal."* Indeed her beautifully rounded ass was carried like that of a centaur; as though she had been built to walk on all fours, but with the spine bending just above the sacrum to allow her to walk upright. Standing straight, this emphasized the contours of her breasts. It left the impression that she had been built to mount from the rear.

Reneé, as she was introduced, rushed about the parlor picking up copies of *Paris Match*, French movie magazines, and *Allo Police*, while Jeanine took their coats. In the kitchen, with the deft motions of years of practice, the spotless table was wiped off, meat unwrapped and laid out attractively, with fresh French bread, pickles, cheese, and a small centerpiece of artificial flowers, heavily scented. Jeanine called upon the men to be seated. Reneé produced a bottle of red wine, which, Burns noted, was the best vintage carried in the cellars of Cafe Este. Jeanine excused herself to change from her cafe uniform and to have her bath before dressing for mass. Before leaving, she rummaged in her large purse for some pencil notes written on the backs of menus and placed them on the table beside Burns' plate.

"Wen you 'ave eat, you come in. I esplain you out of my batt. I write Engleesh not so good." Her accent was charming, old Quebec. Connors leaned over to peer at the notes. Burns folded them but not before Connors had recognized what they might contain.

"What the hell is that? I suppose it's a list of clients that all of your competitors took to dinner or lunch at Cafe Este. Does she make notes about what we talk about while she is serving us?

She probably reads lips from the kitchen. You bastard, Burns!"

Burns grinned, glancing at Hal, who, it seemed, was directing furtive, hungry looks at the movements of Reneé's curves under her soft pyjamas.

With the last of his meal, Burns took the notes and entered the bathroom. There, he settled on a low stool, while Jeanine relaxed in her tub. She replied to his questions as he attempted to translate her French scribbling. She filled him in with what she had heard discussed over highballs and meals. It is surprising how far a key word may carry across a dining room. He handed her a large European-style bath towel when she stood up, without modesty, and stepped from the tub. She dried herself facing him, still answering questions in a low voice. She turned while he toweled her back. With breasts cupped in her hands, she faced him again.

"You doan' feel to make lov? No?"

"You will be seeing Rosaire tonight after midnight mass."

"You know Rosaire, he doan mine. E connetre. E know I know you beefore heem. I ave plentee for heem when he wants. E mus go to ee's familee Chreestmas. E mus ave present for ee's femme. Is true."

They heard the doorbell ring and Reneé answer it. She called out, "Eet ees Fathaire Romeo!"

They could hear the priest stamping the snow from his feet. Unbuttoning his black coat, he removed his black hat, as Reneé introduced him to the men in the parlor. She poured him a glass of wine and he sat down, addressing a few solemn words to Reneé, as he spoke only French. It was obvious, from the mumbled acknowledgments of the introductions, that the men spoke English. Burns followed Jeanine out of the bathroom. She had the large, damp towel draped around her trim figure and caught under the armpits.

"Joyeux Nöel, Mon Pet. You 'av met Messue Burns."

She stood on the toes of her bare feet to kiss the tall priest on the cheek, still holding the towel about her. The priest looked from one sister to the other. He spoke quietly in French.

"These are married men."

"Peut etre, perhaps, yes."

She stood before him, mischievously defiant and opened the towel to reveal her naked body. She spoke slowly in her English so that all could understand.

"Regardez-vouz, mon pere, I 'ave over tirty year. I 'ave no man, eh? But a woman, oui? I 'ave bodee needs man sometime, eh? Wat you tink I do? You wan I go peek op sailaire boyee at docks? Weeth disease, peut etre, yes? Doan worree," she patted his ruddy cheek, "I tell all about in confession, maybee."

The priest smiled at last. He had heard her confessions for years. He would have to keep on warning her again and again, but it would be useless to try to change her. He finished his wine. With an admonition to the two women that they refrain from becoming so involved with affairs of the flesh that they might miss midnight mass, he blessed them all and left.

Hal Ives had not said a word, but he observed all that went on. He continued to watch Reneé hungrily, especially as the girls started to strip on the way to their bedrooms to dress.

Pete dropped the women at the church, then delivered Ives to his hotel. At Larry's suggestion, the limousine took them to his house first. Burns turned on the rear seat radio control and they listened quietly to "Silent Night." In the midst of "Jingle Bells," Larry snapped off the radio from his side.

"We'll hear that stuff all day tomorrow. Right now, I'd like to talk to you about Matt Marra. You scored good with him today, Alton. Our people in Pittsburgh have been working on him for years. They think that they have him in my pocket. I have been thinking about it all afternoon, until I got drunk. It's the deal of a lifetime, Alton. I knew that I could not handle it alone. Since we would have had to share it with someone, I'm glad that it will be with you."

"Thanks, Larry. That is like you."

At Connors' house, all in darkness, Larry fumbled for his keys. They tiptoed into the kitchen, without removing their coats. Connors had a drink, which he needed like a hole in the head. They talked in whispers.

"Don't want to wake Greta until I take up a snack. She's

cranky when she wakes up hungry." Connors got to another thing that had been on his mind. "Tell me, Alton, how did you really make out with that oriental siren, the 'cat girl,' you call her."

"To tell you God's truth, Larry, I don't know."

"She was friendly. You bussed her, but she left with a couple of other guys."

"All that I can say, Larry, is that we have not seen the last of her. I like your term 'Oriental siren'—'Siren of the Rails,' perhaps."

"Merry Christmas, and good luck, Alton, you bastard."

Chapter 9

Most products that the Acme Supply Company manufactured and sold to Canadian railroads were developed in the United States. Large firms in railroad centers such as Chicago, St. Louis, New York, Buffalo, and Cleveland were able to maintain research and development facilities which a Canadian company could not afford. In return for designs, constantly improved, and know-how in manufacturing. Acme paid a royalty, or a share of its profits. This necessitated constant contact and frequent long trips involving air travel that the older officers of Acme had been unwilling to endure. Also, serving thousands of miles of the Canadian transcontinental rail systems demanded frequent vists by air to regional railway offices. Local officers could exert pressures on the head office to purchase products of preference. A superintendent in Edmonton, two thousand miles from Montreal, could demand the purchase of an Acme product, after a quiet evening with Burns over several martinis at a party in his hotel room, ending with a steak, and, if worth it, even an out-of-town girl. This could be much appreciated in a quiet provincial town.

Henry Hopkins avoided air travel. If he felt it an absolute necessity to make an infrequent trip, he traveled surface—by train—no matter how long it took. In hiring Burns, he recognized that more travel on behalf of the firm was necessary. He did not question the cost when Burns traveled first class and billed the cost to the company. Burns spent many hours each week in air flights. He did not consider it a hardship. Away from the eigh-

teen hour-a-day schedule in Montreal, each trip provided a chance to think, to plan, to recap.

The trip to Mobile would be a long one. The double bulkhead seat on the right-hand side was selected, as usual. In the double seat opposite, the stewardesses had deposited their things. They would sit there after the stop at Toronto and he would gossip with them about businessmen traveling recently.

Right now, Burns' mind was on Precision Bearings. The proposed split in the order at the A. & P., as well the immediate problem of Morton's bearing order from Waldorf. A loss of the whole order by Morton would make it more difficult to deal with the A. & P. at home. Canadian railways officers were often influenced by the award or loss of a large order to a railroad in the U.S.

Doodling on the pad in his lap, he sought a common denominator, some way to tie the order in the U.S. with the one in Canada. What about that useless Zerk-fitting idea that he had patented for Edger Hays. Hays had been so enthusiastic about it, but since all U.S. railroads considered it of no value whatever, it had never been used, and Hays had derived nothing from it.

Burns made his decision. He decided upon a change in his approach to Lou Waldorf when he arrived in Mobile. If it worked, he might get all of both orders. It was a heady thought. He put it out of his mind and reflected back on the events of the day before.

Few people were on the station platform at Mount Royal. It was Boxing Day, an old English holiday, celebrated in Ontario, but not in Quebec, where Saint Jean Baptiste Day was observed instead. As most Montreal firms were English, with connections in Ontario, it was a sort of unofficial holiday. Missing, taking full advantage of this, were the stenographers, secretaries, and clerks, with their official-looking briefcases packed with lunches and a pair of shoes to be half-soled. By habit, he looked for her, but did not expect to see the "cat girl." She was not on the platform at Portal Heights, either.

With no one standing in the aisles to block the view, no one to talk to or observe, he could study every detail of the interior of

the railway car. They were familiar details. Burns recalled how he had designed the car with the help of Hal Ives. From the number stencilled over the vestibule door, he identified it as the fifth in an order of fifty built by Dominion Car Company.

There had been a wreck on the line at the afternoon rush hour. An old day coach, built fifty years before, had been relegated with others of the same vintage to the unprofitable commuter service. As the electric locomotive accelerated faster than the steam locomotives with which it had been designed to be used, it jumped the track at the first curve inside the Mount Royal Tunnel. The old car collapsed, several passengers were injured, and two were killed.

This came as no great surprise to Burns and Ives. As engineers, they had warned top management again and again, as more powerful engines were placed in service, that the old cars would not stand the acceleration. Their recommendations were ignored when funds to construct new, modern coaches were not made available. At the same time, there were government funds appropriated for the design and construction of other equipment, considered more urgently required. Burns' staff was assigned to the design of palatial new, all-steel business cars, rolling palaces for the private use of top railway officials, cabinet ministers, the prime minister, and a whole fleet for the governor general to entertain the Royal Family every five years or so.

When the president of the government railways saw the newspaper headlines the next morning, he called in his public relations department. He issued a news release at once. It was announced that the crack engineering staff, assembled since he transferred from the senate to his present position, had the matter completely in hand. For the past year, the president's release went on to state, his research staff had been working on original all-Canadian designs and specifications for the replacement of all of this type of rolling stock. The new cars, for safety as well as sheer beauty and comfort, would represent the very highest state of the car-building art. The designs would do justice to the most progressive government-owned railway in the world. If orders had not already been placed by the vice-president of purchases,

he continued, it was only because bids were being sought competitively to insure that the taxpayers of Canada received the very best value at lowest cost. He promised that construction would start at once and new cars would be placed in service shortly. Simultaneously, he released a letter to his vice-president of purchasing. It was subtly dated two days before and delivered by hand directing that orders be placed, at once, for fifty new coaches of "approved" type. This shifted responsibility from the president to the vice-president.

Even before the news release reached the daily papers, the vice president called upon the engineering department, also by hand-delivered letter carefully predated, to furnish designs and specifications within twenty-four hours. This passed the buck one step further down the line to Alton Burns.

There was neither the time nor the staff to even adapt designs used by other railroads in the U.S. to Canadian conditions. Selection of most economical materials, distribution of stresses to achieve optimum operating weight, and other studies necessary for even the minimum of efficiency, economy, and safety were out of the question.

Burns closed the door of his office. From his Railway Association files, he selected an arrangement drawing of one of the safest, heaviest, most expensive mainline coaches built recently in the United States. On his table, he carefully cut out from the center of the drawing, sufficient seat space to reduce the capacity to forty-eight, the length of car that could be accommodated at Canadian loading platforms.

Splicing the two ends of the drawing together with Scotch tape, he blocked out dimensions and title plate. He carefully rolled up the drawing and took it personally to the blueprint room in the basement. A white-line vandyke from it was converted to a brown-line vandyke, prints from which would appear to be from an original drawing. Back in his office, with door closed again, new dimensions and title plate were inked in. Draughtsmen were selected to make tracings of floor plans, cross sections, and details, similarly cobbled together.

Alone all afternoon and all night, Burns worked on the mod-

ification of typical specifications, as the draughtsmen, working on overtime, delivered drawings. Maggie stood by to type pages of transparencies. They were careful to add "or equal" after every requirement, so that each could be reconsidered later when the inevitable political pressures were brought to bear by suppliers who could not comply. Burns was aware that this would greatly increase the price of the cars, as the carbuilders fully protected themselves against every unexpected change. There was no alternative in the time allowed.

The overtime draughtsmen finished, one by one, during the night. The staff was trooping in next morning before Maggie and Burns had finished printing copies of the specification in the blueprint room. The drawings were a counterfeit work of art. When Maggie had typed the covering letter to the vice-president, tacitly implying that they were original designs based on "months of study and research," it was almost noon.

That same afternoon, tenders closing in only fifteen days were solicited from three carbuilding companies "quoting independently." Considering the size of the contract and the firm price required, the carbuilders took no chances. They met secretly in a hotel room to decide who should be the low bidder by a few dollars and some odd cents. Of course all would share in subcontracts, anyway. The vice-president would do his duty and haggle the low bidder down by fifty dollars per car, which they had allowed for from past experience.

Almost every item of finish on the inside of the coach revived a memory. There were the simple coat hooks. A vice-president had insisted that they must be different. Cast specially from a complicated mold made the cost of each about twenty-five times that of a similar item purchased retail in a hardware store. The same applied to the ash trays, designed for cigars, not cigarettes. The tassel of the emergency brake cord was hand-loomed from the tail of a virgin Quebec province lamb or something. At a cost of about fifty dollars extra, the wife of a French-Canadian member of parliament had insisted upon it, suggesting that it must reflect French-Canadian culture.

A piece of unfinished masonite covering an opening in the

wall of the ladies toilet room contrasted with the mahogany of the rest of the finish. When the carbuilders had tendered their prices, the vice-president had requested appropriation from the Minister of Transport of about fifty thousand dollars per car. This was based on the cost of the last commuter cars built thirty years before for steam locomotive service. Now the lowest bidder wanted two hundred thousand per car, rock bottom, take it or leave it. With the news releases and all, the railroad was on the spot.

Before relaying this shocking news, the vice-president looked over the tenders in desperation. An item that took his eye was one of three hundred and fifty dollars for a sealed electro-mechanical drinking water cooler in each car. He recalled that many years before, when he was head of the yard foreman's union, he had ridden in a caboose. The water cooler consisted of a simple galvanized iron tank with two compartments, one for water and one for ice. He estimated that the cost would not exceed fifty dollars. This might save three hundred dollars. Not much on a two hundred thousand dollar car, but it would be his personal contribution to economy.

So, the old-fashioned water coolers were set into the walls of the ladies toilets. A spigot at the bottom was accessible from the corridor outside. At stations, the cooler was filled with water and ice by removing a simple lid inside the toilet room. When the first of the new cars went into service with appropriate publicity, newspapers were furnished with photos of the various employees carrying out their duties to insure the ultimate in safety and comfort for the traveling public. One of the press photos showed a health department inspector testing the drinking water at the end of the first run. Results of the test, later acknowledged, showed the water to be contaminated. A full investigation disclosed that someone in the ladies toilet room on the first trip must have been at a loss to dispose of a soggy Kotex pad. An out-of-sight repository was suggested by lifting the lid of the tank. The reddish hue of the drinking water was explained in headlines. As a direct result, Board of Transport Commissioners issued an order equivalent to law. All ice-activated water coolers must be removed from

all railway rolling stock within one year and be replaced by a sealed electro-mechanical type. With coaches, sleeping cars, diners, cabooses, and locomotives to be refitted, the purchase of over thirty thousand new coolers at a cost of about one million dollars had to be made within a year.

Acme had hoped to furnish at least a part of the order with Frigidaire models made under license. However, a corporate decision, prompted no doubt by fear of restraint of trade investigations in the U.S., caused Frigidaire to withdraw from this field. They withdrew the rights granted to Acme to use their designs, but agreed to furnish components for any other design under another name, if required, in not less than carload lots. No other tried-and-proven designs were available to enable Acme to participate.

Burns held season's tickets to the Alouette football team home games. They were of most value in entertaining executives in the final games of the season, when interest was at its height. In mid-season, Burns used them to entertain junior engineers or office assistants, with some useful knowledge of new requirements and competitors' prices. These games developed into more of a drinking bout than a spectator entertainment.

Kent Colby was office assistant to the vice-president of purchases. It was the final quarter of the game with Calgary and the Alouettes had done badly. The score was 31 to 1. The Montreal fans were disgusted. Burns and his guest had given up long since on the practice of reserving drinks from the thermos and a swig from the forty-ounce bottle of Bacardi rum for a home team score. Colby was feeling mellow and magnanimous.

"I felt sorry for an old guy that came in to see my boss this morning. He was sitting on a million dollar order and couldn't take it. He looked as though he could use the money, too."

Burns was all ears, but tried to sound only mildly interested.

"Yeah, what did he have to sell?"

"He had spent a lifetime as a refrigeration engineer for Pullman Standard. They retired him, or fired him. While working for them, he developed a water cooler, sealed, electro-mechanical type. They wouldn't push it. They had friends in the supply busi-

ness, particularly Frigidaire. You used to handle their line before they pulled out, didn't you, Alton?"

"Yeah! Go on, Kent." Burns took a small swig of the increasingly potent remains in the thermos, in an effort to appear only casually interested.

"The boss had our engineering and research people look at his drawings. They reported that his was a radical new development, simpler and cheaper than anything offered for our big replacement program. The old man claims a patent in the U.S., but he has neither the facilities or the capital to make it in Canada. The only moving part is the small compressor. Frigidaire makes it, but they refuse to supply less than carload lots to him and then only on a C.O.D. cash basis. The boss checked with the A. & P. He had been in to see them, too. Their engineers said the same thing. He could have had a million dollar order with a little financing and the right connections. He left for Chicago at noon, when we refused to take out a license from him to manufacture it ourselves. He just wanted a little cash, one dollar per unit for his designs. The boss advised him that our directors' policy was to refrain from manufacturing ourselves. The A. & P. told him the same thing. Poor old Shafer!"

"What was his first name, Kent? I have heard of a Shafer at Pullman. He was supposed to be a very smart inventor for them, once."

"I think that his first name is Frank. He has a little office on LaSalle Street, in the Loop. Shafer Agencies, I think he calls it."

Burns excused himself to go to the men's room below the stands. Instead he went straight to the nearest pay phone. He instructed Pete to pick them up at the stadium entrance in twenty minutes. Next, he called air Canada and made a reservation to Chicago. He made one more call—to a house on Peel Street.

The empty rum bottle was at Colby's feet. He held the empty thermos while he watched, with little interest, a disappointing play on the field.

"Well, Kent, the Alouettes got a fucking today. We might as well do likewise. Let's drop in on Lucille."

Colby was interested, but pessimistic.

"No use. I've called a couple of times since you took me there last year. Someone else answers and says she is out or busy. I called at the door the last time and she answered it herself. When I told her that I was alone and you were out of town, she said that her relatives were staying with her, or something. I got the impression that she did not want to see me again, even though she was so randy for me the night that you took me there."

"She works very hard, Kent, and, sometimes, she's tired. I happen to know that she had the day off today, so she will be in good shape tonight. Let's go. Pete's waiting at the gate."

At the house on Peel Street, the door opened, while Burns' finger was still on the bell giving his special ring. Lucille answered it herself. She was dressed in a see-through negligee. She was a short girl, in her twenties, with dark eyes and swarthy skin. While her hair was blonde, the part was dark, as were her brows, lashes, and the triangle of hair that showed clearly through her gown.

Burns took her hand and while he leaned down to kiss her cheek, she had already counted the three ten dollar bills that he had left in her palm. Turning from Burns she placed her arm around Kent's waist, drawing him in, while she closed the door, snapping the two locks.

"I am so 'appee to see you, Ken. Eet ees Ken, yes? I jus' 'ope you come. I 'appen to be lonlee, ce soir."

Colby looked happy. Burns followed them into a shabbily furnished sitting room, with a bed in one corner.

"You are alone, Lucille? No girl for me?"

She took the cue at once. She feigned sorrow. "No, I am so sorree, Monsuer Alton."

"Oh well! That's the story of my life. I'll try somewhere else. Pete will be back for you in an hour, Kent. Where I'm going, I'll stay the night. Be nice to him, Lucille. He's a good customer. Don't bite him or scratch him up. And don't keep him up too late." Burns winked at Lucille. Inside a half hour, Colby would be anxious to have her check him for lipstick before leaving for home.

Burns sensed a million dollar order.

There were only three businessmen spaced, silently, about twenty feet apart at the long mahogany bar of the Drake Hotel. It was the only hotel bar in Chicago that opened at seven in the morning to allow businessmen the fortification required to face another day. One of the patrons was tall, about six feet six. He was expensively, but casually, dressed, clean-shaven, with a tan which suggested hours on the golf course. His prematurely greying hair was crewcut. While he must have weighed over two hundred and twenty-five pounds, he was not fat. His weight was well distributed over wide shoulders and a big frame. The large well-manicured hands that cupped his glass were those of a former star fullback at Notre Dame.

Before enlisting in the Marine Corps, immediately upon graduation from college, Tom Cable received many decorations in the South Pacific theatre. He became a national hero. Seriously wounded twice, he was returned to the U.S. as a U.S. Marine recruiter in the Los Angeles area. With his clean good looks, his physique, and his ready wit on a platform or in a group, he was very effective. Assisted by the PR department of the Marine Corp, he became well known after a few months on the West Coast.

Cast in several movie shorts for the recruitment program, his courtship of a movie starlet was headlined in *Variety*, and mentioned in all of the movie magazines.

When his assignment was terminated and he was sent back to his unit in the South Pacific, she was already recognized as an actress destined for stardom. Much to the distress of her very ambitious mother, who felt marriage to a director or producer would insure her career, she slipped away to San Diego and married Cable the day that he shipped out.

During another year of duty, Cable recklessly survived more heroic actions and won more decorations. Much to the chagrin of her parents, he survived without another scratch. Meanwhile, in Hollywood, she was a star and her name was linked romantically with several famous figures in the industry. In spite of his love of fun, Tom Cable was a good Catholic and divorce was furthest from his mind as he happily headed home to her.

On the trip back, Tom spent one night on the town in San

Francisco, a last good-by to the loyal, good buddies in the good old U.S., after months of steaming, sodden, most often lonely, fearsome jungle. On arrival next day, to a cool reception at the home of her parents in L.A., Tom faced a situation more confusing to him than a formation of Jap fighters. While he grasped for a few moments alone with his wife, her mother went through his duffel bags. She selected a pair of his underwear shorts with stains on them. She sent them to a laboratory for analysis. In a matter of hours, he was confronted with the allegation that the stains were menstrual blood, grounds for divorce.

After drifting aimlessly for a couple of months, Tom, changed somewhat from the carefree, returning hero, settled down and took a position as salesman with Pullman Standard Car Manufacturing Company in San Francisco, where an old alumnus of his alma mater, Elmer Layden, one of the famous Four Horsemen, worked. The railroads' in the west were in dire need of new equipment after the war. It was good training for Tom and he made the most of it. A lucrative offer from River Rouge Steel, subsidiary of Seaway Steel, attracted him. Acme was the representive of River Rouge in Canada.

Burns and Cable had met at railway conventions in San Francisco and Chicago, where not only a common business interest but hobbies of fishing, football, etc., whatever rhymes, brought them together, often. While Cable remarried, he retained his affection for his first wife. He met her frequently when in New York, where she performed on Broadway and on TV.

"Bring another martini for my Canadian friend, Bobo."

This was Cable's greeting, as Burns swung a leg over the bar stool next to him. He expected Burns to drop in as though Montreal were next door to the Loop.

"Better call Faye over at Pietro's Club, old buddy. She thinks she's pregnant."

"So what's really new, Tom? Why should I call her?"

"No reason, except she thinks it was some Canadian stud that you paired her with when you entertained your Canadian customers at the convention last October. She said that this guy had a tool as big as an ear of Indiana corn and she should know.

She was born in a Hoosier cornfield. I was at the club last night. She told me that it was my last chance to lay her. I told her I had gone modern, turned queer, that I now considered old-fashioned fucking only good for truck drivers."

They both laughed and shook hands.

Burns explained the reason for his trip to Chicago. Tom knew Shafer well. He mentioned several patents that Shafer had developed when Tom worked for Pullman. He had been offered early retirement after the death of his wife, because of alcohol addiction. He maintained a small office, from which he solicited odd consulting assignments, not too successfully. Cable offered to call on the old man with Burns.

They found Frank Shafer, a wizened little man in a dirty white shirt, frayed trousers, and a stubble of beard, in his dingy, little office, cluttered with blueprints. A tattered sofa looked as though it might be used as a bed. Brewer's ash trays were loaded with butts. There were empty bottles in a corner under some old newspapers and trade magazines, but the old man was sober.

He greeted Tom Cable as an old friend, and, on hearing that Burns was Canadian representive for Cable's company, on a routine visit to confer in Chicago with Cable, he told of the disappointing trip that he had made to Montreal. He was discouraged and expressed doubt that his water cooler would ever be sold in volume. When Burns mentioned that Acme had represented Frigidaire quite successfully and still had access to the Frigidaire compressor in Canada, the old man spent the next half hour attempting to convince Burns that Acme should handle his device, on a very reasonable royalty basis. Burns allowed himself to be convinced. The royalty was established at fifty cents per unit, payable in cash on receipt of the first firm order from Canadian railways. Most important to Shafer was the fact that if Canadian railroads used the design, some U.S. railroads would do so.

The three of them crossed the Loop to the Wrigley Building and the office of Bevis L. Buckley, vice-president of Eagle Steel Foundries. There, Buckley had Eagle Steel's legal department draw up the agreement, as dictated by Burns, in legal form for Shafer's execution. While it was being typed. Buckley joined

them for lunch, as Tom Cable's guests at the Chicago Athletic Club. They were careful to limit the drinks to Shafer so that he would be in shape to sign the documents and deliver all of the drawings and specifications for Burns to take back to Canada with him.

Three days later, Burns delivered a quotation to both Canadian railroads on thirty thousand electric water coolers. The drawings that accompanied the tender bore Acme's label, but were traced from Shafer's drawings by the same engineers that were called upon to approve the purchase. Acme received an order worth nine hundred and fifteen thousand dollars, to be delivered over one year.

Henry Hopkins would notice the invoices as deliveries were made from month to month. He would enter them in his little black books. He would rub his hands gleefully as he totalled up the profits, alone in his office, at the end of the year.

Chapter 10

It was possible to review further the significance of events of the day before, as the 727 jet thundered south.

Al Lette was the only regular staffer to come in on Boxing Day. The fat little man was at his desk. While Burns organized material that he would need to pack for his Mobile trip, Lette bustled back and forth between his outer office desk and the file room. Vivian Stuart phoned in from Sainte Saveur Ski Lodge at nine ten. She offered to be there within a couple of hours if needed. Burns thanked her and suggested that she enjoy her holiday, as he expected to spend several hours with Henry Hopkins. Any time left him would be spent in dictation on tape which she could transcribe while he was in Mobile.

As expected, based on the experience of the past years, the old man arrived about eleven o'clock. The snow had stopped over the holiday, but it was very cold in Montreal. Hopkins must have walked from the station. He stopped inside the general office to wipe off the fog which had formed on his spectacles when the warm air met the cold glass. His face was red from the cold and his eyes were watering. Burns took the usual thirty minutes Hopkins required alone to review, once more, the scrap tapes that Lette had provided.

Gathering up several files, he knocked discreetly before entering the big office. They chatted about Christmas day, the antics of the Hopkins grandchildren on Christmas morning, and the bullshit in the Christmas broadcast by the queen. As they

talked, Burns arranged his files on his side of the big, black desk. Hopkins' wispy, grey hair was still molded to his head by the band of his hat. He fished the black notebooks from the big brief-case, before beginning his yearly lecture.

"Y'know, Alton you've been in the business less than three years, now. I've been in it for thirty-five. One year business is up; next year it's down. Y'can't do much about it, except stay on your toes and get as much of it as you can. It just depends on how the railroad traffic is; how many new cars and locomotives they can buy. Same with the repairs and renovations, even. If they got the traffic, they'll buy: if they haven't got it, they won't.

"Now, you have been lucky enough to see two good years in a row, each year better than the one before. But don't let that fool ya. We're probably due for a bad one next year. Never saw three good years in a row since Sir Giles' day. Why, I remember one year, let's see, it was the first year that I was a vice-president, we did almost two million in sales. That was twenty-three, twenty-four years ago. I had been with the company only about ten years, then. Sir Giles was president. That was the year he died while grouse hunting. The profit for the year was almost a quarter of a million, and there was no God-damn income taxes then. My salary was five thousand a year and no bonus. There was no big office staff; no God-damn accountants looking over your shoulder. The profit was all gravy. The next year, after Sir Giles died, we dropped to about a million and a half, and we hung around that, give or take a hundred thousand, for the next twenty years. The profits kept coming down, though. We had to have more God-damn staff, with accountants making things com-plicated. Working our God-damn heads off, we got down to mak-ing only about fifty grand profit, and the taxes cut into that.

"The last three years have been lucky ones. This year we hit the jackpot. Don't think you will see these figures again in my time. I don't want you to get any wrong ideas from one fluky year. I thought my figures were wrong when I first totalled 'em. But I've double-checked with the bank statements. We did three and a half million in round figures last year. The profit before taxes and bonuses. . . ," and he looked at Burns over his glasses

to observe the effect of his announcement, "will be about one hundred and fifty-five thousand. Not bad, eh!" He beamed across the desk, expecting Burns to look astounded.

The figure that Burns had derived from Al Lette's trashbasket tapes was more like one hundred and ninety thousand profit on a volume of three million, seven hundred and sixty thousand. Still, Burns managed an expression that satisfied Hopkins.

"We got a lotta breaks, this year, like those water coolers in the last half and the way Jules Lamont swung those spring orders over to us. Now, I figure that you are entitled to a bonus of. . . lessee. . . had it here. . . yeah, here it is. . . seven thousand two hundred fifty-six dollars and forty cents. Pretty good, eh, for a guy who has been in the business only three years? Wish they had given me that when I was your age, thirty years ago. But as I say, Alton, you can't expect that every year. Don't you go living high just because you got this big bonus this year. If we can just hang in there around two million to two million and a half, we'll be OK."

When Burns had agreed to join the firm, Hopkins had hoped to control expenses in bad years by offering the lowest salary plus a bonus in good years. The salary was only ten thousand dollars yearly, about what Burns was already earning. The bonus was the carrot that Hopkins held out. Burns may have known more about the potential for increased business than Hopkins did, at the time. Burns accepted an incentive bonus to be paid at the end of each year, equal to five percent of the gross profits of the company, before taxes and other bonuses. A contract was drawn up accordingly. How this figured out to seven thousand two hundred and fifty-six dollars and forty cents, Burns did not know. From the calculations on Lette's scrap tapes, it should have worked out closer to nine thousand five hundred dollars. While it was not in accordance with the contract, Hopkins may have deducted all of the staff bonuses, including his own, before calculation of what was due to Burns. However, Burns decided to make no show of disappointment. There would be another year. Instead, he held out his hand to Hopkins.

"Thanks, Henry. I can use it. I am quite sure that we can

come close to doing as well next year. There's a few new things coming up. The new Char Lake thing . . ."

Hopkins interrupted. "Yeah, you mentioned that, but don't bank on these new schemes. Just stick to the old business, boy, and you won't be disappointed. Just keep it around that two-and-a-half-million mark. Now, I suppose that you need the cash. I'll have a check for you before the end of the month."

"No, Henry, as a matter of fact, I think that I should exercise my option and become more involved in the firm this year. It is only fair to you and will conserve cash to finance additional business, if we can get it next year. I'll take twenty shares of the company stock and the small balance in cash, if it's OK with you."

Hopkins was pleased. He never liked paying out cash. It was just with this in mind that the clause had been written into Burns' contract, permitting him to take all or any part of his bonus in any year in company stock at three hundred and fifty dollars per share. This figure was based on the book value of the company at the date of his employment.

It was arranged that Burns' pay check on January first would include the balance of the bonus, amounting to some two hundred and fifty dollars and forty cents. Burns was quite sure how the forty cents was included. How the full bonus was calculated would remain a mystery. Hopkins had always refused to answer any questions about the accounting, while he was the sole shareholder of record. He did not have to. The books were audited for tax purposes around the first of March. Only Hopkins was entitled to see the report. However, when Hopkins participated in making a quotation, he insisted upon adding a few odd cents to it, even if the total ran in the hundreds of thousands. "Makes it look honest, you know. Looks like you figured it down to the last cent."

Hopkins was not surprised that the younger man did not want cash. While Burns' salary was modest, his needs were also modest, when he was not on the expense account. He worked long hours, seven days a week, and he traveled or entertained much of that time. His opportunities to spend his own money

were limited. The first year Hopkins had worried about paying Burn's expense accounts. However, they were so detailed that he did not feel able to question them, particularly with the orders coming in. Hopkins did so little entertaining and traveling himself, he was never sure what was reasonable.

Hopkins did inquire casually about the Christmas expense.

"You had enough in the kitty to give some good presents to your railroad buddies this year, eh?"

"Yes, they were will taken care of, thanks to Edison."

The reference was to Thomas A. Edison of Canada, a company set up by Acme many years before to manufacture the Edison nickel-iron-alkaline storage battery in Canada. It was operated out of a small converted garage in downtown Montreal. When Burns had suggested some more personal or cash gifts to men credited with helping Acme to secure some large order, the problem arose as to where to get the cash without showing disbursement in the books of the company. Burns suggested that the Edison battery manufacturing operation be placed in his hands. This activity generated a great deal of valuable scrap in the form of nickel, lead, and steel, which just seemed to disappear, before it could be accumulated in salable quantity. For the past two years, Burns had insisted that the shop foreman keep the valuable scrap under lock and key. Each November, he had been able to locate a scrap dealer of questionable ethics who would buy the scrap for cash, no questions asked. The funds from this amounted to over five thousand dollars. As it was revenue that had never been recovered before, Hopkins preferred not to be told the amount involved, or what was done with it. This was the source of the "goodies" in the sealed envelopes that Burns delivered on Christmas Eve.

Hopkins had the expression of someone who was having difficulty containing some real big news. Finally, it came.

"Now, I've got a surprise for you, boy."

For the fifth time, he reminded Burns that he had been with the company only three years. "Thurston is pulling the pin at the end of the year."

Burns was supposed to look surprised. He did his best.

"Y'know what I'm gonna do, boy? After only three years, I'm gonna make you a vice-president. How do you like them apples?"

Burns wondered what he was expected to say. They both knew that George Thurston had been coasting for years. He feigned surprise and thanked Hopkins for the wonderful opportunity.

"Now we have to think of the money, I suppose."

This was the part that Hopkins did not enjoy. Burns made him feel better at once.

"You know that my personal needs are not great, Henry. I am in my thirties. I have accepted this company as a career. My prime interest, at this time, is to see it successful and grow, if possible. As long as I have enough to finish putting my two kids through another year of college, with what they earn in the summer, I can wait until later to acquire a nest egg, just as you did, Henry."

"Y'know, Alton, you think like me. That's why I picked you out of that rut you were in on the railroad. If you can help me to keep our sales at two and a half million with profit around a couple of hundred thousand, like this year . . . uh, I mean around one hundred and fifty thousand." Hopkins looked embarrassed as he caught his slip too late, but he went on. "Cut your cloth to suit your garment, you know what I mean, when it comes to your expense account and the office overhead. We'll get along fine. You'll be happy and I'll be happy. I won't interfere with you and you won't get in my hair. My wife wants to do some traveling in Europe this year, maybe around the world this year. We can afford it. You will be on your own a lot. Personally, I'd rather take it easy in the garden, but you know women, always wantin' something different." Hopkins caught himself. "Sorry, Alton. How's the wife?"

"Seems to be doing fair."

Burns did not elaborate. He shuffled some of his papers and Hopkins changed the subject.

"Oh, yeah, I fergot to mention, the wife and I made you a director at our annual meeting."

Burns knew that there was no annual meeting, as such.

Hopkins had another afterthought. "Yeah, and I guess you will be entitled to a little dividend, too, when, and if, we decide to declare one."

Hopkins was still skirting the salary matter. Any increase in Burns' salary he saw coming right out of his own pocket, as it were. Burns saw his opening.

"I was hoping that you might defer the annual meeting until I got back from my trip. I may have some news that will affect our plans for next year."

Hopkins was frowning as Burns went on. He did not believe in new railroads, new products, new schemes. He preferred to deal with things that he knew about and understood.

"If you really want to declare a dividend based on the earnings of last year, you may wish to make it a deferred dividend. We may need a little extra working capital next year, and I know how you like to avoid bank loans. As a matter of fact, I was going to bring this up in connection with the increase in my salary. I feel that the company will want to recognize the promotion with an increase, but I am as interested as you are in keeping the overhead down, particularly this year."

"Good thinking, boy. My own thoughts exactly. We'll have another annual meeting when you get back, not that your vote will mean anything. Twenty shares against nine hundred and eighty, eh?" Hopkins softened the remark with his nervous guffaw. He was, as usual, anxious to keep the young fellow in his place.

Burns, however, was determined that there should be a formal annual meeting this year for another reason. As a bona fide shareholder, he wanted to make sure that responsible accounting was set up. At the end of next year he did not want to be at the mercy of Hopkins' black books when bonuses were calculated. Hopkins would undoubtedly oppose the move, but under law, a minority shareholder had more rights than Hopkins might realize. Burns continued, with one sweet and one sour.

"I would like to attend, Henry. One motion that I will place on the record, as your baby shareholder, is that the company purchase a new Cadillac for its president. Since I am going to ask

for a basic salary of only twelve thousand five hundred, I think that the company should be able to afford such a prestige item. It will reduce our taxes, as we can charge it off to sales expense, advertising, or whatever. You know, Henry, I can look after the vice-presidents, but you, as president, should keep in touch with the railway presidents. I think that a Caddy would help both you and the firm.”

Burns knew that Hopkins had always had a weakness for a good car. He had often indicated a desire to drive a Cadillac, but his own background, as much as anything else, had made him reluctant to acquire one. Hopkins’ younger wife had mentioned, after a few drinks at a cocktail party, that she had urged him to buy one. He could have afforded it. As for entertaining or associating with railroad presidents, Burns was quite sure that Hopkins would avoid this. As a former mechanic, he was much more at home with the railway shopmen. He avoided dealing with executives whenever he could. Nevertheless, Hopkins was obviously pleased with the idea. Burns could see him explaining to the neighbors, in the working class district where he still lived, “Aw, I didn’t want the God-damn thing, but the boys in the firm insisted.”

Burns’ mention of the salary he expected relieved Hopkins greatly. While he was quite sure that his own salary was confidential, since he signed his own check, he was afraid that Thurston, at some time, might have divulged that he was paid eighteen thousand. Hopkins had been concerned that Burns might expect as much as twenty thousand, considering how hard he worked, and the responsibilities that he had assumed. The old man was surprised and relieved, but Burns had a bomb to drop now, and he did it carefully.

“Henry, I realize that in the past couple of years you have given me a chance for a satisfying career and a chance to show what I can do with this company. I think that I have made some money for you. I am not too concerned about my personal earnings at the moment. I’m interested in the future. I want to see this company grow. Some ideas are crystallizing in my mind as to how this can be done. What the company was when I came to

it is a credit to you and your staff, not to any effort of mine. On the other hand, I will expect some credit for significant improvements in yearly results over and above that. I intend to work my ass off to effect expansion of profits. Rather than a big salary now, I would like to talk about earned incentives."

Hopkins was looking more and more apprehensive at this talk of new ideas and expansion. However, he told himself, there was little need to worry about it now. The salary matter had been settled. He would put a stop to this increased incentive business.

"Don't tell me y'want more bonus. Y'got over seven thousand this year. You've only been with the company three years and you get five percent of the profit, on top of your salary. What more could you want? No soap, young fellah! Your bonus contract is a God-damn good one. We signed a five-year contract, remember! You are not suggesting that we tear it up, are you?"

"Not at all, Henry. It's a good contract for both of us. I made over seven thousand, by your figures. The stockholders, you and your wife, made one hundred and forty-three thousand, less taxes, when it is distributed. I'm happy with that and, I am sure that you are too, right?"

Hopkins nodded, mollified, as Burns went on.

"I know that you consider this a sort of freak good year; that we may never reach this volume again for awhile, if ever. If we don't then I am not suggesting that we change a thing. I'm happy to work under the present bonus contract. The only thing that I am going to ask is some additional incentive, if, by some superhuman effort or some good break, some year, I can increase the profit over one hundred and fifty thousand."

Hopkins was thinking of the Cadillac, as Burns continued. "As I said, Henry, I am not suggesting that we change a single word in the contract. I would just like to add an addendum to it, providing for an additional twenty-five percent of our company profits over and above one hundred and fifty thousand in an exceptional year. This only means that if we ever do better than this year, the additional bonus will not cost a cent. You just make seventy-five percent of the additional profit. You can't lose, Henry."

Hopkins thought it over. He was conscious that he had understated the profit this year, and if they did as well next year, and Burns had the correct figures, Burns' bonus might be five or six thousand more. How would Burns find out anyway? He was sure that it would not happen again. Why worry about it now? His mind wandered back to the Cadillac. He was anxious to get home and break the news to his wife. Would she select blue or white? A friend of hers had a white one. A little too flashy, but she liked it.

"OK, Alton, it's a deal. If you make this company over a hundred and fifty thousand in any year, before taxes and bonuses, you will deserve something extra. As a matter of fact, you would probably take the extra in the form of a few more shares in the company, wouldn't you? We'll write that in. If you draft up what you want and leave it on my desk, I'll have the lawyers draw up your addendum first thing tomorrow. I'll sign it so you'll have it as soon as you get back from that wild goose chase to—where is it? Mobile, yeah! And be sure to put it in a sealed envelope. Your salary is your own business, you know."

They shook hands cordially, Burns picked up his papers and went to his own office. He accepted a short typed message from Lette. There was a party waiting for him in the Red Lantern Bar on Stanley Street.

Chapter 11

The girl sat alone in the dimly lit room. She glanced frequently at the door, as she toyed with a glass of wine. Her dark coat was thrown open. From the door she appeared as a blurry, seated figure with large, luminous eyes and a narrow gleam of white teeth.

A man entered from Stanley Street. He stood a moment at the door while his eyes adjusted to the darkness. He saw her eyes and selected the aisle where she was seated. He stopped at her table and spoke to her in a low voice. She looked directly at him and said nothing. He hesitated then moved on to speak to two girls seated near the rear. They accepted his offer and he joined them.

The girl twisted her glass without drinking. Eyes accustomed to the darkness, she could see quiet figures in other booths without being conscious of them. When the man approached, she hardly knew that he was there. She felt that her chance of a lifetime was at hand and she felt desperate. She rehearsed again what she would say. She knew that she was attractive. She liked men and she knew that she had a power over them, but those she met were of the wrong kind. Would she have the confidence to handle the right kind?

Coming in from the afternoon light, reflected off an icy sidewalk, Burns could see nothing at first, except the brightly lit check room at his right. Burns recognized the check room girl as a luncheon waitress from Desjardin's Seafood Restaurant. Like many waitresses, she probably spent evenings at the Red Lantern, turning a trick once in awhile to amuse herself and pick up

an extra buck. The location was good, next to a second-rate hotel known in Montreal as the riding academy. Off duty firemen from the firehall on the other side acted as bouncers so that a businessman could feel assured of safety and privacy at the hotel.

"Allo, Monsieur Burns." She took his coat. "Tird boot on your right, somebodee waits you." Without looking in that direction, she joined her thumb and forefinger in an "O" sign.

As he came close enough to see her distinctly, he marvelled again at her attractiveness and animal beauty. He wondered about her choice of a meeting place. She smiled at his approach, but made no move to make room on her side of the table, so he seated himself opposite. She said nothing as he ordered a drink from the waitress who followed him to the table. When they were alone, she spoke in the husky voice that he recalled from their first meeting in the Pick.

"I suppose that you worked all through the holidays."

His eyes still not fully adjusted to the darkness, he could see, first those slanting cat's eyes, the wide mouth framing white teeth, then, the high cheekbones, and the red dress, gradually separating itself from the olive skin at the deep cleavage between her breasts.

"Do you know my name, Mr. Burns?"

"No, should I? I've admired you a hundred times on the train, and, by the way, I looked for you this morning."

"I did not go to work today. In fact, I have not been home since you saw me in the Pick. We stayed in the hotel that night and then I stayed with my sister at her apartment on Colonial Street."

Her eyes searched his face for a reaction to the reference to one of the worst streets in Montreal's red light district. She continued, still speaking very slowly, "Tonight I must be home early. I told my father that I was visiting friends over the holiday. He will be worried." She was making it clear that this meeting would not be prolonged.

After a pause, she looked into her glass and continued, "I am called Sandra Sands, but my real name is Casandra Sandosi. Does that mean anything to you?"

"Should it?"

"Perhaps not. It is a long story. I will tell it in a little time, if you are not in a hurry. It will explain why I wished to talk to you."

She was not being coy. Her tone was friendly, but businesslike. In spite of her cool appearance, her slow, studied sentences gave him a feeling that she spoke under tension.

"It seems that I know more of you than you do of me. I know that you are an engineer. In the old countries, you would be called *doktor*. You know all of the important men on the railways here and you know important Americans who do business with railways here. Executives of foundries and factories are your friends. I know, because you entertain these people a lot. They mean much to you. You work very hard. You entertain these men at night and then at lunch, too. Your home must not be happy, because you always entertain alone, even when your friends have their wives. I have my information because I know the night people of Montreal and they tell me. Am I right so far?"

"One hundred percent."

"You often use girls to entertain. That is not a question for you to answer. Sometimes they could help you more if they knew how. You treat them well, right?"

Burns nodded. "Go on, please."

"Then, I think that I can interest you. I will not take long. Years ago, your company, Acme Railway Supply Company, had a president called Sir Giles Humbolt. It began as a very small company, but he was a very big man and very clever. He made the company rich and much bigger. He did much entertaining, as you do, but he did it better, I think, if you will excuse me, please."

The waitress brought Burns a double Scotch and a bottle of soda water. The girl took the balance of the bottle of soda and added it to dilute her Dubonnet, before resuming. She still talked slowly, as though she had rehearsed.

"My father was Roumanian. His family operated iron foundries in the old country before the First World War. He was big and handsome, six foot, eight inches, and almost three hundred

pounds. He was a metallurgist. He was the sales manager for the family. He sold castings and steel all around southeastern Europe, in Turkey. He was very successful. He liked fun, liquor, beautiful women of many countries. He met my mother in Ankara. Her mother was Turkish. Her father, that she never knew, must have been Mongol, because my mother, like me, had Oriental looks. But, of course, she was much more beautiful. She was a girl of the streets and cafes. My father loved her. He brought her to Bucharest. My sisters and myself, we were born there. In the war my father's family lost everything. He brought us to Canada, with no money and no English. The only things that he knew about were steel and iron foundries. He hung around the gates of Standard Steel Foundries waiting for a job. He did something for Sir Giles. I think that there was a fight at the gate, a strike or something. Sir Giles was trying to get Standard Steel to make castings for Eagle Steel Foundries in the States. He asked the president of Standard Steel to give my father a job. He still works there, but they no longer make Eagle Steel castings. You have some other foundry now. My father was sorry about that, but he will retire next July with a pension.

"While my father looked for work, and even after he started to work for Standard Steel, he earned little. My mother went back to what she did in Ankara to feed and clothe us. My father did not approve, but she was still very beautiful and brought home much money. She loved my father and served him always, when he came home from the hot foundry. He went to bed early at night because he got up early. Then my mother went out. With the money she brought home, my father bought the nicest houses of any of the immigrants in Rosemount. We grew up speaking Roumanian, then Italian, and later French. After we moved to Outremont, where we live now, we learned English.

"Sir Giles had no wife. When he met my mother through my father, and found what she did, he asked her to work for him, entertaining railway officials here. My father accepted it, as they were gentlemen and treated my mother well. She liked to wear nice clothes and to be with important people. Sir Giles employed her most of the time when he was in the city. She brought

enough home that we were able to get a good education. We moved to a better neighborhood.

"My mother was not only beautiful, but she was clever. She listened and she understood big business. Sir Giles told my father that she was his best salesman. Even though I was very young, I can remember her telling my father of the big deals that she helped Sir Giles to make. She would often read to us references in the paper. My father never learned to read English. It was all very romantic to us. We were proud of her. Mother received large cash bonuses sometimes. She brought everything home to my father.

"When I was twelve, my mother died, after a terrible illness. My father hired the best doctors. It took most of his savings. Sir Giles would have helped, but he died in Scotland that year. There was no one else to help.

"After that, my father went to pieces. The foundry lost Sir Giles' account. My father never had the same interest. Times were bad at the foundry. He worked only part time. He began to hang around the rough bars on St. Laurent Main. We were left to look after ourselves, my two sisters and I. My father stayed drunk for a whole week once and married a very bad French-Canadian girl, only three years older than my sister. He brought her home to live with us. She just went on doing what she had done before in the cheap bars. We hated her. She was not like my mother. She did not know nice people. She was not pretty. She did not make meals or keep the house clean. She brought no money home. She dressed badly and sold herself for whatever she could get. I think that she went with men for nothing when she needed a drink, which was always. She started selling my older sister when she was only fifteen. When my father found out, he beat her. He was afraid for my younger sister.

"My baby sister looks different. She is blonde, like my father's people. She was always his favorite. She was not as strong as my sister and I. Because of her, he kicked the woman out. She hangs around the bars yet, but she stays away from my father. He does not go to the bars anymore. He is a good man. When he leaves his work, he will die.

"My oldest sister lives with her pimp on Colonial Street. He takes all of her money. I feel sorry for her. He is a bad man. He is a runner for a gangster. He runs the *barbotte*. He sells drugs. My sister is still pretty, but she has no future at all. My father does not talk to her.

"My younger sister married very young to a French-Canadian boy, whose family has a poor farm in Gaspe'. They have four children. They live with his family. They have no money. She cannot bring her children to see their grandfather. My father would like to see them.

"As for myself, I have tried everything. I have no special training, even though I speak four languages well. I have worked as a waitress in the Downbeat Club. That is not much better than being a street girl. I like clothes and I can wear them well. I have tried being a saleswoman. I have worked as a model and still do sometimes. It is not steady work. I work in a garment loft in the East End as a receptionist-model. The money is poor and I have to fight off the foreman, the fat Jewish owner, and his son every time I change clothes. They threaten to fire me when I do not feel like cooperating. I take the occasional date from a call girl madame if I know something of the man. I do not mind. My body is mine and I have no pimp, but I have to split fifty dollars with the madame.

"I like men, and they like me. They never treat me badly. I think that I have some brains up here as well as down there, Mr. Burns. I think that I could do for you what my mother did for Sir Giles. With my knowledge and education, I could do better. My requirements are not much. I love my father, but I do not want to live with him until he dies. He has a Roumanian friend that he can live with. I need an apartment downtown, where I could bring my sister to live with me. I would need about two hundred a week to be available whenever you needed me. I would like a bonus when I help you to make a big deal, to save for a dowery, perhaps." She spoke a little wistfully.

Burns listened, hypnotized by the direct gaze of those extraordinary eyes. Her proposal, he now realized that was what it was, made him think of the possibilities. He was paying girls

now, cigarette girls in nightclubs, call girls, often more than two hundred dollars a week. The difficulty was that when he needed someone to help in a deal, the right type was not available and he had to settle for less suitable and sometimes dangerous types. She was right when she suggested that some girls that he used were not as helpful as if they knew what they were doing and why. Most could not be depended upon to understand how to further a sale by a subtle word or a come-on at the right time. If that big Char Lake job did materialize—if it did—this girl might be very, very helpful.

Burns was silent. She sipped her drink, put it down, pulled her coat tightly about her generous breasts, symbolically wrapping up the merchandise that she had offered. She put it frankly.

"That's why I thought that we should have a talk, Mr. Burns. Do I interest you?"

She was more at ease now. She had made her pitch and was ready to leave. At the last question, there was a glint of an invitation in those inscrutable eyes.

"Can I have a week to think it over, Sandra?"

"This is strictly between us, Mr. Burns. I have told you that I have no pimp. I will deal with no one but you. I work for only one boss at a time."

"I understand. Can I drop you off somewhere? It is very cold outside."

"No, thank you. There is a train in a few minutes. I will call you next week. You can't call me. Say a week from today at four o'clock?"

"A week from today at four. I'll be waiting for your call. Good-bye, Sandra."

She left him to finish his drink. The bar felt empty.

Chapter 12

After the dull skies and bitter cold of Montreal, the weather in Mobile was like spring. The sun was low over the live oaks of the tree-lined streets as the Gulf station wagon twisted and turned toward the Mobile Arms. The top coat, slight protection against the cold enroute to the airport in Montreal, felt heavy here.

Burns was too busy, silently rehearsing, again, his presentation to Lou Waldorf, to talk to the driver. At the hotel, he pressed a ten dollar bill into the hand of the mildly protesting chauffeur. He might need the man again. If Waldorf reacted as he hoped, he would leave town quickly, before Waldorf could think up a compromise. Whatever happened, he knew that he must meet Buckley in Chicago Firday morning, at the latest. Perhaps Joe would offer the use of a U.S. Motors plane, if he obtained a favorable response from Waldorf.

Finding his way to the small hideaway on the third floor, Burns was greeted by a swarthy short, heavy-set man with a bristling black moustache and wavy black hair.

"Well, well, well, Alton, you surprised the hell out of me when you phoned. Take off your coat. Take off your shoes. Mine's been off all afternoon, while I waited for you. Have a drink, I'm about six up on you. This my cheese? I'll take it. Scotch and water, no ice, right? Never forget a friend's drink, especially when you've had about ten thousand with him!"

Six drinks never showed on Waldorf. He acted the same after a dozen as he did after his morning eye-opener. Burns noted that he had gained weight. Waldorf had always bragged that there

was more cloth in the ass of his pants than it took to make Burns a suit. If the lower part of his body grew any more, it occurred to Burns, that could well be true.

"Good to get away from winter and see you at the same time, Lou."

"You turned out to be a lifesaver for me, too. No chance at all to get way from the old lady this week. I couldn't even dream up an emergency. She knows all the wives here. You can't get away with a God-damn thing in a small railroad town like this. I was bored shitless. You can always get lost in Montreal. Remember our last convention there. What was that little French broad's name, Veronica, Vera? It doesn't matter. She could work up the greatest blow job.

"I told the wife that you were coming in on urgent Railway Association business. She always thought you were some kind of goody-goody guy, bringing your daughter along to those conventions. You always looked as though butter wouldn't melt in your mouth, always had to leave those God-damn boring mixed affairs early to put your daughter to bed. They didn't know what you did when you sneaked out afterwards with the stag guys. She told me to go ahead and meet you alone. Only thing is, I have to bring you over to the house later."

"I don't know how much time that you can give me, Lou. I do know that I have to get to Chicago, but I had to see you first. Something came up last week that is very important to my career as a supply man."

"You know, Alton, I'll help any way I can. Let's talk. Couple of girls from the office pool are coming over for a drink after work—but you can't tell about them. They won't be like those broads in Montreal. Best I could do in this fucking town. Last time I invited 'em they didn't show. They're not so hot looking either but they don't talk. I have ways to make sure of that. Now, what's the panic?"

"I'll get right to it, Lou. You can solve my problems in a minute—and you are the only guy that can help me in this."

A wary look crossed Waldorf's face.

"No, Lou, I don't want to sell you anything. I don't operate

in the U.S., only in Canada. It's that good memory of yours that can help me."

Waldorf looked relieved and poured another Scotch, as Burns continued.

"We manufacture and sell Precision bearings for railway cars and locomotives in Canada . . .

"That's U.S. Motors, the chiseling bastards."

"I don't know why you say that, Lou. Joe Morton has been a good friend of yours and mine. He heads up the Precision Bearing Division. You and I know that each division of U.S. Motors operates independently. Joe Morton has to produce, and I have to produce in Canada, regardless of what the other divisions do."

Waldorf started to say something, but Burns went on, before he had the chance.

"The Canadian A. & P. Railroad buys Precision bearings from my company in Canada. They are budgeting a million dollars to buy bearing replacements next year. As a new representative, I've got to get this order. You can help me in Canada, Lou, regardless of what you think of the people at U.S. Motors in the U.S."

"But these bastards at the Locomotive Division . . . "

"I don't know anything about the Locomotive Division, Lou. I do know that you and I, Lou, we are both on record as stating that the Precision hearing is the best design available in the U.S.A. or Canada. Four years ago, after tests with Eagle Steel's test train, you, as chairman, made a report to the general committee of the Railroad Association. Do you recall that? You signed it and I signed it. We agreed that the cylindrical bearings gave the best ride, the longest life, and resulted in least wear to other running gear parts. We submitted this confidential report to the general committee. It was not published because Precision was the only supplier of the cylindrical-type of bearing and still is, although several other manufacturers are trying to develop one now. The general committee was afraid that publication of your report would put other bearing manufacturers out of business.

"Now, Lou, the president of your own railroad was a member of that general committee at that time. I presume that is

why you always bought Precision bearings. The A. & P. Railroad in Canada did not have a member on the committee. They know nothing of this report. They may consider using some other types. All I need to convince them to use all Precision bearings is permission to show them that confidential report that you signed. That is why I had to see you face to face, Lou."

"Lemme see that God-damned report. You got it there? Yeh! I did sign it. Bloody well forgot about it, to tell you the truth, Alton. God-damnit, don't tell this to a God-damn soul. I was about to award all of the bearing business on our new program to another company. I just wanted to get even with those bastards in the Locomotive Division."

"Jesus, you couldn't do that, could you, Lou? Suppose your president remembers your report. We would both look like some kind of nuts."

"Guess so! Guess I'll have to use Precision, God-damnit!"

"Can I tell the A. & P. people that, Lou, and show them this report?"

"Yeah, God-damnit. What else can I do? We'll be using Precision, but don't tell those guys at U. S. Motors, yet. I want the bastards to sweat a little. Now, let's do some serious drinking. Glad you came down, Alton. God-damnit, I would have looked a little stupid, wouldn't I?"

"Just one more little thing, Lou. Would you object if Precision bearings were furnished with a small Zerk fitting set flush in the middle of the cover. It will not cost you one cent extra. When the cover is painted, no one will know it is there. It will never be used."

"Why in hell would you want a Zerk fitting in the cover of a sealed, grease-packed bearing."

"Look, Lou, I said that it won't cost you a cent. It won't do any harm; it won't do any good. No one will know that it's there, but it will help solidify my order from the A. & P., you understand, Lou. I may be able to do the same with some useless patent for you some day. You don't have to ask for it, just accept it, will you, Lou?"

"I get it. You are learning the peddlers' game fast. Some-

body's personal idea. Somebody gets a little grease in the form of a royalty. I understand. No skin off my ass. More power to him. I think that I know who it is. Let's drink to him."

"Here's to you, Lou, and your help today. You've made me happy. I don't really care whether your girls come now or not. There will be plenty in Chicago. Since you solved my problem, I just want to get the first plane out. I've got a tight schedule. We'll celebrate another time, after I get my order."

Waldorf looked relieved. He had done his best to arrange entertainment for his friend to repay him for accommodations in Montreal. He had, as Burns suspected, had difficulty convincing office girls to devote an evening fighting off a couple of older men in a hotel room. Burns had long since given up on using unpaid office girls for entertaining businessmen. You were never sure that they would please the right man in the right way at the right time, leaving him feeling that he was God's gift to women.

After another drink, Burns offered best wishes and thanks for Waldorf to take home to his wife. He insisted on going to the airport alone to wait on standby for the first flight north. Waldorf objected, but finally agreed to have his driver take Burns alone.

As he stood at the ticket counter in the airport, he felt a heavy arm about his shoulders. Joe Morton was hatless, his tie askew, his suit wrinkled, and his eyes bloodshot.

"Y'know old buddy, you told me about what time you would arrive here. I got in an hour later from New Orleans. I just sat in that lil' ol' bar over there where I could see out the glass doors if you arrived alone. I reckoned I'd wait until you came to take a plane, even if it was tomorrow morning. My big worry was that ol' Waldorf might come to see you off. How did you make out? Are we getting some of the order? Or is he still going to cut us off for a lousy bottle of booze?"

"Just a minute, Joe. I haven't had a chance to say a word. You will get the whole order, with one little stipulation."

"That's OK! Do I have to suck his ass around a city block or something. I'll do it. I'll do it, to get that order."

"Calm down, Joe. You will get the order, all of it, with one little stipulation."

"Give it to me. We'll do it. What the hell is it?"

"All you have to do is furnish a fifty-cent Zerk fitting in the cover of every bearing furnished from now on in the United States and Canada."

"For that order we would put his fucking name on every bearing in nineteen karat gold leaf, but what in hell would he want a Zerk fitting in a sealed, grease-packed bearing for?"

"He does not want it, I do, so that I can sew up a big order for Acme on the A. & P. I want the fitting on every bearing furnished from now on. It will only cost you fifty cents for the fitting, and a dollar per bearing royalty on the patent."

"No problem. A lousy dollar and a half a bearing. We could afford five dollars on the volume we're talking about. But what's this patent bit? You can't get a patent on a screwy, useless idea like that."

"You are right, Joe. There is no patent and none will be granted, but there is a patent 'applied for' in Canada. For my purpose, that is as good as a patent granted, for the next three years. The patent situation is different in Canada, you know. I can apply for a patent on a piece of shit twisted like a pretzel. I can say that a patent is 'applied for' and no one can find out on what grounds, until the application is rejected. This takes about three years."

"Meanwhile, you're going to give someone a royalty, as long as you get an order from him. I understand. Enough said. You get your God-damn useless Zerk. You can decorate the bearing with ten of them, if you want."

"Good deal! Now, what are your plans, Joe. I want to get out of town before Waldorf finds out that we met here."

"We're going to New Orleans, rat neow, old buddy."

"Why? You said that you just came from there."

"I left my hat, coat, and briefcase in a lovely bar there, when I got to thinking and decided to come up here to meet you. I gotta go back to get them. I got a U.S. Motors plane here ready to go. Tomorrow morning we fly to Key West. I got a friend there I want you to meet. You see, I've been working for you while you were working for me, ol' buddy. My old friend, Jim

Murphy, is spending the holidays at Marathon and he has invited us to visit him there. You know who he is don't you?"

"President of M.A. Marra. Wonderful! Let's get out of here."

"We'll get our pilot out of the coffee shop."

As they walked, Morton filled in some background on Jim Murphy. "As you know, Marra has interests in steel companies. They have specialized in recent years on pelletizing poorer grades of iron ore. Recently, they have been working on the ore body in the Iron Mountain of Venezuela. They have another operation going in São Paula, Brazil. Most of their operations involve the building and operation of mining railroads. Most of the companies sell steel to U.S. Motors. U.S. Motors sells finished products to them. Our division sells them bearings, railroad and industrial types. Our reciprocal trading runs to many millions yearly. We scratch their backs, they scratch ours. One of our directors is on their board; one of theirs is on ours.

"This has made it easy for us to work with them in Venezuela. The Iron Mountain has been Jim Murphy's special baby. The Char Lake operation will be his, too, although he is supposed to be getting ready to retire. He is grooming young Matt Marra to take his place. Matt is a nice guy, but hard to get close to at this point. He is a grandson of the founder of the company. While we have not been able to get to Matt, the old man and I have spent a lot of time together. He is more my age. Most of their engineers are rammy, young types, so Jim and I spent many evenings together in Venezuela, playing rummy in the company club or just getting quietly drunk together.

"You will like him. He tries not to look it, but he is a mining man's man. Likes work, bourbon straight, and to hunt and fish, while he is thinking out a new deal.

"He bought a retirement home in Marathon, near Key West. He has ordered a custom-built sport fisher; intends to do a lot of fishing, like Hemingway, when he retires. But until the day he does, he will be the undisputed head of the company. Marra and all the rest take his orders. When I told him on the phone what you told me of young Marra's visit to Canada, we discussed your background. It was his idea that I bring you down to see him.

We are to stay at his place tomorrow night. We can stay for a week if we want to. He is a bachelor, never married. He would sure like it if we went fishing with him."

"You say that he does not have a boat yet. What does he do, charter?"

"He says that he has a large sport fisher being built at Rabovitch in West Palm Beach, but he is not rushing it, as he is only able to spend a few days at a time away from Pittsburgh until he retires."

"You have just given me an idea, Joe. Tom Cable, our good friend from Seaway Steel, is spending some time in Pompano Beach, at the Barefoot Mailman. He will be there now. He is sort of lost between wives. He's in the steel business. I'm sure that he knows Murphy. He loves deep sea fishing, and he is good at it. He has a friend who is one of the best sailfish captains in the Keys, Bill Brighton, out of Matecumbe. I'll call Tom. He will line up Brighton to cruise down to Hanlan's at Marathon for fishing on Thursday. He will give Murphy the sailfish experience of a lifetime."

"Sounds good! The old man will like that. You go phone. I'll pick up some bourbon for the road. There's probably lots on the plane, but we can't take chances, you know. You gotta be sure. When you finish phoning, go right through that gate. The U.S. Motors' Lodestar is on the first ramp to your right.

"OK! You haven't forgotten anything, have you, Joe?"

After some delay, while Tom Cable was paged and located in the bar of the Barefoot Mailman Hotel, Burns found his way to the Lodestar. Morton, already in his shirtsleeves, was pouring drinks for takeoff.

"Put your bags anywhere, Alton. We have the plane to ourselves. We'll stay at the St. Charles tonight. Company keeps a permanent suite there, you know. But when we land, we gotta go to Loie's Bar first. I gotta get my hat and coat and briefcase. Lovely place. You'll like it. We can pick us up a couple of lovely warm octoroons. Gets cold at night if you sleep alone in New Orleans."

Chapter 13

Jim Murphy was a tall man. His bovine head, his heavy, bushy, grey eyebrows, topped off by a full head of snow white hair, matched his imposing frame. His face was tanned and lined. His blue eyes were alert but kindly. In his shapeless corduroy slacks, sweat shirt, and sneakers, he looked the part of the retired godfather rather than the powerful figure of the boardrooms of Pittsburgh.

When Burns and Morton pulled up to the gate in the taxi from Key West, he handed a rake to the black man beside him. He walked briskly across the grounds, planted informally with colorful shrubs and tropical trees. The handyman put away the rake and followed him to the gate.

Murphy had been alone at his Florida villa since the day before Christmas. Today, he had been putting in time impatiently awaiting the arrival of his guests. He was tired of inactivity. He wanted to talk. Roughly taking the key from the servant, he unlocked the gate himself. After directing the man to take the bags, he turned to his visitors.

"What in hell delayed you guys? I've been waiting for you all morning. I can't stop thinking, and when I think something out, I like to be able to give some orders or, at least, talk it over with someone. Old Jeremiah thinks I'm going crackers when I start giving orders to palm trees."

He shook hands with Joe Morton first and then, extending his big hand, he looked at Burns intently.

"You don't need to introduce this guy, Joe. I place him now.

I wasn't sure when first Matt and then you described him. I did not know he was a Canadian. He gave a talk to the Association of Pneumatic Engineers at the Duquesne Club in Pittsburgh a couple of years ago. Dynamic braking on long trains. It was in connection with that wreck on the horseshoe curve. I was there when you spoke."

"Yes," Joe broke in, "Alton was chief mechanical engineer for the government railways in Canada, then. He was vice-chairman of the Railroad Association car construction committee. He is now vice-president of Acme Railway Supply Company up in Montreal. Acme has represented U.S. Motors since before there was a U.S. Motors. In fact, since the days when your old friend Morgan Hamilton was struggling with the first diesel locomotive in Cleveland. Precision Bearings Division was a small independent company then."

"You have a lovely, quiet place here, Mr. Murphy."

"Too quiet sometimes. But let's use first names. I'm Jim. Glad you could come down, Alton. I'm always glad to chin with Joe. Funny how all the good engineers seem to come from Michigan."

Burns said nothing. To mention that he had received his engineering training at night school from an obscure Canadian college would not enhance his credentials in this company. Nevertheless, he felt completely at home with the old man from the start. Like so many important people, he had the faculty to put others at ease.

"I instructed Matt to look you up in Montreal last week. He tells me that he talked to you. You see, I talk to Matt two or three times a day, wherever we are. He's a good boy, smart engineer, but he still consults with the 'old man' on anything important."

"Yes, I saw him, Jim. We had met before. We are to meet again next Tuesday, in Montreal. I did not expect that I would be meeting you beforehand."

"Good! Let's go in to get you two settled. The sun is not over the yardarm yet, but I'm sure that you can ignore that. I can."

Shown to their rooms in the rambling old house, they changed into bathing suits. The sound of ice clinking into tall glasses led them to the patio. Except for the side facing the pool, it was completely enclosed with bougainvillea and flowering vines. The pool looked inviting after the taxi ride. However, Murphy motioned to the marble-topped table where he had placed juleps of his own making. They pulled up chairs. He seated himself with his back to a long marble bench on which charts and maps were laid out. It was evident that the old man had been working during his holiday.

"We'll relax later. Try my juleps for size. I'm anxious to get some things off my mind. I'll fill in a little background so you will understand the situation now facing me.

"About twenty-five years ago, a trapper named Leduc was traveling over land by foot from Eskimo Point on Hudson's Bay to the Royal Canadian Mounted Police post at Char Lake in the North West Territories of Canada. This is just about one hundred and fifty miles from the Arctic Circle. It was just a trading post, an Eskimo village, of course, with an abandoned World War Two prisoner-of-war camp."

Murphy unrolled a large map and pinpointed the location on it.

"It was early July. That is the start of the short Arctic summer, when the days are twenty-four hours long. The snow was pretty well gone. The summer vegetation had not yet covered the rocks. About here, he came across a large outcropping of red ore. There had been copper finds to the southeast. Leduc thought that he might have one here. He registered a claim.

"An assay revealed that it was iron oxide. Even though it was shown to be about one hundred percent pure iron, he was disappointed. He turned the claim over to a Toronto mining promoter, who chose to ignore the fact that the ore body was too far from steel mills to be of any economic value in the forseeable future. The trapper got the price of a new grubstake and forgot about it.

"Many years later, the assay came to our attention. It was one of the highest grades ever found on the surface anywhere in the world. It contained less than one percent silica, the impurity

most troublesome in iron oxide. Unfortunately, the ore was still almost two thousand miles from the nearest steel mill. The Steep Rock mine at the Canadian Lake Head, while inferior in quality and covered with considerable overburden, was still producing. As it was brought up from greater depths and hydraulic mining was necessary, it was becoming very expensive. The Labrador and Carol Lake Mines, much closer to ports on the St. Lawrence Seaway, were producing ten million tons a year, but the ore had to have beneficiation. The U.S. mills were still getting about ninety percent of their new iron from their old 'sleeping giants,' the Mesabi, the Hibbing, and the Marquet ranges, all near to U.S. Great Lakes' ports.

"Mining operations in the Mesabi were becoming very costly, as silica ran to eight percent. We felt assured that there were always the Venezuelan deposits controlled by U.S. mills, and close to a seaport. The silica content was low. There seemed no real need to bring in Char Lake.

"Up until a matter of a few months ago, U.S. steelmakers had complacently relied on forecasts of reserves made forty years ago. No one sounded the alarm when three wars bit deeply into our reserves. The danger facing us was recognized when it was realized that scrap iron, old iron, we call it, is not being used in the same proportion today as when the old forecasts were made. As we dug deeper for lower quality, as inflation and labor costs mounted, there had been a gradual conversion of mills to processes requiring less scrap and more new high grade iron. While technological breakthroughs have permitted us to refine lower grades of ore-bearing materials, taconites and jasperites, this requires more lime, and more important today, more energy. The energy needed for beneficiating lower grade ore alone may be a critical factor, as we deplete our oil and gas reserves. Do you fellows follow me?"

They nodded and Murphy continued, "Now we face the fact that U.S. requirements ars being obtained only by depending upon twelve percent from Venezulea and eight percent from Canada. The Venezuelan situation could be dicey. We could be cut off at a critical time. The energy needed to make our own

ores, eighty percent of our requirements, usable was suddenly uncertain.

"The American Iron and Steel Institute rushed out a new survey. It indicated that the U.S. will require one hundred million tons of new high grade ore per year by 1980. We will have to get thirty percent of this now and forty percent, or forty million tons, from outside of the U.S. by 1980. With only ten million tons available from Canadian working mines now, and allowing for minimal depletion, we will have to get at least thirty million tons, each year, from new sources, starting next year.

"The steelmakers, including the three Canadian mills, are alarmed. First, we considered building a huge new beneficiating plant at Hibbing. The cost of over two hundred and seventy-five million for the first stage would be shared. This scheme had several disadvantages. There was the huge energy requirement. There was no hundred percent assurance that the reserves remaining at Hibbing and Mesabi would hold out the life of the facilities. The Canadian government, with its balance of payment problem, would not welcome a large investment by Canadian mills in a foreign country, not to mention the continuing drain of Canadian dollars to import the treated ore.

"I won't say how, but M.A. Marra now controls the Char Lake ore body. We will be the developer-operator for the consortium of steelmakers and bankers. We will be a major partner. We have fifteen trillion tons of proven good ore, literally lying on top of the ground. There is no overburden to remove. Mining costs will be cheapest in the world. The infrastructure is there. There is a townsite, built by the Canadian government during the Second World War, when it was the headquarters of the Keewatin Division of the Royal Canadian Mounted Police. There is a good Eskimo labor pool nearby. The Royal Canadian Airforce maintains a good airport for Arctic Patrol. Last, but not least, there is a hydroelectric power plant of 1750 killowatts, little used now, operated by the Northern Canada Power Commission arm of the Canadian government. The Canadian government is willing to increase capacity, as we require it.

"Now, gentlemen, we come to the problem, transportation to

Lake Head. Once there, we're home free. We have the Marra ore carriers to divert, as needed, from other ore operations. We have to get ore from Char Lake to Lake Head before the end of navigation next year, or some U.S. mills will close. Money is no problem. The budget is two hundred million. As I have said, gentlemen, money is no problem, time is."

Murphy laid out another map.

"The government railway has a line from the port of Churchill to Lake Head. While they don't want our trains, they are a common carrier. They have to take them, as long as they are safe and of the weight that their roadbed and bridges can handle. We must haul our own trains on our own tracks from Char Lake to Chruchill. We have to lay the rail line, but that is no problem. The route was surveyed before the panic and we have already laid half of the track on the frozen tundra. We can finish the line in a couple of months. Our problem is to get suitable cars and locomotives, and to get them fast. You designed the Steep Rock cars, Alton. We would like to use larger ones, because of the vast distances. But, as I have said, the capacity will be limited only by the maximum weight that the government roadbed and bridges can support at high speed. This, again, you must be most familiar with, Alton. Now you can see why we have picked you as the key to this operation before we even talked with you.

"However, I must caution you, frankly. Matt and I have discussed this matter. We intend to offer you a proposition to be our consultant on a temporary basis, until orders can be placed for the rolling stock. In doing so, we are very much aware that you will have a conflict of interest, which all three of us must handle very, very carefully. Specifications must be written so that all suppliers with good products or services to offer us may be considered—not just those products or services in which Acme has an interest."

Murphy hestitated and looked directly at Burns for a long moment.

"I, Jim Murphy, might personally prefer to deal with certain firms. M.A. Marra may have interlocking directorships with certain firms but there will be directors on the Char Lake board who

will have their own preferences, for one reason or another. We must never risk criticism for partiality. Do you understand? We are dealing with big business and powerful interests!"

Murphy looked Burns directly in the eye, again, as he stopped to finish his julep. All three men were silent as they contemplated the conflicts which could occur in the awarding of a two hundred million dollar order.

"Do you have a time schedule, Jim?"

"Yes, we do. Our critical path schedule calls for specifications and drawings to be ready, approved, and in the hands of the builders by February fifteenth. Orders must be placed by April first. This whole project will be in the hands of Matt Marra, reporting to me. Matt is a mining engineer and a good one. He is not a railway car or locomotive engineer. I am empowering him to hire a Canadian general manager and staff to get out the specifications and drawings at once. We hope that you will be able to help him, Alton.

"We will require about ten thousand cars to be delivered within one year, for the first stage, depending, of course, on the tonnage per car design selected, ninety tons, one hundred tons, or one hundred and twenty-five tons. We will need approximately one hundred locomotives in the first stage, depending again on the tonnage of the trains to be hauled.

"The first things to be decided are: one, size and type of car; two, design of car; three, specification and specialties. All of the specifications that we have used in the past were based on I.C.C. regulations. In Canada, there are corresponding Board of Transport Commissioner's regulations. We will want our equipment to conform to both. Here is another area in which you can help us, Alton. We understand, too, that you may have in your files, designs and details developed by the Railroad Association Car Construction Committee, published and unpublished. These will be invaluable to us."

After a pause, Burns felt obliged to comment.

"I certainly relish an opportunity to be a part of such an ambitious venture—not, as you say, simply as a supplier. This could be a chance of a lifetime to help design equipment to be proud of

in years to come. I have just the man for Matt, as general manager. I will recommend him and present him to Matt on Tuesday. He worked with me for years. He will rise to this challenge. He is good and he is honest. His name is Hal Ives."

A maid had been laying out cold cuts, cheeses, and fruit in the Florida room. Taking cold beers with them from the patio bar, they helped themselves, talking as they ate.

Jim announced that he had heard from Tom Cable at Pompano. He would arrive later. Jim finished his beer and excused himself, explaining that he was an early riser, and, when on vacation, he took a short nap after lunch. He invited them to do likewise, if they felt like it, otherwise, to make themselves at home around the place.

Burns and Morton spent the next couple of hours walking around the gardens, out of earshot of the house, talking of their own special interests in this deal. They discussed particular wording of specifications that would give Precision Bearing advantages which anyone unfamiliar with details of running gear parts would not recognize. They discussed savings in costs to Precision Bearing, if parts adhered to fundamentals of design of the American Railroad Association.

They had a swim in the pool and discussed the role that Tom Cable could play in assisting them. As president of River Rouge Steel and an associate of Seaway Steel Corporation, a member of the financing group for Char Lake, he was bound to be useful. However, the particular product line that Acme manufactured in Canada for River Rouge had no application to these cars, so neither Cable nor his division would benefit directly.

Chapter 14

Tom Cable arrived from Miami in a self-drive Cadillac, at about four o'clock. They were on their second drink when Murphy joined them. Cable needed little filling in, as he had investigated the matter with Seaway Steel officials, after talking to Burns by phone.

Jim suggested a game of poker. All except Burns joined in. The others were aware that he probably could not afford the stakes and understood. Jim gave him some confidential Char Lake reports to read and the rest played three-handed, until dinner was served.

Tails of fresh-caught Florida spiny lobster and stone crab sent over from Hanleys across U.S. Highway 1 were laid out on a table beside the pool by a maid. With some of Jim's vintage white wine, the meal was delicious. After liqueurs, in the cool of the evening, the three-handed poker was resumed. At nine o'clock, Jim looked at his watch.

"If you young fellows will excuse me, I think I'll go to bed, read a little, and see you early in the morning. I'm really looking forward to that fishing trip."

Feeling the effects of two nights in New Orleans without sleep, Joe Morton decided to go to bed, too. All agreed to be up at daybreak for the deep-sea fishing that Cable had arranged with Bill Brighton.

Enjoying a cigarette, Burns and Cable poured another drink. Cable was restless. Burns recognized the symptoms.

"Getting itchy nuts, Tom? What are you going to do? Make some long distance calls? You know a woman in Hawaii perhaps! We could settle for a visit to a bar. We can go across the highway to Hanley's, or use your self-drive to go up to Roxy's Green Turtle!"

"Let's go to Hanley's. We won't have to worry about driving back over those causeways. If there is no stuff around the bar, we can always go upstairs, visit with Ziggy and gamble a little."

Hanley's dining room was empty. A group of guides and fishermen were huddled at the bar engrossed in their own stories. Burns and Cable crossed the room to look out the glass doors at the flood-lit fishing charter fleet at the marina docks. Beyond, across a stretch of lawn, were the outlines of the guest villas against the night sky.

Tom Cable called the bartender by name and whispered to him. Saying nothing, but with an eye on the fishermen at the bar, he pushed a button under the bar top. A door behind the bar led to a staircase. A man at the peephole in the door at the top of the stairs recognized Cable. The brightly lit room inside contained two blackjack tables, two crap tables, and a small bar at one side. The half dozen players at the tables were all men, served by a topless waitress, who also doubled as bartender. This was reputed to be the last of the illegal gambling set-ups in South Florida. Ziggy, himself, a short bald man with a crippled right arm, extended his left hand and led Cable to a crap table. Cable was a regular loser at craps. His first bet would be five hundred. Burns begged off and found a place at the dollar-minimum blackjack table.

Burns had lost his limit of about twenty dollars, when Cable, having dropped a thousand or more, joined him.

"We are invited for a drink at the bar. Come on. You don't want to waste time on the penny-ante stuff."

A tall, slightly stooped man, with thinning dark hair and pale complexion, had left the crap table to join two attractive, well-dressed women at the bar. There was a strong resemblance, but one was much younger than the other. She had long dark hair

hanging down her back, while the older woman had short, tightly curled hair.

"This is Ann, and this is Joan, and this is Mark. Did I get it right? This is my buddy, Alton. He's from Canada, too"

Burns tried to figure out who belonged to who. Both women wore wedding bands, as well as other expensive jewelry. After one drink, Mark explained to Burns that they had just arrived from Canada before dinner. He apologized, but explaining that they were tired, he said good night and left with both women.

As Ziggy approached to offer a drink on the house, fearing the loss of two more of his small house. Cable whispered to Burns, "That young one with the long hair, she's raring to go. I gather that her sister, the one with the short hair, is married to that guy, Mark. The young one is alone, with ants in her pants. They have one of those two-bedroom villas with separate entrances. She asked me to wait about fifteen minutes, until her sister and the guy got into the sack, then to come over to see her in number four. Sorry that we could not separate the other one from the guy. He doesn't look with it."

"That's OK, Tom. But get your rocks off fast. I'll throw away another twenty on the twenty-one game. If you are not back in a half hour, I'll walk over to the house."

They put in fifteen minutes talking to Ziggy about the pet raccoons that he enticed out of the palmettos with garbage every morning. Cable checked his watch and left. Burns found a seat at blackjack. When he had lost ten dollars and was playing on a second ten, the entrance door opened and Cable beckoned, urgently.

"Let's get the hell out of here."

"Why? What happened?"

"C'mon! I'll tell you outside. C'mon!"

As they crossed the highway on the run, Cable explained.

"It was dark as hell out there. I located number four—I think. There were no lights. The door was ajar. When I walked up to it, the broad reached for my hand and led me to the bed. Still no lights, but for the second that the door was open, I could see that she was bare-assed naked. We did not say a word. I just

dropped my pants and shorts and crawled into the saddle. I had a bone on a dog couldn't chew. When I kissed her, I put one hand under her ass and one behind her head. God-damnit, Alton, she had short curly hair. It was the guy's wife I was screwing. He may have been lying on the other side of the bed for all I knew. Did you ever see a dude trying to put on pants at a dead run— and do you know what? I forgot my shorts. God-damn shorts may get me killed. A pair of shorts cost me my first wife. All I need now is to be named correspondent in another divorce. I'll never wear shorts again."

Only after they were safely in the house and Cable had downed a slug of Scotch right from the bottle, could Burns stop laughing.

"Wait until you get up to Montreal again, Tom, you horny bastard. How would you like a mixture of oriental and Roumanian, with a suggestion of French, short hair or long hair?

Burns then told Cable about Sandra Sands. They both agreed that with a deal such as Char Lake coming up, a girl as attractive and willing could be a real asset.

Chapter 15

When the alarm sounded, he swung his legs over the side of the bed and fumbled to turn it off. He snapped on the light. It was three A.M. He stood up, stretched, and stood nude before the full length mirror on the door. He pushed back his short hair, but the cowlick at the front sprang right back. He crossed his arms and scratched both armpits. With arms still crossed, he reached over his shoulders to scratch as far down his back as he could reach. With his left hand, he scratched his left buttock; and with his right, he scratched behind his balls. He did not scratch because he was itchy. It was just part of his waking up routine.

He admired his naked physique in the mirror. *Not bad for thirty-six*, he thought. He had broad shoulders and narrow hips. His chest was muscular, and his belly was flat. He had a round, shiny, tanned face, with round, blue eyes, crinkled at the corners by the sun. His forearms were tanned from the elbows, and the tan on his neck extended in a deep vee where he wore his shirt open. Otherwise, his skin was white. He was "well hung." He leaned toward the mirror to examine one buck tooth, white like the rest, but with the corner broken.

This completed his awakening. He walked across the dark sitting-dining room to the kitchen. He removed a dirty frying pan from the bar top. Filling a jigger with rum, he dumped it in a tall dirty glass. He looked at it for a second. *No use changing now and waste booze.* He would strengthen it instead. He poured in some more rum directly from the bottle. That would disinfect anything. He took a couple of eggs from the refrigerator and

broke them into the rum. Adding salt and plenty of pepper, he stirred the mixture and drank it in big gulps. He made a wry face and went to the wall phone, to dial a number. He heard two rings, then silence.

"Hello, Aggie. Aggie, is that you?"

"Yes, Billy," said a sleepy voice.

"Well, knee Hank in the nuts the way you used to wake me when I had an early charter. Get him out right away. I am going out to start the *Rebel* now. I told Hank to meet me at the cut at four. I'll have mullet. Better get Harry up right away, too. He can bring back the skiff. Are you still awake, Aggie?"

"Yes, Billy. I'll get them up. Be careful out there in the dark."

"OK, Aggie. Oh say! There's some laundry and dirty dishes here."

"OK, Billy, baby," she said, sounding more wide awake now.

Bill Brighton gave himself a quick shave and flipped the cordless electric razor into his kit. He brushed his white teeth and tossed the toothbrush in before zipping the kit closed. He looked at the shirt and pants that he had worn the day before and threw them in a corner. He selected a clean suit from a drawer, put it on, and drew on a pair of brown top-siders. He was wondering if Hank would take time to give Aggie a bang before going to the *Rebel*.

Aggie had been hired a couple years ago as a waitress in the Green Turtle. Brighton took her home with him the first night, as he had no other woman at the time. They shacked up together for about a year and a half. They had an understanding that when either found another partner that appealed more, they would split.

Hank had been working mate on the *Rebel*, on and off, for about five years. He had been married up in his native Alabama before coming to the Keys. Shortly after he arrived in Islamarada, he was joined by his seventeen-year-old son, Harry, who loved fishing and the sea. He helped out doing odd-jobs around the fishing docks.

Periodically, Brighton took the *Rebel* to a shipyard in Miami for an overhaul. On these occasions, he stayed with the boat for a week or two, living aboard. While he was away the last time, Aggie, tired of sleeping alone when she knew that he was living it up in Miami, moved in with Hank. She had not bothered to move her belongings to the shack behind Brighton's house, where she lived with Hank and Harry. She continued to act as housekeeper, in her fashion, in both establishments. Bill was pretty sure that she would return to his bed any time that he asked her. Hank would not mind. However, he had not felt the need. There were plenty of women available in the local fishermen's bars every night. Bill subscribed to the theory that they all felt pretty much the same with a sack over their heads. The arrangement was all right for now for the three of them. Tomorrow would look after itself.

Picking up his kit and a large battery-powered searchlight, he made his way through the darkness to the dock at the side of the house. The *Rebel*, a thirty-eight foot sport fisher, was moored in the coral channel between the house and the Gulf, on the inside of Upper Matecumbe Key. Her fly bridge, tuna tower, and tall fishing outriggers loomed against the sky. He snapped on the searchlight and boarded her. He started the blowers and let them run, while he took a quick inventory of his fishing gear, neatly hung in holders and racks.

He started the diesels and left them idling loudly in the predawn silence. Stepping back onto the dock, he walked a short distance to an outboard runabout tied up behind the *Rebel*. Aboard, he checked fuel gauges and bilge. The two one hundred and twenty-five horse Johnsons roared to life one after the other. Pulling slowly out of the channel, around the *Rebel*, he opened the throttles, as he headed south in the lea of the key. A few stars twinkled in the still dark sky. The water was calm. Clumps of mangroves developed out of dark shadows. He passed close to some, sending his wake crashing into the roots. Others, he skirted respectfully. He passed between two larger islands, cutting his motors and lifting them from the water, as the hull coasted across a very shallow stretch. Even in the darkness, he

knew these waters like the palm of his hand.

Sighting Shell Key sitting alone, he turned the boat at full speed across an expanse of open water to a sea of weeds, rushes, and short mangroves. He entered a small tidal channel, slowing his speed to follow the twists and turns of the narrow passage. When it widened into a large pool, he cut his motors and drifted to a silent stop. Dozens of fat mullet swam below the boat in the beam of the searchlight.

Brighton got out a circular drawnet, weighted at the edges. Holding one edge in his teeth, with an expert motion, he threw it out over the water, to cover a circular area about ten feet across. As the weighted edges settled to the bottom, Brighten pulled the draw cords up the center, trapping a half dozen fish. He pulled the net into the boat, plucked the struggling mullet from it and threw them into a tank of seawater. Fish that had darted away quickly returned to the beam of light. He repeated the process about a half dozen times, until he had thirty lively mullet in the tank. The net was laid out on the bow. The motors sprang to life again, and the boat headed out through the channel to the open water.

Straight ahead, to the east, the first streaks of dawn were in the sky. The boat planed toward the lower end of Upper Matecumbe. Moving from the north, around Shell Key, the running lights of the *Rebel* were visible. Brighton set a course to intercept her at the cut leading out to the Atlantic under the causeway high span. He flashed his searchlight and Hank blinked his anchor light in response.

The runabout pulled up to the stern of the idling *Rebel*. With a dip net, they quickly transferred the live mullet to her bait well. Few words were necessary, as the three men did this often. Brighton climbed into the sportfisher's cockpit, while Harry buzzed away in the small boat. The *Rebel* moved under the bridge, turning from the rising sun to the south, outside the blinking light of the seabouy.

Bill climbed to the bridge to glance at the instruments, as Hank opened her up for the trip to Marathon. With the diesels ticking smoothly, Brighton went down to the cabin. He shed his

windbreaker, unneeded now, with the sun coming up. He poured a mug of strong, black coffee from a thermos and unwrapped the tuna fish sandwich that Aggie had prepared, as usual.

By the time that the waving palms of Marathon came into view, fishing gear was all in order. Deboned balao, rigged with six feet of piano wire leaders carefully coiled, were laid on top of a bed of ice. Rigs for the live mullet and blue runners hung on pegs. Three rods, with one-hundred-and-twenty-five-pound test lines, were in place in sockets on the bridge. Three rods with forty-pound test lines were in the cockpit holders. They were already baited with split balao for picking up live blue runners. This would provide sport as well as bait, while they sailed out to sailfish depths. Brighton brought out two large kites, one yellow, one red, which assembled and handed up to Hank on the bridge. He went up himself to check the kite lines on their special rail-mounted reels. He went over the instructions from Cable with Hank.

Jim Murphy would be placed in the starboard fighting chair, directly below and behind the controls on the bridge. With his Polaroid glasses, Brighton would spot any big fish in the area of Murphy's bait. For the fisherman in this chair, Brighton could maneuver the boat so that a strike was hooked. In the same way, he could make sure that the fish was not lost. Murphy might not realize that a skillful boat captain, such as Brighton, by speeding up, slowing down, swinging with the movement of the fish, even reversing, when the tension on the tackle was critical, could have more to do with landing a big catch than the fisherman. Brighton had been instructed that, above all, Murphy must land the biggest fish, regardless of what the others caught. Brighton was to offer to have the fish mounted at no cost to Murphy, on some logical pretext. Cable and Burns would pay for it afterward.

Bill Brighton took a last look around the cabin, as they pulled up to the dock where their party waited. The liquor bottles were in their racks on the bar. The ice bucket was full. The mixers were in their places. The glasses were clean. However untidy his house, his charter boat was immaculate. It was his livelihood and he loved it.

From the glass doors of the bar, Cable had recognized the *Rebel*, as she entered the cut. They had moved out to the dock, mugs of rum-laced coffee in hand. A waiter in a white coat tended two hampers of lunches. Tom Cable stepped aboard first and disappeared into the forward cabin. There he peered from the porthole at villa number four across the basin. He had visions of a man approaching the boat with a pair of shorts in one hand and a thirty-eight in the other.

With Brighton at the helm, the *Rebel* headed out to sea. Hank instructed those in the cockpit on the use of the light rods to catch blue runners for large live bait on the way out to the deep water. The runners were thrilling fighters. Morton and Murphy in the cockpit, with Cable on the bridge, all using flat lines, kept Hank and Burns busy removing live fish and rebaiting.

Hank substituted heavy tackle on a Penn 100 real at Murphy's chair, baiting that line and the port line, where Burns was to sit on the bridge, with live runners. Morton's line, on the port cockpit outrigger, was baited with mullet. Cable tended his own light tackle from the center of the bridge, using deboned balao. As the lines were let out, Murphy's starboard cockpit line was snapped on to the red kite. It rose in the wind above and behind the boat, allowing the live blue runner to swim on the surface about five hundred yards back of the boat. The only other line on Murphy's side of the *Rebel* was a large teaser, which Brighton trailed from the starboard outrigger, controlling it with one hand as he eyed Murphy's bait. Barely fifteen minutes after trolling speed was reached, Brighton yelled from the bridge, "Two sails following. Watch the kite."

Shading their eyes from the glare of the sun, it took a while for the others to make out the two dorsal fins, riding high, relentlessly following the teaser. Brighton slowed the boat slightly and pulled the teaser closer to Murphy's bait. Everyone aboard was quiet and tense, waiting for the strike. One sail seemed intent on either the teaser or Murphy's blue runner while his mate disappeared. It passed up Morton's mullet, and, with a tremendous leap, took Burns' blue runner. The line snapped off the port outrigger. It cracked as it hit the water when the fish took off.

Burns grabbed the reel and raised his rod.

"Don't hit him yet," Brighton hissed, "he's still playing with it."

Now the big sail could be seen falling away from the teaser and closing in on Murphy's runner. The bait was trying to get away, pulling the kite from side to side. The fish finally caught him. The line swished down as the snap let go. The kite went straight up in the wind. The big sail had plenty of time to mouth the runner before Murphy was able to reel in the slack.

"Set him now, Jim, he's got it."

Brighton cut the speed just enough to keep tension on Murphy's line, as he reeled in, raising and lowering his rod to pick up footage. The fish showed his fighting colors in one great leap after another.

Brighton shouted, excitedly, "Reel like hell, Jim, he's a big one. There's sharks out there. I can see them. They can't catch him until you tire him. Then you'll have to boat him fast."

Jim was sweating, working his rod, winding his reel, whenever the big fish would let him. Every few minutes the fish would decide to run and Jim would lose more line against the drag than he had wound in. When the fish ran with the boat, Brighton, with hands behind his back at the console, speeded up the boat. He steered, with the engines, from side to side, throttling one, slowing the other, to keep the fish directly in front of Murphy's fighting chair. On the bridge, Burns fought to keep his fish on the port side, while all attention was directed to Murphy's fight. Only once, when Burns' fish charged under the boat to surface on Murphy's side, did Brighton divert his attention from Murphy. With an abrupt spurt of the starboard diesel, Brighton was able to assist Burns in getting the fish back to the port side, where it would not jeopardize Murphy's kill.

Finally, the big sail gave way. He allowed himself to be drawn up to the stern, only to change his mind and tear off another hundred yards of hard-earned line from Jim's reel. The fish ended his last dash by sounding. In a final, desperate leap, colors blazing in the bright sunlight, he shook his head to rid himself of the hook. Unsuccessful, he gave up and was drawn up

quickly, swimming feebly on his side. Tom Cable assisted Hank with two gaffs in the gills to bring him aboard without marring his beauty.

They took time to briefly admire the colors of the smaller female that Burns held alongside, then turned back to exclaim over the size of the fish that Murphy had landed. Brighton suggested that Burns cut his loose. They would fish for more, but, as far as he was concerned, Murphy's fish was the prize of a lifetime of fishing.

"Jim, that's the biggest sail caught in the Keys this year. I should know. Most have been caught from the *Rebel*. Let's hang it from the jib where we can get some pictures before his colors fade. I have my mounts done by Pflueger. A record such as this they'll mount for free, if you want to hang it in your office or your new house."

Brighton looked at Cable and Burns, who nodded in agreement. Murphy was beaming. It had been an unique experience for him, after a lifetime of fishing for five pounders. It was the first sailfish that he had ever caught. He was sure that it would not be the last.

"Now, when I retire down here next year, I know what I can do with myself when I get bored."

They cut the fish down and slid it into the wet fish well before it lost its colors to become a dirty brown in death. It was only then that they noticed Joe Morton in his fighting chair, tiredly working his rod. He had been fighting a fish all of the time that they were landing the sails.

"What in hell have you got, Joe, the bottom?"

"Hell no! I've got a fish, a big bastard. I'm tired out; need a drink."

Hank slid into the chair to relieve Morton, who stood and rubbed his arms. The line went straight down over the stern. Brighton gave directions from the bridge, motors idling.

"Yeah, I knew he had it. I was worried that he might get in the props while we were getting in the sails. He's a big hammerhead shark. I was glad that Joe kept him occupied while we boated the sail. He did not go anywhere but straight down. I fig-

ured that Joe needed the exercise. Now, we'll just get him up and kill him, to get back my line and rig. Then you'll see a shark picnic. There's about six hundred pounds of him to make a meal for his friends out there."

They took turns reeling the stubborn brute to the surface, where Brighton put three shots in his head with his shark gun. Hank helped Bill to gaff him while the rest enjoyed a cool drink. They turned him over, and leaning over the transom, with a big fish knife, Brighton slashed open his soft belly. As the water at the stern turned red with blood, Bill cut the hook loose. The big creature sank slowly. A half dozen shadowy forms raced in to tear and slash at the carcass and at each other. With Hank at the wheel, they quickly pulled away from the rather terrifying sight.

By four o'clock in the afternoon, the excitement of catching a sail fish had been repeated several times, but each was anticlimactic.

The *Rebel* headed for Hanley's, with eight pennants flying. They did not look at the sailfish when they reached the dock. All of its iridescence had faded out. It would look better when presented to Jim Murphy with simulated coloring. The plastic sails would not fold into the clean-lipped, vaginal-like openings in his back and belly. He would never need to fold them away to flash through the sea again. The attractive plaque on the mount would read:

RECORD SAILFISH
CAUGHT BY
JAMES W. MURPHY
AT
MARATHON, FLORIDA
UNAIDED

Unwritten would be the effect that this fine catch might have on the awarding of a multi-million dollar order, unaided.

Murphy had arranged for the Marra Lear Jet to pick up Burns and Cable at Key West for the trip to Chicago. Murphy's pilot wanted to spend New Year's day with his family in Cleve-

land before coming back to pick up his boss on Monday morning, so this worked out well for everyone.

Tom Cable was last on the dock, staying aboard to make some final settlement with Bill Brighton. When he did get ashore, he walked quickly through the bar to the street, without so much as a glance toward villa number four.

Chapter 16

Eddies of fine snow swirled in the revolving doors of the Chicago Medina Sheraton. The doorman came into the red-carpeted lobby, stamping his large boots, unbuckled over the cuffs of his trousers. He took off his gloves and blew his warm breath into cupped hands.

"Taxis are scarce, sir. If you want one, I'll have to phone. It's five below out there this morning."

"I don't need one. I'm just trying to work up enough courage to walk across to the Wrigley Building."

Burns turned up his coat collar. The icy wind took his breath away as he fought against the gusts coming up Michigan Avenue from the river. Inside the lobby, he brushed back his hair. He took an elevator marked "Tower" to the warm, luxurious offices of Eagle Steel Foundries, Incorporated.

A pretty receptionist sat at a shiny desk, flanked on either side by tall rhododendrons. She smiled, "You must feel at home here, today, Mr. Burns. Is it much colder in Montreal?"

"Good morning, Miss Swatowski. I don't know, really. I came in from Florida last night. It was eighty-five there."

"Lucky you! I suppose that you came in for our party. Isn't it wonderful. Mr Buckley is our new president, but I suppose you knew."

"I am sure that there was no doubt about his election. Is he in or is he keeping president's hours?"

"He's in as usual. Please go in. You know the way. He hasn't moved into his new office yet and I don't think he will. He likes it here with us in this wing." She lowered her voice, even though

there was no one else in the room, "I'll be talking to the Indiana Harbor plant. Want me to tell Mary that you will be at the party? What's your room number?"

"I have suite one-oh-six to eight at the Medina, but I expect to be with Mr. Buckley all day, and I'm going back to Montreal on the first flight in the morning."

Buckley's secretary, a wizened little woman with thirty years at Eagle Steel, rose from her desk. She greeted him by his first name and they went through the "weather in Montreal" routine again. Chicagoans always seemed to think that if it is five below there, it has to be fifty-five below in Montreal. She led him to the door of Buckley's office, as she did on each visit, even though they occurred two or three times each month. Buckley was on the telephone, talking to the Newark foundry. He waved to Burns as he talked and motioned him to a chair. The secretary took Burns's coat.

Handsome at fifty, his physique, smart tailoring, and dark brown hair, with only a little grey at the temples, made him look ten years younger. It was hard to pick out any outstanding feature of his face except for an engaging grin which he often wore. After listening for a few moments, he issued instructions, carefully, and concisely.

Burns and Buckley had met some ten years before. Burns was assisting Lou Waldorf at a meeting in Lafayette, Indiana. Buckley attended as assistant to Gabe Herter, then vice-president of engineering at Eagle Steel Foundries. Herter was a member of the manufacturers' advisory committee. These joint meetings of railway men and manufacturers were usually held at the Railway Association laboratories at Purdue University to interpret the results of tests and research. Herter was respected by the industry. He had served as a foundry engineer in most of the plants under the Eagle Steel banner. He had made patterns. He had poured steel. He had sand in his shoes!

A young engineer just out of the University of Michigan, Buckley had been assigned to Herter's staff. As was his custom, the chief invited the new engineer out to lunch at a pub near the foundry. He wanted to know his staff; to size up Buckley.

"What's your first name, Buckley?"

"Bevis, sir. Bevis Alonzo Buckley."

"Bevis! Who in hell ever heard of a foundryman with a name like Bevis. Your name will be Buck around here."

"But I have a brother called Buck."

"It don't matter. You're called Buck. No God-damn Bevises in our foundries."

It was Buck Buckley thereafter. Few people at Eagle Steel knew what the "B." in his signature stood for.

Since Burns and Buckley were the youngest of the group which met at Lafayette, they hit it off together right away. The friendship strengthened through the years and especially since Burns joined Acme, the Canadian licensee of Eagle Steel. Buckley never ceased to amaze Burns with his careful analyses. Every big contract was carefully assessed. All of the individuals who could be involved were considered from every angle; knowledge, strength, power, weaknesses, preferences, pride, and greed. Then the product offered was evaluated for features which would be most appealing. Presentations were planned, step by step. Every interview was rehearsed. Every question was anticipated. Buckley always maintained that the railway business was no Sunday School picnic. There were often no second prizes. It was usually all or nothing at all.

This was the atmosphere in which Burns produced his notes concerning that Char Lake project, compiled after his meetings in Montreal, Mobile, New Orleans, and Marathon. Buckley instructed his secretary that they were not to be disturbed. He laid out what he had learned from his organization and friends. After hours of discussion, interupted only by the delivery of coffee and sandwiches at noon, policies and procedures were set down in order of importance:

1. While Jim Murphy might like to use larger cars, a ninety-ton-capacity, rather than one-hundred- or one-hundred-and-twenty-ton capacity, must be selected. Cleveland Steel would be the sole competition. They had many large-capacity designs in service in the U.S.A. Only Eagle Steel had furnished ninety-ton

designs. If Cleveland Steel was led to believe that larger capacity would be acceptable until the specifications came out, it might be too late for them to develop ninety-ton designs from scratch. Since the cars must be hauled over government railway lines, and since Burns was confident of his influence over Jules Lamont, the selection of ninety-ton could be assured. The important thing was to keep this information out of the hands of Cleveland Steel as long as possible. Eagle Steel would stand by, ready to furnish patterns and equipment to start production at once. It would take Cleveland Steel months to prepare for an unexpected design.

2. All designs should have the formal approval of the American Railroad Association, either by way of prior use on a U.S. railroad or formal tests. This requirement, if kept secret until the latest possible time, could put competitors off base without time to get back on. Specifications must require proof of satisfactory static and dynamic tests for all running gear and structures. The only machines available for such testing were owned by Eagle Steel. While Eagle Steel could not refuse to test and approve a competitor's products on their machines, strengths, weakness, capacities, and even production practices would be revealed.

3. Cleveland Steel was a threat, not only in the supply of running gear parts, but also they designed and furnished the gear used to couple cars in trains. However, while both companies furnished the regular type of coupling mechanisms used on conventional cars unloaded while upright, Eagle Steel, alone, had developed coupling devices needed when cars must be dumped from the top by turning them over, one by one. It was obvious then that Burns must have specifications written and designs selected for top dumping cars to innocently exclude Cleveland Steel altogether.

4. With Burns likely to influence the overall designs as consultant, it should be possible to arrive at the assembly of a package, including all of the items that Acme manufactures and sells. It would be desirable if a price was acceptable on the whole package, without breaking it down to allow competitors to quote on individual items. Obviously, Burns would have to live with this project day and night for the next few months. He would

have to keep all of the Char Lake group in Canada isolated, at work and at play, to prevent advance information from reaching competitors. Burns told Buckley of his plans for Sandra Sands to this end.

5. While U.S. Motors, Eagle Steel, Seaway, and M. A. Marra would each have a director on the Char Lake board, there would be three other directors. One of the three was likely to be a representative of the bank group handling the financing in Canada. Murphy had indicated that bankers in Canada would be the Empire Bank. Burns would be able to influence this director. The remaining two directors could be interested in Cleveland Steel. This was, no doubt, the reason for Murphy's insistence that specifications must not be written so as to exclude any reputable supplier. Burns and Buckley agreed, however, that certain seemingly innocuous requirements could be written in that would set up barriers, placing Cleveland Steel at a disadvantage.

6. It could develop that two or three of the directors might be interested in the participation of Barton Bearings. Acme would offer Precision bearings, of course. While Eagle Steel normally would have no interest, there was a connection with the parent, U.S. Motors. Eagle Steel would design certain contours into the pedestals of the running gear which would be suitable for the application of Precision bearings only. These contours could go unnoticed until the specifications were issued and it was too late for competitors to adapt their designs.

7. Of utmost importance to achievement of all objectives, of course, was the engagement of Burns's protege and long-time friend, Hal Ives, as Canadian general manager of Char Lake operations. Then, it would fall to Burns to control and contain both Ives and Matt Marra until the contract was placed. It was agreed that Jim Murphy would probably go along with recommendations of his key men in the field.

A recapitulation near the end of the meeting placed a minimum value on the package that Acme would offer at thirty million dollars, more business than Acme had done in the past ten years. The net profit would reach one and a half million for

Acme and about one million for Eagle Steel. With standards established on the first order, the potential was in the neighborhood of one hundred million.

It was after five o'clock. From the tower, the snake of lights around Lake Michigan stretched as far as the eye could see. The staff in the outer offices had left to prepare for the party. Both Burns and Buckley stood up, stretched, and added another two cigarette butts to the heaped ash trays. Buckley reminded Burns again of the many long hours entertaining, suggesting, and coercing by whatever means between the planning and placing of such an order. They found their own coats and crossed Michigan Avenue to Burns's suite at the Medina.

Stiff Scotches and showers failed to halt the discussion. It was only when Buck borrowed Burns's razor to clean up that Burns remembered to call Tom Cable. The latter, in his office further down Michigan Avenue, was awaiting the call. He was anxious to here the results of their conference. They made an appointment to meet at Augustino's later.

The ballroom of the Medina Sheraton was designed for ceremonials of the Nobles of the Mystic Shrine. Once known as the Medina Temple, the hotel had been built by this branch of the Chicago Masonic order. Shriners continued to patronize it and were given certain special privileges. Located across the street from Eagle Steel Foundries, it was used frequently for company functions.

Bright, two-story murals of knights on the Crusades mounted on white chargers and surrounded in battle by infidels on foot, filled the wall panels. Thick Persian-style carpet covered all but the dance floor in front of the bandstand. It was a warm setting for the reception. Members of Eagle Steel's public relations staff were conferring with the hotel's head waiter. Buckley had brought his coat from Burns's suite, anticipating that they might leave separately.

Abe Sinski was one of the first to arrive, since he was staying in the hotel, too. He was chief inspector of foundry operations, with headquarters in St. Louis, where the company maintained its laboratories and research facilities. He was a tall, gaunt man.

He had joined the foundries in the footsteps of his father, when he graduated from high school in Granite City. After the war, he studied metalurgy at M. I. T., under the G. I. bill. Buckley, as vice-president of engineering, had appointed him to his present position.

As soon as the waiters were set up, Sinski brought the first drinks to Burns and Buckley. It was unlikely that they would have a chance to get one later. While the guests were arriving they began to bring Abe up to date on their deliberations concerning the Char Lake project. Burns continued it when Buckley had to break away to join the receiving line at the door. Some new patterns and molding procedures would be required quickly in the Canadian foundry. Abe would be expected to spend a great deal of time there in the next few months. This prospect did not displease him a bit. With Burns, he had sampled what the wide open city had to offer.

The ballroom was filling quickly now. The office girls were collecting in groups around the buffet table, admiring the arrangements of food and complimenting each other on new dresses donned for the occasion. Male staffers lined up at the bars to collect drinks for themselves and the women. The receiving line, in addition to Buckley, included his predecessor, now chairman of the board, and the vice-presidents of finance and personnel.

When the receiving line broke up, Burns noticed the office girls vying for Buck's attention. He found himself surrounded, and he was quite sure that his sudden popularity was largely because of his past friendship with the man who was now "The Big Wheel."

A public relations officer took the center of the dance floor. He introduced "the man that we have all loved as our president for so many years," Mr. J. M. Jenks. A tall, thin, grey-haired man, Jenks adjusted his pince-nez, thanked them, and simply introduced the new president, Mr. B. A. Buckley, with the hope that the staff of some seven thousand, up from some three hundred when he became president, would support Mr. Buckley as they had supported him. There was an enthusiastic round of applause both before and after Buckley's short, friendly speech.

Wishing them a happy New Year, he rejoined the group of executives preparing to leave, so that the staff could enjoy themselves, their own way.

Before he left, Buckley beckoned to Burns. He explained, in a whisper, that he was going to drive the old man home to his north side apartment. They would have a nightcap there with the vice-president of finance. As soon as he could get away, he would join Burns, Abe, and Cable at Augustino's.

Burns invited a few staff members who were often useful to him to his suite for a nightcap. Leaving behind three couples that he knew liked a chance to be together on this occasion every year, he took his hat and coat and said good night to them. On the way out, he looked up the night chambermaid on the floor, gave her ten dollars, and asked her to change the sheets on his bed when she was sure that his guests were finished with the suite.

Abe was already at the North State Street bistro when Burns arrived. A waitress was serving him an open-faced steak sandwich in a booth at the end of the long bar, at which there were only a half dozen hookers nursing drinks.

"Hadda get some meat on my stomach," he explained, "Those horses' ovaries do not agree with me when I'm drinkin'."

Abe talked about the party as he ate, "That gal from Hammond, what's her name, Hilda? Yeah, tha's it, Hilda. Now that Buck's president and she thinks we are his pals, she'd do it on the dance floor. Last year she couldn't see anybody but Carter. She figgered because he was VP in New York that he'd get the top job. She didn't go near him this year."

The hostess who had brought Abe's sandwich brought a Scotch for Burns. She was a tall, attractive girl in a skin tight evening dress with a neckline that plunged to her belly button. She kept her job with her quick wit, her memory for names and faces, and her knowledge of who was who in the railroad and steel industries.

"You guys out ruttin' tonight?"

She included Tom Cable, who had just arrived. He gave her a peck on the nose and slid into the bench next to Burns.

"Where's Buck? I suppose he's too fucking big for Augustino's now. It will be the Union League Club or the Chicago Club, I suppose."

"Because you're his pals," the waitress said, "the rest of you will act like stuffed shirts, too, including you, you son of a bitch, Cable."

She shoved him over on the bench with her hip and perched on its edge with her arm around his waist. "You told me to keep it warm for you one night about a month ago and it's been simmering ever since. His God-damn office is only five minutes from my apartment, and I have to use a vibrator when I get up in the afternoon."

"You're living in the past, sweetheart. Old-fashioned fucking is for truck drivers. You've got to get with it, Kay. There are more sophisticated ways of doing it now."

"Bull-shee-it, Cable. I heard that you spent every night for a week with a fat Syrian dancer in Detroit. It doesn't take a bushel of tits to make a good screw, you know. By the way, Abe, your competitor, that candy ass vice-president of Cleveland Steel, was in three times last week with that purchasing agent for the St. Paul Railroad. They did a lot of talking about a big order for newsprint cars. Better get with it, baby."

"Two questions, Kay. Which purchasing agent? There are three on the St. Paul. And why do you call John Kelley a candy ass? Is there something about him that I don't know?"

"Cable, are you buying me a drink, you son of a bitch? It's the best that you can do since that Syrian broad wore you out."

She formed her lips to make a hissing sound that carried to a waitress at the other end of the bar. She ordered a martini for Cable and a champagne cocktail for herself. Then, spotting Buckley at the door, she called the girl back and ordered a Scotch on the rocks for him.

Leaning foreward as she slid out from the table to greet Buckley, she exposed both of her breasts as part of her regular come-on. She hugged Buckley, congratulated him on his appointment, and when he was seated next to Abe, she squeezed in beside him.

"We've been bullshitting, Buck, but I'll be serious for a mo-

ment. It couldn't have happened to a more regular guy. I'm sure that I am not the only one around the Loop who will help you in any way we can—and I mean *any way* we can. Here's to you."

She hugged Buckley again and kissed him on the cheek.

"Now Abe, I'll answer your questions. I was telling Abe, Buck, this guy John Kelley has had this purchasing agent of the St. Paul in here three nights last week. He's a skinny, little, old guy, named Wardstrom. It must be a big deal. They keep talking about these seventy-ton newsprint cars with Cleveland trucks and disc brakes and, oh yes, hydracushion."

"Did Kelley and Wardstrom do anything exciting? I mean like get drunk or something? Kelley can screw himself up when he drinks."

"No. The candy ass didn't get drunk. One night they did have a lot of drinks and the old man wanted a girl. I set them up with a couple that were in that night. Kelley haggled about the price in advance. He wouldn't pay more than twenty-five bucks. Well, the girls were having a slow night so they took it and delivered twenty-five bucks worth, no more, no less. Gert took them to the Wacker Hotel and gave them fifteen minutes. The old man liked Gert. all right, but it wasn't long enough for him. He wasn't very happy. If you want to treat him right, I've got the right girl for him. Has a nice apartment near here—bar and everthing— and she'll take her time. Give you plenty of time to talk when he's mellow."

Kay stood up and shoved her champagne over to Cable.

"You can drink it for me, lover boy. I've made my commission on it. I can see that this is a pre-arranged pow-wow and I have other customers to look after now. Oh, yeah, I call Kelley a candy ass because he thinks so much of himself that I'll bet he gets out of the shower to pee."

"I don't even get out of the bath for that," Abe said, as Kay left.

"Is that supposed to be a Polish joke, Sinski?"

"Naw! I don't tell Polish stories. Some of my father's people come from Poland, but both my mother and father were born in Roumania."

"When you come to Montreal to start production on the

Char Lake order, Abe, you'll be right at home. I expect to have the most beautiful Roumanian girl that you have ever seen working for Acme. She is part oriental. Her father is Roumanian. He holds the same position that you do, chief inspector for the foundry that will make Cleveland Steel castings in Canada, if we lose all or part of the Char Lake order, God forbid!"

That brought the conversation around to decisions made that afternoon. Buckley explained that Burns would try to influence Char Lake to decide upon ninety-ton capacity cars in order to place Cleveland Steel in the position of having to get approvals on designs that they had not furnished before. Sinski, completely sober now, agreed that this was good strategy. He told them about a recent test of a Cleveland Steel seventy-ton design that they had not made before. The castings failed the tests and redesign took months. The trouble was simply that sufficient chiller nails had not been used to control cooling of the metal at a change in section. Cracks, too small to see with the naked eye, had formed as the metal shrank on chilling. The castings failed. Three extra chiller nails in the mold, in Sinski's opinion, would have prevented the failure. He agreed that it was too much to hope that reputable foundry people like Cleveland Steel would make the same miscalculation twice, but it was possible. Then, if there was not enough time to retest, they would be out of competition.

As Abe finished his story and took a swig of his beer, a short, plump, cheap looking girl, who had been sitting behind him at the bar, tapped him on the shoulder. He turned to look at her, inquiringly.

"Scuse me, Gemmen. Ah's uh stranguh heuh. Jes arrive las' week. Ah'm fum Lil' Rock, Aukansaw. Don' know nobody heuh. You gemmen fum Chicago?"

"Nah, we ain't from Chicago."

"Ef'n yore on a convenchun yuh mus' be docters. Only convenchun this week is a few docters at the Ambassador East. Yuh docters?"

"Yah. Yah. We're doctors. That's what we are all right. This is Doctor Burns, this is Doctor Cable, this is Doctor Buckley, and I'm Docotor Sinski."

"Muh name's Janie. Ah'm jes a lil' ol' hillbillie fum Aukin-saw. Mebbe yuh all bein' docters yuh cud hep meh. Yuh see, ah ben heuh all week an ab ben goin out a bit, yuh know. Ah'm jes afraid ah miat be pregnant rat naow. Cud you all tel me rat off if'n yuh examined muh?"

"Sure, I'm staying at the Median. Goin' there now. C'mon along. I'll examine you and then later on Doctor Burns here can collaborate with me to back up my diagnosis. He's staying at the same hotel."

After Abe left with the girl, Buckley lifted his eyebrows and grinned, "If that little girl is not pregnant now, she will be when Abe completes his diagnosis."

Chapter 17

Dear Dad:

Happy New Year!
If you get home by New Year's Eve, I hope that you will have someone to be with so that you will not be alone.

I wish you a very successful new year. I hope that you keep your health. Above all, I hope that we can be together more often, next year.

Brother George phoned twice for you during the week, but, like me, he did not know whether you would be back for New Years' Day or not—or even where you were. I could not tell him where to find you. While we see you so little any more, Dad, we do love you and we are both lonely for you.

George said that since he had not heard from you, he would stay with some college friends in Toronto. I really have no close friends here in Montreal, since I have been away at university. It was terribly lonely here in the house all week, waiting for you. A few of the foreign students are staying in dorm over the holidays and there will be some sort of party. While it will not be like being with the family, it will be better than being here alone—so I'm taking the train this afternoon.

My current college boy friend is going back, too. He is in much the same position as me. His dad and mother broke up years ago. He came home to be with his dad but his father has gone to the mountains to ski with a friend

over the holiday. I thought of you every night, dad, waiting for a call or something. Please take it easier, won't you, and make one little New Year's resolution for us, please—to spend a little time with us, next year.

With a little tear,
Love,
Linda

P.S. Some girl named Sandra called twice. Said she'd see you Monday.

Alton Burns reread the note that he found on the dining room table. He wiped tears from his eyes before taking off his coat. He stood at the window and looked out at the dreary winter scene. The sky was dark. There was no sun. It was calm and cold. A boy trudged along Graham Boulevard, dragging a sled. A car crunched along on the opposite side of the street, only the top visible over the banks piled high on the median by the snow blowers There was a Christmas wreath hanging in a silent window of the house next door. He looked around his modest semi-detached home. It was clean and tidy. Linda had worked hard while she spent her holidays here alone. There were no decorations—nothing to give the house any holiday atmosphere. It was quiet and lonely.

He took his bag to his room and began unpacking. He removed his jacket and tie and put on a dressing gown over his trousers. He avoided looking outside. It made the house seem chilly.

There was an old photo album laid open on his desk in his bedroom. Linda must have been looking at it while she waited alone. For no particular reason, he took it with him to the small bar in the basement playroom, empty and silent. He poured a stiff Scotch, one of many that he would pour that afternoon and evening.

He sat at the bar and opened the album at random. He studied a picture of his son, a smiling boy of sixteen in a hockey uniform. He realized that the picture was over two years old.

How did it happen that he was lonely and alone on New Year's Eve, a night of celebration for his friends and at his clubs? He could recall being alone on the last three, at least. One he had spent all night in his office. Another, in a desolate hotel room in Ottawa, after test riding a train overloaded with revelers.

Did it really matter, that Char Lake contract? Was it worth sacrificing two good children who offered their love? Was it worth wearing himself out over? Becoming an alcoholic? He poured himself another drink.

As his morbid thoughts revolved in his brain, tears welled up. He thought of the futile attempts of his old mother and father, before they died, to give him love and affection, which he rarely had time to acknowledge. How many painful rejections had he inflicted on these loving old people?

It grew dark early, and he did not bother to turn on lights. He toyed with the idea of phoning for fried chicken, simply because he knew that he should have food. He forgot about it and took another drink instead. He raised a wry toast, to a selfish son and parent.

Hours later, he awoke to the eerie wailing of a locomotive's whistle in Outremont Yard, saluting the new year at exactly twelve midnight. He had been sleeping, face down on the old album, at the bar. He imagined the echoes of those whistles off the snow drifts at Char Lake, with the northern lights in the grey Arctic skies. He poured a toast to the new year, downed it, and went to bed, alone.

The outlook on New Year's Day was as gloomy as the night before. It was still dark outside. Under streetlights, which seemed dim before dawn, the snow looked grimy and dirty. Burns made a pot of coffee. He added Scotch to his cup. He wandered about in his robe, until he could stand the house no longer. He bathed, shaved and called the limousine service. A silent, sulky driver, filling in for Pete, took him to the dark offices on St. James Street.

He began a review of car construction committee records taken from his locked files. He selected various designs of ore cars, laying each out on a separate desk in the outer office. Going

from desk to desk, he selected two that he would propose for Char Lake. They were of the ninety-ton, top-unloading type. He selected two designs of larger capacity, which were obviously unsuitable because of wheelbase or height restrictions of the government railways' Churchill line.

He made a pot of coffee in the women's lounge amid stale smells, women's smells. They stirred him a little. He found a bottle of Scotch in his own office to sweeten the coffee. He sipped all afternoon, as he selected confidential test data to support the selection of Acme's products, discarding test records that gave any indications of weaknesses. He made copious notes and summarized them for his meeting with Matt Marra.

From time to time, he thought of phoning his secretary. Funny how a man missed having his secretary around, he thought, even though he hardly knew her socially. About six o'clock he gave in to the impulse. A man's voice answered. Her boy friend, he thought. He could hear Vivian Stuart being called to the phone.

"Oh, Mr. Burns, you are back. I expected a call yesterday."

"Just wondering if there were any important messages while I was away, Miss S."

"None that you will need until tomorrow, but I'll be glad to come downtown, if you need me."

"No, please don't bother. I'll be leaving the office, soon," he lied, wishing that she would insist.

"There was a Sandra called. Sounded real sexy."

He ignored the curiosity in her voice.

"That's all right. I can attend to that tomorrow. Happy New Year, Miss S."

"Have fun yourself, Mr. Burns."

He felt disappointed when she hung up.

He was hungry now. He hadn't eaten since noon on the day before. He could notice the effects of the Scotch that he had been sipping all day. He unlocked the staff cafeteria, found some cold roast beef, and made a sandwich with some stale bread and mustard. He ate it as he picked up the drawings and test data, arranging them in the order of his notes and summaries. He was

restless more than tired but felt that he could do no more. It was nine o'clock. New Year's Day was just about over. He felt lonely at the prospect of going back to that dark house again.

He ordered a taxi, put on his topcoat, and waited for it on the windy steps of the bank building. Getting into the cab, he still did not know where to go. He found himself telling the driver to take him to the Red Lantern, where he had met Sandra. Perhaps there would be something to cheer him up there.

In the darkness of the lounge, he could discern only the bartender listening to a portable radio. The cheerful little checkroom girl was doubling as waitress. She recognized him again and when she brought his Scotch, she sat down with him while he sipped it. She made him feel a little better. However, when a single man came in, she left to take his coat and accompanied him to another table. Burns drained his glass, helped himself to his coat, leaving a five dollar bill for her. He went out into the cold again.

He walked up to Ste. Catherine Street, hands in coat pockets, shoulders hunched against the wind. He turned east, thankful for show window alcoves where he could warm his ears from time to time. Deep in thought, he turned on Bluery Street. At Sherbrooke Street, the neon sign of Ninia's Algiers was lit. While he frequently entertained at the place, he had never visited it alone. He had chatted often with the Egyptian belly dancer, who operated the place, while his customers dallied with some of her dancers.

Ninia's blue Cadillac was at the door in the no parking zone. He noted that the dent was still in the hood where Ninia had christened it with a bottle of champagne the night that she took delivery of it. She said that she wanted to be the first to dent it. Burns had paid for the champagne for the entertainment of his customers that night. Ninia billed herself as "One of King Farouk's Harem Dancers." She was the star of her own show. Burns had found her attractive in her abbreviated harem costume, undulating her bare curves in her suggestive harem dances. There had been times when he had been tempted to accept her offer to entertain him privately, in deference, he suspected, to the amount of money that he spent entertaining in her

club. There was always a client whose desires came first, and then there was the sobering fact that the man who claimed her as mistress was a well-known Mafia figure in Montreal.

She was on her way out when they met at the door. She was in mink coat and evening dress.

"Alton! Darling, what do you do here on New Year's Day, all alone? It should not happen like this. I must go to dinner. There is no business. I gave the girls permission to have a few drinks and close up. The girls be glad if you join them for a little, but me, I must go. I am so sorry, darling." She proferred a heavily made up cheek, carefully protecting her elaborately made up lips and her false eyelashes.

At the bar, there were four girls, three in filmy harem costumes, and one in yellow halter and pantaloons. The chubby, fat queen with them, Burns recognized as Ninia's choreographer and costume designer, Aboud. The queer swung on his stool and asked if he could get Burns a drink, addressing him as dearie in a high pitched voice. The girls greeted one of the club's frequent patrons in a much more restrained manner than usual when they were working.

Without the garish red candles that usually provided the only lighting, the ceiling lights revealed all that was shoddy in an empty nightclub. The table cloths normally looked rich on tables covered with glasses and gilt candleholders. Now, the stains, worn spots, and patches could be seen. There were scars on the table legs. The varnish on the bar was cracked, bleached, and streaked. The carpet was stained and dirty. The heavy velvet curtains around the stage were faded, and the wood floor was worn and splintered. Burns wondered how the girls could roll their bare breasts over it in their exotic dances without injury.

The girls themselves looked different. One had a long, hooked nose that Burns had not noticed before. Another, a very busty girl who did an act with tassels tied to her nipples, had unbuttoned her halter for comfort. Without the uplift harness, her breasts were so pendulous as to be almost flat. The third dancer, a short girl with a chubby face and heavy mascara around her eyes, was billed as Myriam of Morocco. She was really a

French-Canadian, whose real name was Marie. The girls were paid a commission of twenty-five percent on drinks that they influenced customers to buy. Burns had found Marie less greedy than most and he usually requested her when a client showed an interest in having a girl in the party. She affected an Egyptian accent ordinarily, but now she spoke to fat Aboud as a French-Canadian.

"Aboud, get hoff your fat hass and get Mister Burns a double to take wit' him. We are closing, han' we are taking him wit us. He is not doing anyting tonight, are you, Mister Burns?"

"I'm on my own tonight, Marie. Where are we going?"

Aboud moved quickly and gracefully for a man so big. With many flourishes of his limp wrists, they watched him pour a large Scotch. He brought it around to Burns's side.

"See, Mister Burns, you are such a dearie for coming to see us tonight, I'm giving you a big one. Not that you need it. I'll bet that you have a monster of your own, but you never offer it to me."

"No, Aboud, you're not my type." Burns grinned good-naturedly at the suggestion. "All of those jocks that I see hanging around you should have enough for you."

"Oh, when I work them up, they're all right. Where are we going?"

"We're all going to a special party at the gay bar. I want you to meet my butch, Mister Burns. You know her. She will be glad to see you."

"The gay bar is closed. There were no lights when I came in here."

"It's locked up, but not closed. They are having a quiet little party tonight for gay girl singles. Married ones are 'ome wit dere 'usbands an' family tonight."

"I didn't know that you were gay, Marie. I know that many of the night people are, but you put on a good act with men. Won't I be out of place?"

"No. You are jus a fren' of my dyke han me. Jus' min your own business han no one will notice. Leave your coat here."

She led him by the hand to the kitchen at the rear. They

entered a concrete service and utilities tunnel where Burns had to walk at a crouch. The tunnel led to the rear of the gay bar, two doors away on Sherbrooke Street. The club room was small and tastefully decorated. Chairs and love seats were clustered around low coffee tables. There were blacklight spots over the tables. A low background music throbbed, muted. Burns could see that the room was about half filled with couples of girls, some of whom he recognized from clubs and cafes. Most couples seemed intent on each other. Conversations were in whispers, or low voices.

A tall girl, waiting alone near the door, looked inquiringly, if not approvingly, at Marie with Burns.

"You know Josephine from Martin's, Mr. Burns. Joey is my dyke."

Josephine extended her left hand to Burns and took Marie's arm with her right. She seated them at a table so that Burns faced away from the room. She spoke to Marie in a whisper. "You really shouldn't have, Marie, dearest. You know how some of the girls are."

"It's all right, Joey. Mr. Burns is a good friend. He doesn't want anything. He's been aroun'. He knows duh score, and, to-night, he is alone. Aboud is coming over, too. He will sit with us."

Burns could see Josephine's point. He was not comfortable.

Fat Aboud waddled in. He recognized someone and moved out of sight. He appeared seconds later with a tall, clean looking, moustached man in the evening clothes of a maitre d'. Aboud in-troduced him, "You all know Rejean."

Joey and Marie resumed their whispered conversation. Burns spoke to Rejean in a low voice. "I knew that you were gay, Re-jean, but I did not expect to find you at a lesbian party."

"You puzzle me, too, Mr. Burns. You are neither, and I find you here." Rejean excused himself, saying that he had a noon shift next day. He mentioned that he was driving to Park Exten-sion and asked if he could give anyone a lift, taxis being scarce. Burns accepted gladly. The town of Mount Royal was on the way. They left Aboud and the girls to go back through the tunnel for Burns' coat.

The snow on the deserted streets squealed under the tires of Rejean's drafty M.G., as they drove up Bluery Street to Park Avenue.

"Did you ever meet a girl named Sandra Sands, Rejean?"

"Oh yes! She is a beauty and a nice girl. If I were the kind of man that needed a woman, she would be my choice, let me tell you. I know her sister, Magda, well, too. She has a bad pimp. He does not work. He is a runner for Ninia's friend, drugs, betting, and all that."

Burns made a mental note and said no more.

Turning on the lights in the house in Mount Royal did nothing to dispel the gloom of it. In bed, with too much alcohol poisoning him, he found it hard to get to sleep.

Chapter 18

Vivian Stuart rose just before six A.M., strangely excited about going to the office. She had not really enjoyed her New Year holiday. She drew a tepid bath and languished in it. Her muscles were stiff from the skiing and the cold of the mountains. The warm water felt good, as did the brisk toweling afterward. She was of a sensuous nature. Now she admired her own nude body before her mirror, as she dusted with powder, applied deodorant, and perfume. Somehow, she felt, this would be a good day for her. Her horoscope, if you read it right, said to "take advantage of any new opportunities today."

She knew that the new promotion for her boss would be announced. Instead of being secretary to an assistant vice-president, she would be secretary to the executive vice-president. There would be a raise in salary, perhaps enough that she could afford an apartment downtown. On her own, she could do what she liked, whenever she wished, with whomever attracted her. No more parked cars or drafty or hot ski lodges. She felt quite up to making sure that she remained Alton Burns' secretary, even when . . . an executive vice-president was in line to be president. She could see Maggie's face.

Arriving at the office a half hour early, she proceeded quickly to make Burns' new office ready for him.

Henry Hopkins had called her into his office while Burns was away.

"Where's Burns?" he bellowed before she closed the door.

"I think that he is in Mobile, Alabama, today, Mr. Hopkins."

"What the hell is he doing down there?"

"I believe that he is doing something for U.S. Motors, something Mr. Morton asked him to do last week. Didn't he tell you?"

"Oh, yeah, but he should be here. We've got no bloody customers down there. Are you sure that he is not at Eagle Steel in Chicago?"

"I don't think so, although I know that Mr. Buckley asked him to attend some affair on his way back; but that would not be until Friday. Do you need him, Mr. Hopkins?"

"Nah, it ain't urgent. Just tell him that I wanta see him as soon as he comes into the god-damn office."

Hopkins' face was dark with anger as he reread the telegram in his hand. He held it as though he did not know what to do with it. While Vivian Stuart wavered, not knowing whether to leave or not, he crushed the telegram and hurled it into his wastebasket. Then he retriveved it and held it out to her.

"Do you know anything about this, Miss Stuart?"

She straightened out the paper and managed to read it. "Please convey best wishes to George Thurston on retirement and be assured of our full support of Alton Burns as he assumes responsibilities of executive vice-president, signed, Eagle Steel Foundries, B. Buckley, President."

"No, I don't, Mr. Hopkins. Mr Burns did not discuss this with me."

He reached for the telegram, crushed it again, and threw it in the wastebasket.

"God-damnit! I made Burns vice-president, not executive vice-president. They may be our biggest account, but they can't tell me what to do. They don't own this God-damn company. Tell Burns to see me just as soon as he gets back."

"Very well, Mr. Hopkins. I'll tell him."

When Burns arrived in the office, a little later than usual, he hurried straight to his old desk. Vivian Stuart appeared before he hung his coat. She was thinking of the conversation with Hopkins but thought it best not to mention it. Burns seemed to have overlooked the fact of his promotion and that he would be moving into Thurston's office.

"Welcome back. Mr. B. I've moved all of your things into your new office. I'll show you where everything is. Mr. Hopkins wants to see you as soon as he comes in."

"Thank you, Miss S. Did you have a good holiday?"

"Not particularly. I was glad to hear from you, although you didn't sound as though you were enjoying yourself. At the risk of being improper, I was tempted to phone you back, but I assumed that if you were at loose ends, Sandra would take care of you, whoever she is. She called twice last week or did I tell you?"

He ignored her curiosity.

"When she calls, tell her to meet me at room 15 at five o'clock sharp. Tell her how to get there, please."

"Would you like me along as chaperone? She sounds dangerous."

Ignoring her curiosity again, he followed her into his new office. He placed his briefcase on the modern excutive desk and looked around the spacious room. He rearranged an arm chair before a long coffee table and patted the center cushion of the large red leather sofa.

"Nice and firm, Miss S. Think we can make use of it?"

"Is this Sandra a secretary? You are not thinking of replacing me, are you, Mr. B?"

"No, Miss S., Sandra is not a secretary, but we may have some work for her. You will know all about it. Just be patient and I'll satisfy your female curiosity in due course. Now, let's go over the program for today."

She seated herself and laid out her notebook.

"As soon as I am finished with the old man, I'll go down to Lamont's office. You can make a luncheon appointment with Edger Hays, room 15 at twelve fifteen. Locate Hal Ives and have him meet me here at two thirty. Make a reservation, a penthouse suite, at the Laurentien, for Mr. Buckley and Mr. Cable, arriving tomorrow morning. Have the switchboard look out for a call from Mr. Matt Mara, and have it relayed to me, wherever I am. When you leave the office, have the switchboard give the message to Sandra, if you haven't. We can't call her. As soon as Ives comes in and we get into our meeting, you go up to Cantlie House,

that's the new apartment building just being completed at the corner of Peel and Sherbrooke. They are renting now. There is an office on the ground floor. I want to rent two efficiencies, unfurnished, one on each of two floors, at least four floors apart. They must be suitable for draughting offices, with space for four drawing boards and a desk in each. I will need them for two months only. On still another floor, I want to rent a one-bedroom unit, unfurnished, for one year. I will furnish it from the house in Mount Royal. I will go up to sign the leases myself tomorrow morning. I want to occupy all three apartments by the end of this week. Any questions, Miss S.?"

She looked over her notes and shook her head as she thoughtfully left the office.

Henry Hopkins looked up from his black notebooks and began talking before Burns sat down.

"I've been thinking some since we talked, Alton. I've decided to make you executive vice-president, OK? Of course, we have already settled the matter of salary and bonus. Right, so, here's your contract, ready for you to sign."

"Thanks, Henry. Titles don't mean too much to me. The contract looks OK. I'll sign it and return a copy tomorrow."

Hopkins was relieved. His attitude was more friendly now that he felt that there was no plot to extract a higher salary.

"Ya have a good trip?"

"Yes, I think that I told you. Joe Morton was having a little trouble with Lou Waldorf of the Gulf Railroad. Waldorf was browned off with U.S. Motors and wanted to get even by refusing to buy Precision bearings. There was nothing in it for us but I thought that I could see a way that Waldorf's decision could fit in with a plan I have to get all of the bearings purchased on their replacement program at the A. & P. this year. I'm seeing Hays at lunch today. If I play my cards right, Acme could get the whole order this year."

"As I have told you before, Alton, there's no way they can give us all of the business, but no harm in tryin'. Oh yeah! Here's your twenty share certificates and the check for the balance of

your bonus. Put those shares away in a safe place. They might be the controlling shares in the company some day. Haw! Haw!" Hopkins used his loud guffaw to soften the sarcasm. "While the wife and I were signing 'em, we figured that we might as well hold our annual meeting of shareholders. Maggie has typed up the usual minutes along with the minutes of the director's meeting that we held the other day. Hope you don't mind. As holder of only twenty shares, your vote don't count for much anyway, but if you want any little change in the minutes, just add 'em in."

"Yes, there was something that I wanted to talk to you about in that connection, Henry. I have talked to Hector Muir at the bank. New corporate taxes this year in a firm of our size can get pretty complicated, especially if we should get some extra profits, which I am sure now that we will. I hate paying more taxes than we have to and I am sure that you feel the same way. Hector thinks that we could save his fee many times over, if we hired W.D. Byers as tax consultant and auditor. The bank uses him as a consultant. You know him. He is a Shriner."

Burns was prepared for an objection, but Hopkins was so satisfied with the way that the matter of title and salary had been settled, without extra cost, that he readily agreed.

"Good idea. Let's do it. If it takes a resolution or something just write it into the minutes. The wife and I will sign it."

Burns chose to walk to the offices of the government railways. The January sun was warm enough to begin melting of the ice crust on the snow-packed sidewalks.

The young, gum-chewing receptionist in the offices of the vice-president of operations and maintenance summoned Florence Ridout as soon as Burns entered the reception room. Florence appeared at once.

"You have some tan, Alton. It looks good on you."

"Yes. I had a day's fishing in Florida, Florence."

"Want to see his nibs? He's in his usual bad mood."

Burns nodded and as she turned to announce him, she hesitated and came back to whisper, "I'll bet you forgot cigars, again."

Burns nodded and grinned when she disappeared into La-

mont's private office. Lamont did not smoke cigars, but he felt strongly that the gift cigar from a supplier was due him as a symbol of respect. It pleased him if it was a certain type of dollar cigar that fitted into a case that he had been given. He accumulated the cigars in the top drawer of his private filing cabinet. When he inspected a railroad facility he was fond of flashing the case and dispensing one of the expensive cigars to the superintendent or foreman at no cost to him.

Burns never felt this tribute necessary, in view of their special relationship. However, Florence Ridout thought that it was better for him to conform. So, whenever he called, she went into the private office first, on the pretense of looking for a file. With her back to Lamont, she filched a couple of cigars. She slipped them to Burns as he went in, enabling him to give back to Lamont a couple of his own cigars. Everyone was satisfied.

"Well, what's the trouble now," Lamont growled.

"I just want to invite you out for dinner tomorrow night, Jules. It won't be in public. It will be in a suite at the Laurentien and I'll arrange a little private party for you afterward. You can be home early."

"Yeah! I'm due. You can get Gaby. What do I have to do?"

"I'll see that Gaby is available, but before that I will need your help again, with the guy that we met with Connors, Matt Marra."

"Yeah, the man with the pipe dream about hauling ore from Char Lake over our Churchill line?"

"Right, but no pipe dream. They are going to do it. Now I've got to see that they do it with ninety-ton cars and all parts approved by the Railroad Association. We can't let them select one-hundred-ton, or one-hundred-and-twenty-ton, or seventy-ton. They must be ninety-ton. This will give Acme the advantage in obtaining the order for all of the running gear at a good price. At least thirty million dollars is involved, Jules. Now you know how important this can be for me."

"Yeah. What do you want me to do?"

"Just make sure, in advance, that nobody, but nobody in any department of your railway, agrees that you can move a car over

this capacity over your Churchill line without damage. Who can prove otherwise? Right? Cover everybody, Jules. Mechanical engineering, civil engineering, and research departments. Brainwash them all. You are the boss. I must get the matter settled at dinner tomorrow night."

"I don't know. Perhaps we can handle one-hundred-ton."

"Not if you say that you can't, and if you prepare all of your experts to say that you can't."

"Who will be at the dinner?"

"Matt Marra, Buck Buckley, Tom Cable, I hope, and Hal Ives, if I can get Marra to engage him as project general manager. He is going to leave your railway, anyway. I was sure that you would not stand in his way."

"OK, I'll be there. Where do we meet, and where will I see Gaby?"

"It's a new set-up, Jules. We will meet in the Boulevard Room, about five. Buck will have a penthouse suite at the Laurentien. We will meet some women in the bar, by accident. From there, we will play that part of it by ear. All that you have to do is get your message across, loud and clear. Then, after dinner in the suite, you can move off to Peel Street and Gaby. You can be home by ten."

On McGill Street, Burns hailed a cab. He arrived at room 15 in time to read the financial page of the *Montreal Gazette* before Edger Hays arrived. Over a drink, while they waited for lunch to be sent up, Burns brought up the reason for the meeting.

"I took the liberty of acting on your behalf and made some money for you over the holiday, Edger."

Hays looked alarmed. "What do you mean, Alton?"

"Remember the idea that you had last year. You proposed using a common Zerk fitting in the face of the Precision bearing housing for emergency lubrication. Everyone, including your own people, denounced the idea. I applied for a patent on your behalf, anyway. Lou Waldorf of the Gulf Railroad has a big program of bearing purchases this year. He has decided to use Precision bearings exclusively, provided that—and get this, Edger—provided that every Precision bearing is furnished with your

Zerk-fitting idea. Of course, he does not know that you hold the patent. U. S. Motors has agreed to furnish it at no extra charge to get all of the Gulf business, and they are allowing a royalty of fifty cents per bearing, which I will pass along to you. When I told Lou that you would require this feature on all of the bearings that the A. & P. purchase this year, he was relieved. The fact that you were requiring the same improvement justified his choice. I have advised U. S. Motors that we will furnish Zerks on all of the bearings purchased from Acme by the A. & P., at no extra cost. I knew that you would agree."

Burns looked at Hays for confirmation.

"Oh yes, of course. I must get out requisitions for this year's purchases as soon as I get back to the office. With this modification, we can justify the purchase of Precision bearings exclusively."

As the orders for bearings came in to Acme in February, Henry Hopkins did not question Hays' departure from the long established policy of splitting the business between two bearing suppliers.

He rubbed his hands together and gleefully recorded the profit.

Chapter 19

Hector Muir had just finished trimming his close-clipped moustache, when the phone rang in his bedroom. The head office branch general manager of the largest bank in Canada placed the razor neatly in its case before answering. He recognized the voice, at once.

"Did I wake you up, Hector?"

"No, I'm up, Alton, but I'm half asleep yet. What can be troubling you, so early, fellah?"

"No trouble, Hector. I've just had a very interesting week and I want to tell you about it. Can I ride downtown with you?"

"Fine, fellah. Want me to pick you up as I go by your place about eight-thirty?"

"Good, Hector. I'll be on the sidewalk, if I can find it in the snow."

Muir was an imposing figure at any time; polished, urbane, and suave, his black homburg was always at the right angle; his perfectly tailored clothes always fit. He had not been born to this station in life. For three generations, his family had lived in a rural settlement in the Ottawa Valley. They had been lumbermen, until the trees petered out. His father, a locomotive fireman, died of a heart attack shoveling coal into the fiery maw of a steam locomotive. His only brother, somewhat older, had been a telegrapher and was now nearing retirement as a divisional superintendent on the A. & P. Railroad. Hector, himself, had worked as a railway call-boy before starting as a junior in the local branch of the Empire Bank. He was still a railroad buff at heart.

When he had worked up to the position of manager at the McGill Street branch of the bank, he met Burns. The head office of the government railways was across the street from the bank. The railroad payroll account was maintained at the branch and Burns had his small personal account there.

They fell into the habit of walking together from their offices to the weekly luncheon meetings of the Young Men's Board of Trade. On other days, they lunched together at a nearby tavern. They took night courses in public speaking and finance at McGill University. Before Burns joined Acme, Muir had advanced to his present position at the bank's head office on St. James Street. It was a coincidence that Acme had enjoyed a long association with the Empire Bank, long before Burns joined the company, with offices in the same building. They were neighbors in the town of Mount Royal. Both were Masons. Both joined the Engineer's Club, nearby on Beaver Hall Hill.

Burns was intensely interested in Muir's activities in the world of finance, and Muir was no less interested in Burns's experiences with the railways. In Muir's car that winter morning, and later in Muir's office before the bank opened, Burns's new contract with Henry Hopkins was discussed. With rapt attention, Muir listened to the information that Burns had gathered on the Char Lake project. He was not without some prior knowledge of it. The Empire Bank had been approached to participate.

"Do you realize, Alton, that this deal, under this contract, could put Acme in your inside pocket, lock, stock, and barrel, and make you filthy rich at the same time?"

Burns was frank in saying that he had not really considered that. All of his concentration had been on the engineering aspects, to secure the most of the order for Acme.

"Leave the contract with me, Alton—and those minutes of the so-called annaul meeting. I'll have our attorneys look them over and get them back to you this afternoon. These may be the most important documents that you will ever sign. We'll make sure that there are no loopholes. I'm telling you, Alton, this looks like the opportunity of a lifetime."

"Your assistance may be very important, Hector. This deal

may take more financing than Acme has ever faced before. I may have to go into hock myself, as Hopkins will never understand the expenditures that I may have to make, gamble, perhaps, to wrap it up."

"No problem, fellah. As a matter of fact, I have some confidential news for you. I was advised at the president's New Year's reception, unofficially, of course, that I will be appointed VP and general manager of the bank at the end of February. That carries with it a directorship. When you need financing, just let me know. The main thing is to keep us advised every step of the way. You always do, anyway." Hector Muir assumed the official attitude of a bank executive for a moment. "You know, Alton, our best security is the assurance we have in the ability and integrity of the individual. I know you. I know how you work."

"Thanks, Hector. Your elevation is not much of a surprise to me. It's been in the cards ever since you moved here to head office. My sincere congratulations."

Like conspirators, they went over Burns's course of action, starting with the recommendation of Hal Ives to be Canadian general manager. Above all, Muir agreed, the more confidential the specifications were kept until issued, the more chance for success.

It was finally agreed that Hector would set up a line of credit in Burns' personal account for up to twenty-five thousand dollars. Burns offered to take out an insurance policy that would protect Muir and the bank to some extent.

Hal Ives was waiting for the call from Burns' office. He had risen early at his sister's home in Verdun. He bathed and dressed when his turn came to use the one bathroom. He offered to stand aside and read the paper while the two children used it to get ready for school. He said that he was in no hurry. He was, and the situation annoyed him. As usual, he hid his feelings.

It had not been a happy holiday for him. The new opportunity, whatever it was, that Burns had mentioned, was the only pleasant thing that he had to anticipate. He wondered if it would mean working with Burns again. He had hinted once that he

would like to work at Acme, but he had not followed it up. Perhaps Burns had consolidated his position now and could bring him in. He would like that, at this time. He was sure that Burns could use his talents as he had in the old days on the government railroad.

When Vivian Stuart called, he left at once for Acme's offices. Burns described, at some length, the Char Lake situation and the recommendation that he would make to Marra. He inquired if Ives was sure that he wanted the position of Canadian project general manager. Ives did not even inquire about salary. He wanted it. With that settled, Burns suggested that Ives prepare himself for an interview. Ives was handed what appeared to be a huge collection of files and drawings.

"My complete confidential files of reports to the A.A.R. Car Construction Committee on ore cars," Burns termed them.

Ives would spend the rest of the afternoon studying them so that he would be prepared to make knowledgeable recommendations when asked.

Of course, the reports and data included were actually only those carefully selected from Burns's much more voluminous files. In most cases, there were two sides to an evaluation. The vast majority of the reports given to Ives favored the products that Acme offered.

Several files from different railroads concluded that ninety-ton capacity cars offered most in economical maintenance and versatility. There were a couple of files which mentioned unsatisfactory service with one-hundred-and one-hundred-and-twenty-ton Cleveland Steel running gear. There were many reports describing satisfactory performance of Eagle Steel's ninety-ton designs.

There were many good reports on Eagle Steel's clasp-type brakes. Cleveland Steel's one-hundred-ton equipment was designed to accommodate disc-type brakes. There was correspondence describing difficulties with this arrangement.

Cleveland Steel's designs included a lateral motion device to protect wheel flanges when negotiating curves, such as would be encountered on the Churchill line. Eagle Steel did not provide

this feature at a considerable saving in manufacturing costs to them. However, if U. S. Motors' Precision cylindrical-type bearings were used, the lateral feature was provided in the bearing. Several reports indicated that this combination was most satisfactory. There were no favorable reports on service provided by competitive types of bearings.

An even dozen analyses pointed up the advantages of an ore car which emptied from the top by turning the whole car over rather than dumping through doors in the floor. Several files from nothern railroads described problems with doors freezing shut in cold weather, such as would be encountered in the Arctic. With the top dump design, an expensive rotary coupling and cushioning device was required between cars. Only Eagle Steel offered such a device.

Explaining that he had an important meeting at five o'clock in room 15 at the hotel, Burns suggested that Ives order a sandwich or whatever he needed from Vivian Stuart. Burns promised to be back in a couple of hours. Ives was glad to be left alone. With access to "all" of the A.A.R. confidential files on the subject, he would be well prepared for his interview with Matt Marra.

Chapter 20

The Boulevard Lounge was a large room. Window boxes of plastic greenery behind drapes with dim indrect lighting gave a feeble imitation of windows looking out into the darkness. This helped patrons to rationalize drinking in the early afternoon. While it would be much busier later, there were few drinkers at five o'clock.

Two tables were occupied by men in conversation, probably salesmen and clients who had been there since lunch. At a table half way to the rear on the left hand side, three girls were seated. When the waiter approached, he was advised, in French, that they were waiting for a friend and would order later. They sat silently, glancing toward the door from time to time. One was a buxom blonde, quite attractive. She had a sort of peaches-and-cream complexion, with a suggestion of olive. It was heightened by her dark almond eyes, black lashes, and eyebrows, carefully arched suggested that her hair was bleached. The other two girls were obviously French-Canadian.

The blonde wore a red dress, classically cut to show off her generous bust. The others wore dark dresses, inexpensive, but tasteful. Rather expensive looking fur coats or imitations were draped over the backs of their chairs. Aside from the oversized purses, a badge of their trade, at the sides of the chairs, they could have been taken for young housewives gathered for a drink after shopping, before leaving on the train to the suburbs.

Three waiters terminated their heated discussion of last night's Canadien's hockey game to stare, as the tall, striking-

looking girl entered the room. She walked directly to the girls' table. Her fur coat, thrown open, did not appear expensive, but her simple black dress could have been an original designed for her perfect figure. Her eyes were unusual.

The men at the table stopped talking in mid-sentence to follow her movements. One waiter approached the table. Without looking at him, and without hesitation, she ordered four orange juices, plain. She seated herself, tossing her jet black, shoulder-length hair. She sat with her back to the door. There was no conversation while they waited for service. When the men came in, the peaches-and-cream girl confirmed it with a glance at Sandra. She nodded silently, that she understood.

Burns selected a table at the right of the entrance without waiting for the head waiter to seat them. With the exception of Lamont, who they had met in the lobby, they had left their coats in Buckley's suite.

"Bring three martinis, very dry. These are Americans," Burns pointed out to the waiter. "I'll have Scotch and water without ice, and my father here," Burns nodded toward Lamont, "will have Walkers premium black label straight. What will you have, Hal?"

Ives hesitated as usual when a decision was to be made in front of Burns, looking for advice.

"You have to have something, Hal. This is your night. We have to toast to your new career as project general manager, Char Lake Mines and Railroad."

Ives ordered a rob roy, uncertainly.

That morning, after intoducing Ives to Matt Marra, and spending about a half hour in Acme's offices discussing Ives' qualifications and experience, Burns had left them alone, while he went to the airport to meet Buckley. It was no surprise to find Tom Cable on the same plane; Burns had asked for Cable's support at this crucial meeting. They lunched together at the Mount Stephen Club. Cable went shopping for a couple of hours, while Marra, Buckley, Burns, and Ives met in Buckley's suite.

By the time that Cable returned, the others had discussed Hal Ives' recommendations and examined the reports that he had

selected from the "confidential" files and brought with him to support them. Up to that point, Marra had not indicated that Hal Ives' appointment was definite. Now he stood up, stretched, poured a cup of coffee from an urn on a side table, and, for the first time that day, relaxed and walked around the big suite.

Back in the sitting room, he addressed Hal Ives. "Why don't you and Alton leave us for a few minutes. You can get me a couple of cigars downstairs. I'd like to have a little talk with Buck and Tom."

Tom Cable was examining the stock of liquor on the bar which had not been touched all afternoon.

"Nothing here will make a good, dry martini. You guys really do not need me, but I'll stay and drink some of Burns's garbage, if I'm not in the way."

Marra spoke softly to Cable.

"I wish you would stay, Tom. You may not be interested directly in this project, but your company does have a director on my board. I have a very important decision to make and I may need your support. Anyway, you were present when these matters were discussed with the old man in Florida. You know his views and that will help. This is a big thing, Tom."

Downstairs, Burns and Ives bought the cigars, then walked aimlessly around the lobby. Ives was jittery. He wanted this opportunity like he had never wanted anything in his life before; a new job, away from Edmonton, with all of the bitter memories of his wife's illness, suffering, and death. It was what he felt that he needed, now, to get a new lease on life. He liked what he had seen of Matt Marra. He would be working with Alton Burns again, at least until the ore trains were rolling.

"Don't worry, Hal, relax. I've advised them what salary to offer—just three times what you are getting now. You will be able to live on your expense account, since you will be traveling a lot. It's a good deal. Both Buck and Tom are behind you. That's at least three directors out of seven. Joe Morton praised you most highly to the old man in Florida. Matt has no choice. He's got to take you."

When they returned to the suite, exactly one half hour later, Ives was met at the door by Marra, hand outstreched. "Welcome,

Mr. Project General Manager, Hal Ives."

"Congratulations!"

"I'll add mine downstairs. Let's get out of this hovel. They make beautiful dry martinis in the Boulevard Room. We have only booze, here. It must be the 'happy hour.' There is bound to be more sexy scenery than you guys provide up here."

"I'm with you, Tom. Liquor agrees with me more when there are women around, to look at, at least."

Jules Lamont, in his heavy coat and knee-high galoshes, was standing disconsolate in the lobby near the elevator. Sweat was running down the sides of his florid face. A drop hung from his big nose. He was in his usual offensive mood for being kept waiting. He did not like the idea of drinking in the Boulevard Room. He mumbled about going upstairs to get rid of his heavy coat. He would prefer to pour his own drink from a bottle that he could see, but he came along reluctantly, at the urging of Buckley and Cable.

They had just been served the first round of drinks when Sandra arose form her chair and walked toward them on her way to the lobby, noting that there were six men, not the four that she had been told to expect. She looked stunning, the wide slanted eyes turning neither right nor left. Tom Cable gave a low whistle and, out of the corner of his eye, Burns noted the keen interest of Matt Marra. As she passed, Burns stood up.

"Hello, Sandra."

"Why, hello, Alton."

Saying no more, but smiling with those white teeth and expressive eyes, she walked out into the lobby. Tom Cable whistled again. "Lovely, lovely! Who is she, Alton?"

"I don't know, part-time model or something. I met her on the commuter train going to work in the mornings. She's just friendly. Nice girl!"

"She is with three other girls. Did you notice? They all look good. There's got to be some possibilities. Go to work, old boy. You are, at least, a speaking acquaintance."

Sandra returned from the lobby, a package of cigarettes in her hand.

She looked directly at them, now, with a friendly smile. She

gave a slight nod of understanding, as Burns took his cigarette from his mouth with five fingers showing. No one noticed except Sandra. All eyes were on her. Seemingly struck by an afterthought, she stopped near their table and returned to the lobby.

Tom Cable leaned toward the door to watch the movement of her hips as she went out.

"Stop her when she comes back for her coat, Alton. Perhaps she and her girl friends are on the loose. Maybe they will come up to the suite for a drink. For God's sake, don't let her get by again."

"I really don't know her that well."

"Well, for Chrissake get with it, man. The way she looked at you! You're among friends, you know. It won't do any harm to try." Matt Marra was eager.

When Sandra returned, Burns stood and held out his hand. She stopped and took it. She looked at them quizzically. Matt Marra stood up and proffered his chair, but she remained standing.

"Are you and your girl friends out on the town tonight, Sandra?"

"Yes, sort of. It's our bowling club. We had some money in the kitty and we decided to spend it on a dinner. One of the girls has not arrived yet. We are waiting for her."

'If you and the girls are just out for dinner, why don't you join us? These boys are from out of town."

She glanced at her girl friends' table, uncertainly.

"I don't know. It was to be a girls' party. I'll ask them when Mona gets here. OK? If you are not in a hurry, come over and see us before you leave."

The eyes again followed her liquid curves as she left them.

Jules Lamont cleared his throat to break the silence. He griped in his usual complaining tone. He was hot and uncomfortable. He was comparing Sandra's trim, sensuous body with Gaby's pot belly and flabby tits, which he would fondle later while she laid back, her pig-eyes expressionless. Nevertheless, he was impatient to get this part of the evening over with, to get to his own pleasure.

"I understand that you are still serious about going ahead with your Char Lake mine, Mr. Marra."

"That's right, Mr. Lamont. September is 'roll' month for us."

"I want you to know that you are buggering up my budget completely. We will have to work all summer on our roadbed just to take your heavy goddamn ore trains. I am warning you, though, we are not touching the bridges. I hope that you are not planning on using any cars of over ninety-tons capacity. If you are, forget it. I've checked with engineering, operating, and research departments. Ninety tons is the limit. If you build anything heavier, you'll have to build another thousand miles of line of your own. As a common carrier, we are obliged to take your traffic, but we can't take cars that our bridges won't support. I don't want to have to argue the point after you have issued specifications."

"I can put your mind at rest right now, Mr. Lamont. We want to work with you. We have to live together. After meeting with Hal this afternoon, my mind was practically made up. You have cinched my decision. Ninety tons they will be."

Burns drew an inaudible sigh of relief. While the preparation that he had made for Hal Ives to present made him pretty sure that the ninety-ton type would be selected, Marra's definite statement was welcome. Acme had won the second inning. Buckley's eyes conveyed his congratulations. Burns could not help at this moment but wonder if all men in all industries, confident, competent men, did not each have his price. Every decision was bought, one way or another. Lamont had done his part in this struggle for millions, and he would be rewarded like a seal with a piece of stinking fish. In his case, it would be a few minutes of grunting and synthetic groaning, as he forced his half-flaccid, fat prick into the Lysol and Vaseline of Gaby's tired, sideless, and bottomless vagina. He wondered what price they would have to pay to hold what had been gained. Matt Marra looked easy, at this moment. Burns had him sized up to be handled in the same way as Lamont, but it would take better bait and much more finesse. Hal Ives, as a long-time friend with the position that

he wanted handed to him, should already have been bought and paid for. Perhaps something as small as the mounted fish that Burns felt had influenced Jim Murphy, would keep Ives sweet from time to time. He was so naive and honest that he could be dangerous. He must be kept under control, completely, for the next three months. Tonight might reveal what it would take. After the briefing that he had given her, Sandra would be watching and listening. He was sure that she would give anything that she had to help.

Burns was called out of his reverie by Cable.

"There's the girl friend. Not bad, either! Your friend Sandra is filling them in now. Better get over there, Alton. Let's see what kind of salesman you are."

"Yeah! Get going, Alton. They are looking better every minute."

Burns got up, reluctantly, and walked over to the girls' table. They saw Sandra introduce him all around. They pretended to consult together as Burns instructed Sandra further.

"Matt Marra is the most important. He is the one who offered you his chair. It is most important that whoever he selects keeps him coming back. We are going to have to keep him pregnant and tired every night that he is in town for the next three months. He must be relaxed, interested, and happy, and completely under control. I don't want to know what you have to do for him. You get paid as long as he is satisfied and can't wait for more. No phone numbers, of course. Sandra makes all arrangements, so that I know what's going on. I suggest your sister, Magda, if he fancies her. From what you tell me, she knows how to handle men. You will have to play it by ear, and if he insists on guiding you by the ears, that's all right, too. He seems to vibe with women, so he should be easy, but if Magda can't keep him under control, you will have to step in with yourself or somebody else. The sky is the limit with him.

"The next most important is Hal Ives, the quiet one in the grey suit. I've known him for years. He has never shown any great interest in women. He just likes to look. You know the type. However, his wife died just before Christmas, after a long

illness—nothing catching. He may not have had sex for a long time. Whoever takes him, don't push him, study him, console him, flatter him, but keep him interested and occupied whenever he is not with me. You spend some time with him, yourself, Sandra. Size him up tonight. We will see plenty of him for the next three months, as he will work out of Montreal. It could be that he will not let himself go in front of his new boss, Marra, and vice-versa. If you find this to be the case, split them. I don't care how you do it.

"The fat guy is lined up already with a steady. He'll duck out after dinner. That's OK, forget him. The other two men have been around. They know the score. They are already on our side. They are just here to help. We are not selling them anything, but they are important to me in other ways.

"Remember now, the two customers get the royal treatment. They are the great lovers. They are the cleverest. They are irresistible. The penthouse is number eight. We'll go up now. You follow as soon as possible. Check with me often, Sandra, but don't make it obvious." Burns leaned over and kissed Sandra on the cheek for the benefit of the men watching and the curious waiters.

Back at his own table, he did not bother to seat himself. The men looked at him, inquiring without asking. He picked up the check and signed it with Buckley's suite number.

"Everything is arranged. We have company for dinner upstairs. Let's go."

At the elevator, with the exception of morose Lamont and a quiet Hal Ives, they acted like little boys anticipating a new toy, chuckling, questioning in whispers, excitedly speculating.

"I've got to stop off at my room on the fifth floor. I want to change my shirt and clean my teeth and . . ."

"Don't be too long, Matt," Cable interrupted, "you might get wet decks."

The girls arrived about fifteen minutes later. There was a courteous scramble to take their coats. Marra rejoined them before Cable and Burns had finished serving the first drinks. Marra's first question, in a whisper, was if they made the first drinks

strong enough. A maidenhead melter, he called it. The men, with the exception of a detached Lamont, were soon paired off and feeling their ways with light conversation.

"God-damnit, I'm hungry," Lamont growled. He had mentioned this downstairs. No one had paid attention. "Let's get the fucking room service up here and order something." He said it loud enough for Marra to hear. Matt beckoned to Burns to follow him into the corridor.

"For Chrissake, don't order yet. The girls are just getting mellow. Let 'em have another couple of drinks before we feed 'em. Another drink and mine will be ready for anything."

"I think that Shirley is ready for anything right now."

"Well . . . , I'm not sure. Can't you hold off Lamont for another round?"

"I'll try, Matt. But don't worry. These girls are out on the town tonight. She probably wants just what you want."

"Yes, but I don't want to make a move with this crowd around. I'd like to take her down to my room alone, but I'm not sure that she is ready to go yet. If we have dinner, it will bring out the inhibitions."

"OK, Matt, I'll stall. I am sure that Shirley will stay receptive."

"Thought you had never met her before," Marra looked suspicious.

"I know Montreal girls, Matt. I live here, remember."

With Lamont watching intently, Burns picked up the phone. He dialed room service with a finger on the disconnect button. He waited several seconds while Lamont continued to glare in his direction.

"This must be the busiest hour for room service."

Sandra joined him and he hung up. Lamont grunted in disgust and waddled to the bar, where he poured himself another Scotch. Taking a couple of gulps, he looked angrily at the telephone.

"Lemme see if I can't get those lazy bastards off their asses down there. If they can't serve right away, I gotta go. I'm supposed to be out with Len Bennet tonight. He's with the Vapor

Company. My wife knows that he always goes to bed early since he had his heart attack."

Lamont never told his wife when he went out with Burns. She did not dislike Burns, but when her husband went out with him, she wanted to be taken along.

Six years ago Lamont, separated from his wife because of his closet drinking and bad temper, was enjoying a day of fishing with Burns. They were using Larry Connors's company cottage and boat on Eighteen-mile Lake in the Laurentian Mountains. Connors was not along. Trolling by a private dock, on the otherwise deserted lake, they saw a woman in a bathing suit sunning herself. With the audacity of being half stoned, they invited her to join them. Bored, alone at their cottage, while her mother and father had gone to Montreal for the day, she accepted.

Somewhat obese, a very plain girl, ordinarily very regimented by religious parents, she was flattered by the attentions of the two men on a beautiful, silent mountain lake. After several drinks, the first heavily diluted with flat, hot ginger ale, at her request, she agreed to lunch with them at Connors's cottage. The lunch consisted of mainly more and stronger Scotches, urged on her by Lamont. When Burns disappeared discreetly in the woods, the girl found herself in bed with Lamont.

A short time after returning to Montreal, she discovered that she was pregnant. She refused to consider an abortion, on religious grounds. Lamont's wife gladly agreed to divorce. They were married just before the baby was born, much to the chagrin of her parents, torn between having a divorced son-in-law or a bastard grandchild.

Lamont was built with a penis as thick as it was long. After the hurt that she suffered, mentally and physically, that afternoon, when the Scotch effect wore off, she was passively frigid. While they were reasonably happy with their young daughter, Lamont now preferred his sex with prostitutes, who did not draw the line at a little oral stimulation for some of his extraordinary sexual desires.

While it was Lamont's nature to distrust anyone and everyone, he felt safer with Burns than anyone else. When he was

with Burns, it did not cost him anything. Frequent meetings for any purpose made it possible for Burns to know of every confidential development on the government railways that interested him. If there were competitive quotations required, he knew what price he would face. If he wanted an order, a few cents lower gave it to him. Neither trusted the other completely. Burns protected himself by maintaining a pipelone through junior employees and secretaries on Lamont's staff. Lamont knew it. Burns made him aware of it when Lamont delivered inaccurate information.

Room service answered the call at once. Lamont handed the phone to Burns, with a baleful scowl. Burns passed it to Sandra and watched how she handled the situation. She finally ordered New York strip steaks, with baked potatoes, for all, except two girls who wanted Quebec smelt. With more discussions in French, she ordered two bottles of Nuit St. Georges, room temperature, and two bottles of Ontario champagne at eight dollars a bottle. No one would know the difference by the time it was served, she explained, as the waiter would serve it in a napkin. She took more time to discuss a cheese tray and desert.

She left them to join her sister and Matt Marra. Hal Ives left Mona. She seemed to be boring him. He took the chair, vacated by Sandra, next to Burns. He whispered that he, too, hoped the food would be served soon. He felt that he should leave early. He nodded toward his new boss. He apologized. He hoped Burns would understand, with his new job and all. It was evident that Mona, whatever she offered, did not interest him. Her face showed her frustration at her failure.

Two waiters arrived, wheeling tables. Sandra joined Burns, as he waited to sign the check.

She reported in a low voice, "My sister is doing well with Marra. He wants her, but not in this suite. He does not want anyone to know."

"Good! He's the biggie. Work it out some way."

"I have an idea, but first, Mona is a turkey. She tried hard with Ives. It didn't work. I'll fix her up tomorrow. She would be glad if we let her go now. The two Americans are happy. I'll try

to look after Ives myself, after Mona goes. I don't think that will work either, tonight. I think that he associates me with you." She gave him an oblique look and squeezed his arm.

"Don't let anything get in the way, honey. He may make out that order. Understand?"

Lamont was already eating his steak, wolfing big bites, before the waiters had finished arranging the tables together. Before Burns had much more than tasted his, Lamont poured all of the red wine that his empty water glass would hold and gulped it down.

"If you're driving me home, Burns, c'mon." Lamont sorted out his hat and coat with some fumbling. On leaving, he confronted Matt Marra. "Remember this, Matt—Mr. Marra. Ninety-ton is the limit if you want us to handle your trains. The board of transport commissioners will back me up. And don't forget, when you are writing your specifications, every part of the cars must be A.A.R. approved. You understand? Every part and the whole car must be tested and A.A.R. approved. When you go bankrupt, we don't want cars left on our lines that we can't use in interchange with U. S. railroads."

Matt Marra reluctantly turned his attention from Magda to stand.

"You have my assurance, Mr. Lamont. We will specify that every detail of our cars be A.A.R. tested and approved."

Another score! Buckley's look acknowledged it to Burns. They had now won three innings. The top-dump, the brakes, and the cylindrical bearings must now be accepted, and that was the ballgame.

Pete was waiting in the limousine. Seeing Lamont with Burns, as they walked down the steps from the hotel, he knew where he would be told to take them. He wished that Burns would select different company. The thought of that pig with that poor French-Canadian girl, who had a no-good husband and six kids to support, angered Pete. It annoyed him when he was told to drive the man to his home in St. Lambert afterward. Tonight it would be the same. Lamont would demand that he stop at the little bar across from the bridge. He would insist that Pete come

in with him. He would tell Pete to pay for the double Scotch and charge it to Burns' account while he went into the washroom to bathe himself again with his little cake of strong Castile soap, before going home to his wife.

At the Peel Street house, the lights were out, but Lucille answered the door while the limousine waited at the curb. In her nylon dressing gown, she reeked of perfume.

"Gaby is waiting hupstairs," she whispered.

"I could use a Scotch. Good disinfectant, y'know."

They could hear Lamont wheezing and grunting as he sat in the dark at the foot of the stairs removing his galoshes.

"Gaby 'as a bottelle hupstair for you."

As soon as Lamont began to mount the stairs, Lucille took Burns's lapels to draw him close, and whispered, "If you 'ave to go, I will look after Gaby."

Burns slid his hand through her dressing gown to cup a soft breast in a good night gesture. She pecked him on the cheek and gave him a grind of her pelvis from force of habit. The door closed silently in the darkness.

Back at the Laurentien Hotel, Sandra was in the sitting room of the suite emptying ash trays and assembling used dishes on the room service carts. Pouring two glasses of the red wine, she led him to the couch at the far end of the room. She turned off a floor lamp and sat beside him.

"Tom and Buck are still here. They are gossiping with the girls, probably about the tricks tonight. We had a little problem with Matt. He wanted to take my sister to his room. She waited for him to ask her. Finally, I ordered a bottle of Pernod, in French, and signed for it in the hall outside. I took him aside and told him that you had left a bottle for him to take back to the states. They don't sell it there. Works like a Spanish fly, I told him. Then I implied that my sister would like to leave and I asked him to take her home. He took the bottle of Pernod and jumped at the chance. She was telling him how much she liked Pernod after dinner as they left. She will agree to drink in his room. Leave it to her. I'll report to you tomorrow. Magda knows just what to do with him."

Buck and Tom were saying good night to the girls in the corridor. When they left, Cable poured a nightcap and both men joined Burns. Sandra excused herself and when she returned she seated herself in the yoga position before the three of them.

"Sandra is OK. She is going to help us all through this deal. I would like her to listen in now, so that she knows just what we will expect of her."

Buckley, the strategist, took over.

"Sandra, I don't know where Alton found you or what your deal is. You took us in completely tonight, right up to the time Marra left. You handled the show well. Your sister seems to have Marra eating our of her hand. That's good. She will have to keep him isolated every time he comes to Canada for the next couple of months.

"You and your girls failed completely with Ives. He never became involved for a minute, although there were times when he looked interested in you, Sandra. We know that he has been a friend of Alton's for years. He owes Alton everything. But this may not be enough to keep him quiet and away from Cleveland Steel when they hear of his appointment and pursue him.

"We have won all the way tonight. Now, of course, the big thing is to keep the decisions made secret. If Cleveland Steel should get any information, they would begin redesigning at once. They could produce samples for test, submit them to our facilities at St. Louis, and demand to be asked for quotes on approved parts. With two directors on the board, they could not be refused the inquiry. Then it would be dog eat dog, both companies willing to take all or part of the first order for prestige alone. There would be no profit in it for any of us.

"Tomorrow, Alton will place orders for the construction of patterns and tooling. It will cost us a quarter of a million to get ready for production. There will be no indication of capacity on the drawings. If Cleveland finds out that our new patterns are ninety ton, they will get to work at once."

Buck looked from Sandra to Burns.

"I know what you mean, Buck. I have known Hal Ives since we started to work for the railway together. I admire and respect

his ability. He was always loyal when he worked with me. But he does not work for me, now. Every man has a price. Perhaps Hal's price is his friendship and gratitude for what we have done for him, but we must be on guard. There is so much at stake here."

Sandra stood.

"I understand. I will work with Mr. Burns. He has promised me a bonus, and I intend to earn it any way that I can." Sandra pressed Burns' arm again as the men stood. "Do you need me for anything else tonight, Mr. Burns?"

"I know that I would, if I were you, Burns." Cable was walking toward the bedrooms. "Our flight leaves at eight-thirty, Buck."

"Can I send you home in the car, Sandra?"

"No. Please stay with your friends. I'll get a taxi. I'm moving into my new apartment on Chomedy Street tomorrow."

Chapter 21

Sandra surveyed the trays of food set out on three platters in the small kitchen. Spicy, garlic aromas made the apartment smell like the home in Rosemount when her mother prepared for a party with her father's foundry friends years ago.

She interrupted the thoughts of her dead mother and of her gruff bear of a father to gather up some empty cartons from her father's small presents. Through the glass doors of the lobby, returning from the garbage chute, she could see the blackened snow in the street. It had melted during the January thaw, piling up and thawing again in February. It was insulated in layers by soot, salt, and debris, until it looked like dark lava.

The older sister had moved in with her to occupy the second bedroom. It was part of the deal when she began working for Burns. She was to have her sister with her and provide a place where Matt Marra could go for his most interesting relaxation every night on his weekly trips to Montreal. There had been a problem. Magda's pimp, a handsome young French-Canadian, refused to let her leave the crib in the red light district. He had threatened her. He beat her, and finally put a mark on her forehead. Magda, at first, wavered. She was accustomed to his domination. She had heard that he had a stable of two other French-Canadian girls, but he made love to her most nights, when she turned over her money to him. He protected her. He knew important city politicians. She had seen him talk to them at church. Knowing that the pimp worked as a runner for Ninia's gangster boy friend, Burns sought his help. A suggestion from the mobster that legs could be broken easily if he did not leave

Magda alone, solved that problem. Sandra was pleased to have her sister with her and their father was grateful. He welcomed them both now, when they visited on Sunday afternoons.

When Sandra told her father that she had accepted a position with Acme, he did not question her need to move downtown to an apartment of her own. She would often have to work late. When she explained that she would be able to change her sister's life by taking her in, the old man was satisfied. He gave up the house and moved in with an old Roumanian friend, putting the money in the bank for his retirement. His old association with Sir Giles Humbolt made him confident that his most beautiful daughter would be looked after. Who knows? She might become the well-kept mistress of one of the gentlemen of Sir Giles' old company. That would be better than the life chosen by their younger sister, Olga. She was so far away on that poor farm, raising three children, already, grandchildren that he had not seen. With his retirement on a pension, things could be better, but they could be much worse.

Sandra had located the apartment, but it was Magda who took the landlord's fancy as soon as she moved in. She welcomed his attentions in the afternoons when Sandra was out on a modeling assignment or other part-time activity for her old boss. The girls received preferential treatment. Like their father, the landlord understood that he was never to call in before phoning, and never at night.

Burns seemed satisfied with the way that Magda kept Marra occupied whenever he was in town. Sandra held every evening open in case Burns needed them. Several other girls were on standby for a call. At the end of the evening or next day, Sandra paid each girl what she felt had been earned or contributed to the cause. Burns compensated her without question. She was able to retain a few extra dollars for herself. Burns demanded only that his customers were left happy, satisfied, and unworried about anything, including their health, providing that, in addition, the girl had a good report as well, learned in bed or wherever. Above all, there must be no suggestion that money or reward of any kind was involved. Favors must be proffered only because of the client's overwhelming male charisma.

From time to time, over the past few weeks, Sandra was concerned that she was not contributing enough herself. She had never seen such a man at work. She knew that Burns had been at the office from early morning, through lunches and dinners, when he supervised two engineering offices at night. One room in the Cantlie House was staffed with five designers from the government railways, working on the body of the car. The other was manned by five draughtsmen from the A. & P. Railroad, working on the running gear. They were kept separate. Neither group knew of the other's existence. The drawings were checked, titled, and indexed in Burns' apartment on still another floor. After Sandra and one or two of her girls appeared to pour a drink and send the moonlighters home happy, Sandra collected the last of the night's productions and took them to Burns' apartment. Ives and Marra, when he was in town, would be there.

By midnight, the work would be approved. Magda would leave with Marra. Ives would leave, invariabley declining company. Sandra would be alone with Burns until Burns called Vivian Stuart, who had taken an apartment for herself in the same building and on the same floor. Appearing fresh, as though she might have had a nap and a shower, she would be prepared to take notes, from which she would type specifications the next day. It was then that Sandra felt out of place. While she had no designs on Burns, she told herself, picturing Vivian Stuart tucking her boss into bed was not very satisfying. Oh, well, she would console herself on her way home alone in the car. There would be that ten thousand bonus that Burns had promised if the deal went through. When the order was placed, there would be a celebration. There would be no specifications that night.

Spraying deodorant into the black hair in her armpits (Sandra never shaved her body; she had been with a man once who was wildly turned on by the thick growth of hair on parts of her body), she looked at the little clock on the dresser. It was five o'clock. Magda would be meeting little sister Olga at Central Station. What a surprise for her old father on his birthday, when he met his youngest daughter, his favorite, who he had not seen for five years!

Today her father was sixty-five. Sandra had casually men-

tioned that he would like to see is three daughters together. Expressing appreciation for the efforts of Sandra and Magda and understanding her concern for her father, now that she had moved away from him, Burns suggested that Olga attend a birthday dinner for him. He had requested a pass on the government railways and Jules Lamont had supplied it, grumbling that it should be worth a piece of tail, at least.

Sandra phoned *Le bureau de la police* in the small village near Campbellton, New Brunswick. A message was delivered to Olga at the farmhouse. She was delighted at the prospect of getting away from her humdrum existence in the dead of winter. There would be some fun in Montreal. She arranged at once to leave her three small children with her mother-in-law, who still had seven of her own at home.

Sandra allowed herself to fantasize as she touched up her lips and applied perfume before slipping into sheer step-ins and a low cut dress. It was Saturday night. Matt Marra was back at home in Pittsburgh. It was usually the loneliest night of the week for girls like her and Magda. Tonight would be different. Her only guests, in addition to her sisters, would be her father, the Greek Orthodox priest, and Alton Burns. At the end of the evening, there would be no secretary to take dictation. The presents for her father were small compared to that ten thousand dollar bonus . . .

With these thoughts still in her mind, she greeted Burns, first, before embracing her little sister and their father. Pete was bringing in some dilapidated suitcases and parcels. All talked at once. Burns had decided to pick up Sandra's father and to meet the train with him. On the sidewalk outside, they had met the thin, swarthy priest.

The old man was, indeed, a giant, powerfully built through the shoulders. His face was flushed from the beers consumed in the station bar while they waited for the train to arrive. He removed his fur hat. His great domed head was completely bald. His handlebar moustache was white, with two yellow streaks down the middle to his full, red, upper lip. There were creases around his blue eyes, from looking into the glowing furnaces. His voice boomed out when he saw his birthday cake.

"Aha! Aha! My daughter is a good cook, yah!" He gave Sandra a bearhug before she led him to the bedroom with his big, grey coat. She took Burns's coat with her.

Olga was as different from Sandra and Magda as night from day. She was a tiny, fragile creature, weighing no more than a hundred pounds. Her skin was light from her winter confinement. As she took off her French touque and shabby coat, Burns first noticed that her thin, stringy hair was blonde. Her face was small and pinched. She had a tiny nose, but her eyes were very large and light blue like her father's. Out of place on her slight frame was a huge bosom. It was hard to picture her as a farm woman with three children. She looked like an overdeveloped child, herself.

Requiring a great deal of fluid, after a day before the furnaces on the foundry floor, Joe Sandosi liked his beer in a large tankard. Sandra had bought one for him with the word "father" on the side in Roumanian. Burns filled it for him from a large bottle of Molson's. Magda and Olga called back and forth from the bedroom to the bathroom in French, while Sandra talked to her father in Roumanian. The priest sat silent, his black hat on the floor beside him. Sandra poured some Portuguese wine for him. She took his hat and coat. Magda called for two rum and Cokes from the bedroom. Burns poured the drinks and delivered them to her and Olga. Olga had stripped down after her long train ride, but still wore her high leather boots and what appeared to be black leather panties. She turned to accept the drink from Burns without a trace of modesty. Magda giggled at the look on his face. The large protruding, reddish-brown nipples of the round, oversized breasts were surrounded by an aureola fully four inches in diameter. *She must have nursed her children until they demanded steaks*, Burns thought.

Big Joe took a slug of beer from the big tankard, letting fully half of it slide down without a swallow. The Greek priest spoke neither Roumanian or French, but he seemed to understand English, as he nodded and smiled from time to time.

Olga, in a dressing gown, emerged from the bedroom with Magda. She sat on the old man's knee. Seeing the tears in his

eyes, Magda playfully pulled open her sister's robe. "You should see her leather boots and her leather panties, Pappa."

"Get dressed, you," the old man said, pushing her off his knee and turning to Burns seated beside him. "If that one stayed in Montreal, I do not know what would have happened to the Sandosi sisters." There was pride in his voice, with the chastizing tone.

The priest filled his pipe and was puffing contentedly over his fourth glass of wine. They helped themselves to bits of Roumanian sausage. From her kitchen, Sandra monitored the conversation, interpreting in English for Burns' benefit, when it lapsed into Roumanian or French. Big Joe was telling the story of his relationship, years ago, with Sir Giles Humbolt. He repeated the same story that Sandra had told him, how Sir Giles had helped him to get a good job when he and his family were starving in a strange land; how Humbolt had treated his first wife, so beautiful, so clever. He sadly recalled getting the news that Sir Giles had been killed. He told how the Acme business had been taken away then from Standard Steel Foundries. His job had never been the same afterward. They continued to treat him well because he worked hard and knew the foundry business, but it was not the same.

Today, under the rules of the company, he must retire. He would have a pension that would keep him, now that the two girls were working and Olga was married (he frowned at that), but he loved to work. It was his whole life. He was a strong man yet. He did not want to quit and die. He knew everything that there was to know about the foundry. He had taught everyone there.

Burns chose this time to tell the old man of a plan that Sandra was sure would make him happy on his birthday.

"Sandra has suggested that I talk to you tonight, Mr. Sandosi. Acme will be starting on an important large order for castings at Commonwealth Foundries. We can't say much about it yet. We know how capable you are. We will need a chief inspector. When you have the matter of your pension settled with Standard Steel, we will have a job for you at more than you are

getting now. It may go on as long as you feel able to handle it. You will be working for Sir Giles Humbolt's old company again."

The joy in the old man's eyes prompted Burns to walk away to fill his half-empty glass. Sandra sat on the arm of the old man's chair, her arm about his massive shoulders.

"*Mon Dieu!* I am sixty-five and I live again. I wish that I could start with Mr. Burns and Sir Giles's company tomorrow, but only yesterday, I promised the big man at Standard that I would stay on for a few weeks to complete the casting of a very important order for Cleveland Steel. It seems that thousands of new railroad cars are required for a new mine in the north. They are ninety-ton, and we have never made such a size before. We have finished the patterns and molds. Six samples must be poured next week for testing in St. Louis. If they pass the tests, thousands of castings will be needed. They must rely on me to make such important castings, yet they would force me to retire."

Burns froze where he stood in the middle of the room. Sandra understood at once. Her eyes showed it. Cleveland Steel knew. Someone had sold out. Burns' first thoughts were of Jules Lamont. Had one of the moonlighting draughtsmen guessed and leaked information? No. It would take weeks to calculate the capacity from the dimensions of the sections and there were no titles on the drawings. Ives was his man, and he was sure that it could not have been Matt Marra. Now if Cleveland Steel's sample castings passed the tests, and Burns was sure that they would, they could demand the right to quote a price. Certainly, this would force a reduction in Acme's quotation and seriously endanger the selection of all of Acme's specialties, including U.S. Motors' bearings.

The look on Burns' face tore at Sandra's heart. She knew, from the meetings that she had attended, that the big contract was now worth little to him and Acme. The exciting life of the past two months was over. Hope for the bonus that would give her the new start in life was gone forever. Why hadn't her father told her, but then, how was he to know what was most important to her? But, as she looked across the room into Burns's eyes, she felt more for him than for herself. She knew that he had spent his

own money, even gone into debt. He looked tired and haggard as he prepared to leave.

Burns went over to the old man, contented now, after the drinks with his loved ones. He wished Big Joe a happy birthday again, apologizing for having to leave before the dinner. Big Joe assured him that he understood. Burns to him was an important and busy man of a big corporation. In his happiness, he was oblivious to the bombshell that he had dropped in their midst. Silently, Sandra brought Burns' coat and went with him to the door.

"Please go to the Gay Bar on Sherbrooke Street late tomorrow night, Sandra. Check with all of the waitresses and entertainers there. Try to find out who the Cleveland Steel people have entertained. You may have to go gay yourself. If you haven't tried it, don't knock it. It may be more rewarding than trying to sell railway cars." He gave her a wry smile. "I'll start checking with the night people, myself. We will find the son of a bitch that double-crossed us. Not that it will do us much good now." Seeing tears welling up in her eyes, he added, quickly, "It is not your fault, Sandra. You offered everything you had to offer, your sister, your time, and your own body. Right now, though, I just don't know what to do."

With the impulse of the woman that was in her to comfort, she wanted to say, "Stay tonight, please."

While she stood silent, he was gone.

Sandra went quietly to her room to shed her tears alone. She no longer heard the happy chatter between her father and her sisters. Her woman's intuition told her who had done this to Alton Burns and to her. It was she who had failed. She threw herself, face down, on her pillow, marking it with her tears. Gypsie blood throbbed in her brain. She pounded the pillow with her fists. "Kill! Kill! Kill! Kill!"

Chapter 22

The double plate-glass doors of the vice-president and general manager's suite on the executive floor of the Empire Bank opened electronically. Inside, the deep carpet sank under foot. The receptionist, blonde, sleekly coiffured, looked up as he entered.

"Good morning, Mr. Burns. He is expecting you, but he is on long-distance to Ottawa at the moment." She nodded at the red light on a console. "We haven't seen much of you lately."

"Been busy, Joan. How are you making out?"

She raised a manicured hand, tilting it one way and then the other.

"Vivian Stuart had us to her apartment last week when you were out of town. It was nice, as hen parties go. There was myself, the girls from our legal department, and the head teller downstairs, Sara Carstairs. She is quitting, you know. Vivian showed us your apartment, too. Same building, quite handy!" She gave him a suggestive look.

"From a business point of view, of course. Vivian has had her hands full. She has been coming into the office every day and then working on Char Lake specifications at night until after midnight. It's finished now. The specifications, I mean."

"There! He's off the phone, now." The little light had gone off. Picking up a leather folder, she rose to lead him through a mahogany door.

Hector Muir stood to shake hands. Joan placed the folder on the shiny expanse of his desk.

"Hyah, fellah?" He motioned to a conversation corner of the large office, where two sofas faced a coffee table. "Coffee, Joan, I'm thirsty as hell, and I hate to drink alone in the morning."

As Joan left the room, Muir opened the folder and glanced at the single sheet of paper inside. Then he joined Burns at the coffee table.

"A statement of my overdraft, I presume, Hector."

"Yes. But, I'm not worried, fellah."

"That's why I'm here, Hector. I'm worried."

Joan returned with a carafe of coffee, cups and saucers, sugar and cream, on a tray. She placed the tray before them on the table, then quietly unlocked a built-in wall cupboard. She left the door to it closed as she left the room. Muir opened a humidor and each took a cigarette. He went to the wall cupboard and brought out a bottle of Scotch. After filling both cups with steaming black coffee, he topped each off with Scotch.

"Jesus! Hector. It's only 10 AM." Burns glanced at the door.

"Don't worry, fellah. Nobody gets by my Joan when I am having my coffee with a friend. Remember when I had that little heart attack just after my appointment? The doc told me that I had to relax more. He prescribed a couple of drinks before dinner. Remember when a half a martini used to last me all evening? No more of that jazz. I have a few before dinner. I also have a couple before lunch, a couple before I go to bed, and, maybe, a couple in the morning. I never felt better in my life. Remember when I would get all tied up inside? You and I used to have to get away by ourselves to unwind me. No more. I'm relaxed now; but, to change the subject, what's on your mind, fellah? If it's the twenty thousand or so overdraft, I would have called you if I was worried. With that tiger that you have by the balls . . ."

"That's just it, Hector. The balls pulled off that tiger last Saturday night and I'm afraid that we have lost him. I'm afraid that I'm going to have to ask you to wait for about five years of good bonuses to pay off that overdraft."

"What's gone wrong, fellah? Fill me in. I'm sure that we can help. The Empire Bank can swing a big stick and we haven't used it yet, you know."

"I'll bring you completely up to date, Hector, if you have time." Muir nodded and took another sip of Scotch-coffee. "We'll make time, fellah."

"Well, everything was going as planned the last time I reported to you. Sandra was doing a marvelous job. Her sister, Magda had Matt Marra completely under control. He could see no one else but Acme in this deal. Ives was my man. Vivian Stuart finished typing the specifications, all *our* way, ninety-ton, Precision bearings, clasp brakes, top-dump, the works. Only a half dozen people knew what Char Lake would require. We even had an arrangement with Marra, providing no one else had designs ready, to quote one price on our complete package. We would quote direct to Char Lake and they would buy from us directly, and at a confidentail price, cash on the barrelhead.

"Now, we find that Cleveland Steel knew over a month ago that the capacity would be ninety tons. They redesigned accordingly. They have the facilities and the know-how. All that they needed was the time. They got information in time.

"They have completed their redesign and have made patterns already, before the specifications are issued. They are applying for test time on Eagle Steel's test machines. They could be approved in three weeks. They are good foundry people. My guess is that they will be successful. Then, their two directors on the board will insist that they be given a chance to submit a price on a product to specifications, which we wrote so carefully. The prestige involved is so important to both Eagle Steel and Cleveland Steel that either will take all or part of the order, at cost. Acme, as a licensee, could be out in the cold.

"So, Hector, one little leak, possibly unknowingly made, may have wiped out my chance of a lifetime. Now, instead of getting that big bonus, and, possibly control of the company, I'm going to end up twenty-five thousand in debt, and still a small-time railway supply man."

"And who was the God-damn double crosser? Do you know? My guess is Matt Marra. You can't trust any of those Americans with Italian names."

"This time, it did not happen that way, Hector. We canvas-

sed our friends, Sandra and I, at every luncheon club, dinner place, nightclub, and bistro in town. The one who was meeting with a vice-president of Cleveland Steel was my protégé, Hal Ives."

"And he owes so much to you. Why did he give them information?"

"Hector, I thought that I knew Hal Ives. I was so sure. I knew that he was honest and capable. He seemed untouchable. Sandra offered him every kind of attention, women, even herself, to keep him occupied and away from Cleveland Steel. He refused to get involved. Sandra worried. Woman's intuition, perhaps. I was not too concerend. I thought that Hal was my man."

"How in hell did they get to him?"

"Something that I overlooked. We were both farm boys. Hal inherited the family farm outside of Toronto when his father died. He breeds horses there, pacers and trotters. It is his only hobby. A vice-president of Cleveland Steel talked his language. They took him to the horse shows when we thought that he was at Char Lake. They brought him books on the breeding of pacers, Currier and Ives prints, the whole bit. They took him in their plane to the Royal Winter Fair at Toronto. They talked horses and he just talked."

"OK! The worst that can happen has happened. Let's see what we can do now." Muir paused. "U. S. Motors, your friends at Eagle Steel and Seaway Steel, may control only five directors out of seven on the Char Lake board. You may have overlooked a trump card, fellah. Empire Bank is doing some of the financing on this deal. Our wishes will have to be respected."

"Whoa, Hector, you are out on a limb for me already. The Empire Bank can exert pressure, but you must be careful. I can't put you in the posture of shutting out a supplier, if qualified, who could save the company hundreds of thousands. As I see it, there is only one way that the Empire Bank can safely help me now, and this is a very long shot at best.

"Eagle Steel must accept Cleveland's sample castings for test. They must be tested impartially. You must remember that Eagle Steel is already bound under a consent decree in the U.S.

to refrain from restraint of trade in any way. Cleveland Steel have good designers. They will know what they are doing. Nevertheless, there have been instances where a first test of a new design failed because of a small miscalculation. In that case, a second test is usually—almost invariably successful. On the slim chance that their first test should fail, Hector, it would help us if the time limit on the financing is so tightened that there would be no time for a second test in this case. I know that I am clutching at straws, but, as I see it now, it is our only hope."

Hector pensively poured another inch of Scotch into his cold coffee. Burns noted his glance toward the folder on the desk, as Muir spoke. "I know how much you have put out of your own pocket on this deal, Alton. I am not worried about your overdraft, mind you. I know that you will retire it, if it takes ten years. It bothers me that we have so many trump cards that we can't use. I feel for you, fellah, and we will do as you say. By the way where does your president, that old fart, Henry Hopkins fit in?"

"Henry has never taken this deal seriously. He was sure that it would fall through from the start. He will be quite happy with our regular casting tonnage coming in on schedule at our usual profit. He has already rejoiced about some unusual sales this year in water coolers and Precision bearings. These, alone, will give us by far the most profitable year in the history of Acme. He is so complacent that he left last week on a world cruise with his wife. He feels confident that our orders are committed, and our profits for the year are on ice."

Burns sipped his coffee and continued, "This is like locking the door after the horse is stolen, but we are going to make one last try to salvage something. Sandra, in spite of her older sister's success with Marra, feels that she has failed me completely. A woman of her type does not give up easily. She would like one more chance. This will surprise you, Hector. She thinks that she has finally figured out what Hal Ives must have to be controlled. She wants to try out her younger sister, who has just arrived in town from New Brunswick. To you and me, she would be unattractive, a tiny washed-out blonde with big eyes and big tits. She is a farm housewife, more or less happily married to a French-

Canadian farmer. She has three kids by him, presumably. She appears dumb, no conversation of interest, but she loves animals, particularly horses. She wears high leather boots and black leather panties. I have seen them. Stinky, I would think. Sandra thinks that she would appeal to Ives, where the glamour girls have failed.

"Sandra wants to try her out tonight. I am sort of afraid to deny her the chance. She is so frustrated right now, she could commit murder. It is a long shot, too late in my opinion, but it can't do any harm.

"I warned Sandra. 'Your sister is happily married. She has three kids. What if your plan works so good that he wants to go to bed with her?' Sandra says, 'So what? If my sister offers her body without coming, it's just like shaking hands. It is as harmless as a little kiss with his tongue in her mouth.'

"Tonight, we are having another party in the Laurentien Hotel penthouse. Buck is arriving this afternoon to console me. Marra is in town. Ives has agreed to come. We will make no accusations. It would do no good, now. The long chance is that we can salvage something, amicably.

"We will have dinner in the suite. Sandra will have her two sisters, the little one in her leathers. Sandra says that she has a small horsewhip in the bedroom, whatever that means. I would like you to be there, Hector. You will lend a suggestion of Empire Bank power. You can get in a dig about the rigid time limit for financing, no time for a second test if Cleveland Steel fails the first. You can send your chauffeur home. My Murray Hill will be at your service when you have to leave.

"If things work out the way that Sandra predicts, Buck Buckley will have a company plane standing by to take a party to Chester, Pennsylvania, in the morning. Pullman is running a Railroad Association squeeze test on a reserve mining top-dump ore car. It may insure that we salvage an order for the coupling mechanisms for top-dump cars, at least.

"The plane will then go on to a ranch in North Carolina, owned by a vice-president of Eagle Steel, where a pacer will be presented to me for safekeeping at Hal Ives' farm. Sandra's sister will go along, leather boots, leather pants, and all."

"You'll make it, fellah." Muir spoke without conviction. "I'll be there."

"Oh, Hector, one more thing. You know that Tom Cable of River Rouge Steel has tried to be helpful on this deal with nothing to gain for himself or his division. There will be two weeks of waiting while Cleveland Steel submits to tests. There is nothing that we can do in the interim.

"Tom Cable has asked me to help him out with a project to rehabilitate Argentine railroad equipment. It is to be financed by the Canadian government in a foreign-aid plan. Cable's product is excellently suited to applications there where hardwood is scarce and termites are a problem. It could develop into a very profitable contract for Cable's division. There would be a profit in it for Acme, too, as manufacturing must be done in Canada to justify Canadian Government financing. I plan to go to Argentina. I shall be gone two weeks, unless I hear that Cleveland Steel has passed the tests. In that case, I may never come back. I'm kidding, of course, Hector."

"If y'gotta go, y'gotta go, fellah. There will be a few people like me watching the fort here. Incidentally, that guy Ives sounds like a necrophile. Isn't that some kink who would screw the dead?"

Chapter 23

The Pinewell private airport was deserted, quiet. The short, swarthy man bounced out of the ranch wagon. A taller man, in jeans, slid out of the driver's seat and leaned against the top of the car. The short one walked a few steps and squinted impatiently at the sky to the north. There was not a speck in the azure blue.

"Whasamatta wit d'God-damn plane? Shoulda be here by now."

"Yeah."

Herb Capozzi took two large Cuban cigars from inside his windbreaker and held one out to his boss. Mike Lardo walked back and took it. He bit off the end, spit, and crammed it into his mouth. Without lighting it, he began chewing it at once.

Lardo was impatient. He was always impatient. Beads of sweat ran down his wide, dark forehead. His small dark eyes glinted from behind his horn-rimmed glasses. He fished inside of his shiny, silk suit jacket for some notes.

"Shoulda be tree besida da pilot an' a nigger navigator. I'll look after d'tall guy. He's Alton Burns, Eagle's rep in Canada, workin' on dis big deal. I'm supposa be buddy-buddy wit' 'im. Only met 'im wonce at a sales meetin' in Hammond. Other guy'll be medium height in a cheap grey suit an' fedora. Says here, don't talk much, likes nags. Says here, dis's important; he's supposed to be bringin' a horsie little broad wit' 'im. You look after dis Ives and 'is broad but keep near enough t'hear all I wancha t'hear when I'm talkin' to dis guy Burns. If dey wanna get away togedder, we check, see? Says here, he scares easy, mayn't a

been in da sheets wit' dis broad yet. We gotta play it cool and nieve. Says here, if 'ey wanna stay all night, OK; then we got a big deal made.

"This guy Burns. He's supposa be like my blood brudder, so I give 'im Togo, dat pacer outa Suzie Q. If dis does da trick, dey might wanna leave right after some drinks. If Burns says, yes, let'm go. It's some crazy God-damn business, but it's business. Where d'hell are dey?"

Lardo had the title of vice-president of labor relations with Eagle Steel Foundries. He had started out as a shop steward of the Steel Worker's Union at Gary plant. Becoming president of the local, his influence spread to locals in Hammond and East Chicago. Soon, East St. Louis and Newark plants fell into line. If Mike raised a hand, the foundries could be closed down by a wildcat. When he raised the other hand, the workers went back to work. Mike had contacts with the syndicate in the Loop, to make sure that such things happened.

They made him a vice-president of labor relations. It was his principal function to keep labor at the plants under control. Having associated with people who liked horses and gambling, it was natural that he should have a ranch in North Carolina, where he could entertain labor leaders. He was often given special assignments, such as this. The ranch was an ideal, out-of-the-way place to amuse sporting-minded men, important in some way or another to Eagle Steel. Congressmen, senators, and local politicians in cities where their plants were located, could be very helpful. At sixty thousand a year, his unlimited expense account and his race horses, it was not a bad life for an Italian-immigrant laborer. He was worth it to Eagle Steel. When there was a problem, Mike could be depended upon. He could act benevolently or otherwise.

The Lear Jet pulled up to the edge of the old air corps training strip near the deserted control tower. Mike rushed up to it as soon as the engines were turned off. When Burns appeared at the top of the hydraulic steps, he hesitated a moment, mentally consulting his notes.

Mike rushed to the ramp to grab Burns' hand.

"My old friend. You're visiting us at last. A year since you was here when I bought the colt and you named him Togo. You will see him now. He is waiting for you. He cries for you. He is not the same as the others. He turned out to be a pacer. Let's go. I want to show you."

When he spoke quickly, it was hard for him to keep the Italian from coming through.

"An' who is dis beautiful lil' gal. She's dressed for the ranch already. Yer all gonna stay a week. An' who's dis gentleman?"

"This is Hal Ives, the general manager of the newest railway in Canada, the Char Lake Railroad. Olga is with him for today, just to see your ranch, Mike."

Mike gave him another embrace.

"I doan believe it. I taut' you allus have d'beautiful women. Yuh can't win 'em all, huh, ol buddy."

Mike held the girl by the arms and looked at her thin, blonde hair, adoringly.

"Beautiful! Beautiful! Well, les' go. D'wagon's waitin'. Bring d'pilots. Bring ever'body. I wanna show y'all some nag, 'is name's Togo."

On the way to the ranch, along the picturesque county road, Lardo kept up a running commentary about each estate that they passed. While most of the houses were hidden from view, the rolling meadows could be seen bordered and dotted with tall pine trees. Along the road there were neat cedar or stone fences. The gates bore such names as "Sunnymeadows" and "Dappled Hills." Mike rolled off the names of the gentlemen farmers who lived there for a part of the year. Most represented well-known families from New York, Boston, Chicago, Baltimore, or Washington politics. When horses grazed near the road, Mike could identify them by name and owner. Often he could recite their racing records. Burns watched Hal Ives, who was leaning forward in the rear seat to catch every word, Olga's hand in his, sharing their common interest in horses.

Burns could not help but resent Hal Ives for the first time in their long association. He tried to put it out of his mind. He had decided to make the best of this day, anyway.

The winding drive behind huge stone gate posts and a high wrought-iron gate was lined with magnolia trees in early bloom. The pastures on either side were like wide, green, golf-club fairways. Clumps of pine forest stood quiet in the afternoon sunlight. Mike waived the driver on past the portico of the large house, its three wings spreading out like a one-sided star. They passed a neat stable and pulled up to the low cedar fence of a paddock. Mike was talking to Ives, leaning over the front seat back, waving the still unlit but well-chewed cigar.

"Y'know, Mr. Ives, when he was a colt, I was buyin' some horses at a auction. Alton likes this one, see. He was with me see." He continued the lie. "He looked like a winner paw'n d'ground t'get bought. I taut he was a runner an' he turns out a pacer. Shows yuh what I know when y'get me away from d'paramutuels." Lardo paused to point with his cigar. "We'll go up to d'house where d'lil' lady can fresh up soon's we stop for a minute. I wanna show Alton dis mother before he starts sayin' he's gotta go back to d'plane or sompin'. I know him, allus on d'tear. I wanna do somepin' for 'im dis trip."

When they stepped out of the station wagon, Mike moved to take Ives' arm. He guided Ives away from the rest. Olga was dragged along, her hand still in Hal's. Mike was speaking confidentially now.

"Y'see, Chicago tells me Burns has one big deal cookin' wit dis new railroad in in Canada. Coudda mean a multimillion buck order for Eagle Steel. I'm a director of Eagle Steel. Got a few bucks in it, y'unnerstan'. Now dis horse, see, Burns picked him out when he was jus' a young colt. He's a beauty, but dis farm a mine, it's a runnin' horse operation and dis is runnin, horse country. Dis here's a pacer. I unnerstan' dey go for pacers up in Canada, so I'm givin' Togo to Burns. I'm shippin' him up to Canada, for 'im, if he will take 'im. It's nuttin' but right, y'unnerstan? He gets us a big deal, we got suthin' he can use up 'air. Mebbee make hisself a bundle on dos dirt tracks. Watch 'is face when he sees Togo now."

Ives was nodding his head. He looked a little embarrassed, but said nothing, as Mike led the way to the paddock fence. The

big sorrel was a handsome horse, neck arched, taking some sugar cubes from a groom's hand. Olga took some sugar that the groom offered her. Togo moved up to her without a trace of fear and took the sugar from her palm. The powerful muscles in his wide chest rippled under the sheen of his coat when he moved. Ives inspected the stallion almost reverentially.

He could hear Mike talking loudly to Burns.

"What you tink of 'im now, Alton. Ain' he a beauty—and d'mudder knows it. I put 'im out wit' a sulky-track trainer for a mont! Won ever' race he entered. Clocked two-ten on 'is firs' heat. Tink wat he cud do at dos fall fairs in Canada, wit' a little trainin' dis summer. Might make yuh fifty gees in one season, an' you'd have d'mos valuable mudderfuckin' breeder in d'country. Waddya tink? He's yours, Alton. You deserve him as a bonus fer gettin' 'at big order for us up in Canada." Mike spoke the last sentence loud and clear.

"But we don't have that order yet, Mike. Cleveland Steel is preparing to quote against us. We still have hope, though. They have only three weeks to qualify by sending sample castings to St. Louis for tests. If they should fail on the first test, we will have the order."

Ives looked at the ground. He made a circle in the dust with the toe of his shoe.

"Thanks for the thought, Mike. I don't know where I could keep him. I don't own a farm."

Burns looked at Ives. Noting the horrified look on both his face and Olga's, Burns added, "Perhaps you might look after Togo for me, on your farm. I don't know when I would ever be able to use him myself."

Hal Ives' face lit up. Olga squeezed his hand.

"Sure." Ives was enthusiastic. "I can give Mr. Lardo shipping instructions."

Mike Lardo indicated that the matter was settled.

"OK. Let's go get us a drink."

On the patio of the ranch house, a colored waiter served highballs. Olga and Ives lingered at the paddock fence. His arm was arround her. They were in quiet conversation, as they continued to admire Togo's horse charms.

Chapter 24

The phone jangled three times, four times in the sitting room of the suite in the Claridge Hotel. The bedroom was in semi-darkness. The shades were closed. Forms moved in both of the twin beds. The girl rolled out of her bed slowly. As she passed a chair, she grasped a large Europen-style bathtowel. The man in the other bed looked through half-open eyes at the outline of her naked body framed in the doorway against the morning sun streaming in through the wide windows of the sitting room.

Burns lay there, comfortable in the soft warmth, not wanting to lose the feeling of half waking in a dream world. He could hear one side of the phone conversation in the other room. It was in Spanish, a little breathless, high pitched, the way that Spanish women talk when annoyed. The conversation went on. Finally, he heard her cradle the phone and place another call. He did not try to understand what she was saying. It was probably some new crisis at the little bar. It seemed late for that, he thought. From the angle of the sunlight in the other room, he guessed that it must be about seven A.M. The conversation ended in that imperious tone that Spanish women seem to reserve for servants. She entered the bedroom to raise the blinds gently, letting in the sunlight of a fall morning in Buenos Aires.

The white towel was wrapped around her now, tucked under her armpits, and held out from her body by her breasts. The jet black hair was still at its lacquered height of Spanish style. She sat on the edge of the bed and tenderly stroked his cheek to waken him. Her black eyes searched his face. She spoke in English, with

a well-educated Spanish accent. Her voice was that of a little girl now. The imperious, demanding voice was another side of her.

"My darling, there is a radio-telephone call from the United States. Chicago is in the United States, *si*? They say that it is important. You must take it at the Plaza soon, as it is later in Chicago. You must go to the Plaza at once, darling. You are awake? You understand?"

Burns kept his eyes closed as she tenderly stroked his hair back from his forehead. He fumbled around in the towel to caress her body. She raised her arms to let the towel fall free for his convenience.

"But no, no, my darling. There is no time for that now. I am going to make the warm bath. You must put on a towel and take the breakfast that I ordered from Maria. We will have our bath and our coffee. Then you must go to take your call at the Plaza. This must be a busy day for us. We must hurry. Get up, my darling."

"But this is Saturday. No one hurries in Buenos Aires on Saturday. Why do we have to hurry today? I thought that we might go to Mar del Plata and lie on the sand. That call from Chicago I don't need. It can't be anything but bad news. Let us relax and enjoy ourselves today. It may be our last day together. I must leave for Canada. I am not accomplishing anything here. Teevee can run the Playboy alone for one night, even if he steals all the money and serves his own Scotch to the *gringo turistas*."

"No, no, my darling. You do not know Argentina, yet [She pronounced it Arkentina]." There is to be a revolution at noon today. Did you not see the soldiers around the Casa Rosada yesterday and the paint signs on the walls at the American embassy and at the Royal Canadian Bank, where the Canadian embassy is? Could you not read them?"

"I talked to Mr. Rousseau at the Canadian embassy yesterday. He didn't say anything about it. He is leaving this morning for a vacation with his wife. She is meeting him at the Roney Plaza Hotel in Miami. I assume that he is coming back in a couple of weeks." Now that he thought of it, had the Canadian trade attaché been a little vague? He was the only one at the

Canadian embassy who had tried to be helpful to Burns in trying to obtain this order. Yesterday he had not seemed so interested. Burns assumed that it was only because his mind was on his vacation with his wife.

He had touched a raw nerve with Gladys.

"They don't know anything. The American and Canadian embassy people never know anything. They see only a few people who tell them only what they want to hear, the same people at every party. They do not know Argentines. They are stupid people on a holiday. I know. I was married to an ambassador. They spend every night getting drunk [she pronounced it *thrunk*] at embassy parties on Scotch that they get free from Canada. They're so stupid. We do not need them. Now I go to make the bath. You take the coffee from Maria. As soon as we finish, you go to the Plaza. You must walk. My chauffeur is busy with other things today. He is Italian. He must not know too much.

"You walk to the Plaza. You receive your radio-telephone call. You shave [she patted his cheek]. You pack a case. You meet José Miranda and Gussie, the Uruguayan girl at the concierge's desk in the Plaza at ten o'clock. You take a taxi, but not at the Plaza, two blocks along Sante Fe Street. You go to the *aeroporta*. I will have tickets and papers for all of us. We leave on Varig at eleven-thirty for Montevideo. From there, we go to Punta del Este where we stay at my house. Jose wants to talk to you about going to Canada."

"Yes, but José is the son of the Minister of Railways. If there is a revolution, his father will be out. There will be a new minister. My friend in Canada agreed to take José as a trainee only because his father intended to make him manager of the Argentine Railways when he returns. Mr. Rousseau helped with this understanding, too. If his father has to resign . . . "

"No problem. His father was a general before. He was in the government before this one. When it is over, he will be minister again. You do not understand Argentine politics. There is the bell. Take the coffee, *por favor*."

Answering the door was unecessary. Maria, a rather severe looking woman, slightly stooped, had already opened the door

with her passkey. She deposited the tray on a small table in the sunlight near the patio door; strong coffee, wide cups, crescent rolls, a jam bowl, and the inevitable Argentine cheeses. The old lady did not speak. She sought out her mistress. In the bathroom, they talked briefly in Spanish, Maria in the whining tone of servant, and Gladys in her most demanding voice.

Waiting for them to settle whatever it was, he turned to the little bar. He poured from a bottle of Grant's into a goblet used in Argentina for highballs. The Scotch poured slowly through the plastic insert in the neck of all bottles of good liquor sold in South America to prevent substitutions of some inferior liquid.

The old lady returned, still silent. She set about moving the breakfast to a wrought-iron table on the small, grassy terrace outside. She had moved the table and two chairs between two large hibiscus bushes, in the full new blooms of morning. Burns leaned against the parapet, sippping his drink and looking at the city nine floors below. He could see the Casa Rosada to the east, with the bright sun above its rose-colored mass. Three silent tanks were angle-parked across the street from the Royal Bank of Canada, and the Canadian embassy, but there was always the odd tank parked on Florida Street. From his vantage point he could not see the Chase Manhattan Bank and the American embassy. A few boyish-looking soldiers stood in doorways twirling their submachine guns by the trigger guards, but there were always some of those.

When he heard Maria close the door, he tossed off the rest of his drink. He crossed to the bathroom, removing the towel from his waist. Gladys was sitting upright in the bubbles, smelling strongly of the pungent Rosario perfume. She was frowning at him from the level of his knees. She moved forward when he stepped into the large tub behind her. She sat motionless and thoughtful. He had learned in a week to respect her moods. The wrong English word at the wrong time, misinterpreted, could lead to a violent outburst. He said nothing as he let himself down into the tepid water. He slid his legs outside of her thighs, her soft but firm hips in his groin. He soaped his hands, rubbed her back and massaged her breasts, gently, from behind. She toyed with the bubbles in the water before her.

Still, in silence, she turned in the large tub. He turned, too, as they reversed positions. She soaped his back and massaged his neck, thoughtfully. She reached behind her, pressing her coarse pubic hair against him when she lifted the drain. They stood and showered together. She stepped out of the emptying tub to reach for her large towel. She handed him a warm one from the steam-heated rack. He waited for her to speak while they dried themselves, looking at each other's bodies.

In the bedroom, she slipped a black mesh brassiere over her head, leaning forward to nest her generous breasts in it. She put on a warm knit dress, while he pulled on his clothes. He followed her out to the little patio overlooking the roof tops and the streets. They sipped the bitter, strong Argentine coffee in the warm sunlight. Below, the streets were still quiet for this time of the morning.

He wanted to ask some more questions. Her large dark eyes were still thoughtful, avoiding his. He looked at the morning sky. It was a clear, azure blue. It formed a picture background for the flaming red and purple colors of the trees in the park on the banks of the river to the north. It was as if the whole of the most beautiful city in the world was quietly and warmly gripped at the apex before a sexual climax. He loved what he had seen of Argentina and its people. If Argentina and the whole world, for that matter, could be freed from power-hungry politicians. . . .

Still silent, she rose and took his hand. Leading him into the suite, she took his billfold from the table. She fingered the bills in it.

"You have no pesos, only American."

From behind a chair, she lifted her alligator purse. She took out two five hundred peso notes. He picked up the bottle of Grant's, but she took it from him and handed him the two notes.

"My darling, this is more important. One is for the concierge downstairs here at the Claridge, when you go out. One is for the concierge, Luz, at the Plaza, when he gives you your passport. Do you understand? These are important people today. They could have asked for your passport last night. You go now. I will see you at the *aeroporta*."

She closed his hand on the notes, tucked his wallet in his

inside jacket pocket, and gently pushed him to the door. She kissed him firmly on the lips with her hands behind his head. "Go!" The door was closed and locked behind him.

Going down in the elevator, he was not overly concerned. In the past week he had seen so many little crises in the company of Argentine women, when the coffee pot boiled over, when a piece of beef fell into the bar-b-que from the spit, when a hostess dropped the little gift that one always brought when invited into a home. Argentina's women made a great deal of nothing. He would have to play along. Perhaps that was what made life in the Argentine appear so interesting. A shot of Scotch in the morning helped.

As he turned the corner into Florida Street, he met a much smaller than usual number of shop girls going to work in the shops of "The Paris of the Americas." As usual, however, they were smiling and chattering happily in Spanish. Argentina girls were always modestly but beautifully dressed on Florida Street, night or day. Their high heels clicked on the mosaic sidewalks, a different design in front of every store. As he approached the Plaza, the flaming colors of the jacaranda trees in the park opposite appeared like a mirage in their final blaze of a waning summer, blues, yellows, and reds everywhere.

The old, garishly painted taxi cabs were jockeying for positions at the entrance as usual. Drivers tooted their feeble horns and wheeled in "U" turns. A half dozen armed soldiers at the curb in the park seemed more intent on a group of girls than on an impending revolution. Perhaps Gladys was taking the whole thing too seriously. For a girl in her late twenties, she could be so tense, so volatile. Her moods were unpredictable. One moment she could be so soft, loving, even childlike. The next instant she could be a *tigra*, as the Argentines called their cougars, ready to kill.

Before crossing the intersection at the Plaza, Burns looked down the side street toward the river. Outside the little bar behind the hotel, the light on the Playboy sign was still burning. Teevee must have forgotten to shut it off when he closed the bar at five. Perhaps the bar was not closed. He decided to check.

The street door was locked, but he could hear voices and

laughing inside. He went through a narrow alley to the rear door. Unlocking it quietly with his key, he walked through the unused kitchen. He could see the rear of the bar. Teevee was on duty, but he could not see the patrons beyond the bar. Hearing Burns enter, Teevee motioned him back into the kitchen and joined him there.

"Army officers," he whispered. "They want more drinks and I have no Scotch, except what I make with alcohol and flavors." He pointed to some cans, glass jars and a couple of bottles of Grant's with the plastic inserts pried out and laying on the table.

"Is the revolution going to be serious, Teevee?"

"All of our revolutions are serious. But I don't think that anyone will be killed." Teevee spoke perfect English. He was born in Miami, of Cuban parents. "I know that we must have some good whiskey to keep them happy." He nodded toward the bar.

"I'm going to my room in the Plaza now. I have a couple of bottles there. It will keep you going until the liquor store down the street opens. Come and get them when you can leave."

Teevee looked relieved. He asked Burns to wait. He went back into the club and asked his patrons to be patient while he went to the bathroom. There was some laughter at suggestions about what he should or should not do in the toilet. When he returned to the kitchen, they quietly let themselves out through the back door.

The concierge at the Plaza looked a little surprised at their entrance through the alley door so early in the morning. A smile appeared when Burns palmed the five hundred peso note to him. He knew the denomination from the feel of it.

"Senor Burns requires his passport, Luz," Teevee explained. "He must present it at the Canadian embassy today; some regulations that the Canadians have when there is a little disturbance, you understand."

Luz went to the drawer of his desk. He selected Burns' passport from several others and handed it to him, with a bow in deference to the five hundred pesos. He had a little less deferential bow for Teevee.

In the suite upstairs, they wrapped the two bottles of Grant's

in pages of the *Buenos Aires American News*. Burns noticed Teevee, looking tired after working all night, was eyeing some of the sirloin tips and cheeses left from the night before.

"Help yourself, Teevee. You've had a long night. The Playboy sign has worked, Teevee. More tourists come in, now?"

Teevee nodded, his mouth too full for him to speak. As he ate all that was left of the food, Burns recalled how it had all happened during his ten days in Argentina.

A first arrival at Buenos Aires airport at midnight can be an unforgettable experience. A driver who spoke some English offered the services of his 1933-vintage Chevrolet taxi. It had a Ford radiator. Scrolls covering its sides were painted in yellow, red, and purple. Weird designs were painted on the hood. Without lights, and with every revolution that the ancient engine could develop, it careened along the blossom-lined boulevard toward the lights of the city. Headlights were flicked on only at an intersection, when a collision with another car seemed inevitable. The driver explained that the first to flick on his lights had the right of way.

The stern-looking concierge at the Plaza Hotel acknowledged his reservation. He requested Burns' passport, examined it, and put it away in a drawer of his desk. The floor maid was on hand to receive him in his suite. She was very pleasant. She offered, in sign language, to unpack his bag. She took away all of the clothes that required pressing. She had decorated the suite with hibiscus blooms from the bushes on the patio. There was Scotch and soda, but no ice, goblets, and a tray of Argentine cheeses, laid out on a little table.

He had been told that there would be some other Canadian manufacturers that he knew already there, seeking business from the same Canadian-financed rehabilitation program. He was looking ahead to meeting them. Their experiences would help him to make the right contacts in this strange country. He was depending a great deal on that. He was in for an unpleasant surprise.

In the little coffee shop next morning, he recognized a half dozen faces. They were railway supply men that he had known in Canada for years. They were quietly eating breakfast at the small

tables. Some nodded in recognition, but none welcomed him. It was obvious that they resented his presence. He sat alone. It was plain that it was a different ballgame here. There was none of the camaraderie of the railway supply business in Canada, where a man who sold one product often helped a man who sold another product. Here, there were no patents valid. It was every man for himself. The expense of pursuing a large order ten thousand miles from home was a big gamble. Competition was unwelcome.

Eating his steak and eggs alone, he realized that he did not know where to start. Where he knew every railroad official on Canadian railroads on a first-name basis, and knew his responsibilities and authority, here he knew no one. He knew no one in the government ministry reponsible for the national railroad. He had never met the Canadian ambassador, or the trade attaché at the Canadian embassy. He did not know the bankers here. He did not know anybody, period.

At the Canadian embassy in the Royal Bank Building, he drew his first zero. The ambassador had a golf tournament to attend in Cordoba the next day. He would not return for a week. His three ssistants were occupied with some Canadian members of parliament on a fact-finding mission, with their wives and families. There was no time for industrialists who simply paid their taxes. There were cocktail parties to be arranged, paid for out of Canadian taxes. Two Canadian members of parliament wanted to take their wives and families on a charter cruise up the River de la Plata estuary to the Parana. This took the time of all of the embassy staff for the next few days.

Burns left his card for the manager of the Royal Bank of Canada. He was also involved. He had been told by the head office in Montreal to look after a city politician, a bankrupt lumber merchant from St. Henry, who Burns knew. He wanted to investigate possibilities for the export of beaver pelts to Argentina.

Burns went back to the embassy for directions to the Ministry of Railways. The only employees available in the large embassy offices were two French-Canadian women. They spoke little English; one, none at all. The other told him that the ministry of

Railways was in Ottawa and that it would be better if he found an agent who spoke French if he wanted to do business there. He started to explain that he was interested in the Argentina railways, not the Canadian railways. He gave up and asked for a telephone book.

Some weeks later, back in Canada, he received a questionnaire from the Canadian Minister of Trade and Commerce. It inquired of Canadian manufacturers who had sought trade for Canada in foreign countries details of the valuable services extended to them by the Canadian embassies. Burns replied, "I arranged my own transportation, my own entertainment. I arranged my own cocktail parties, and paid for them myself, with tax-paid dollars. I found Canadian embassy officials so burdened with entertaining Canadian politicians that they had no time for legitimate businessmen." This reply was probably filed in the deputy minister's wastebasket.

At the Argentina Ministry of Railways' offices a receptionist was polite and spoke English. The minister was out until seven P.M. He had many assistants, but they were out, too. Perhaps one would return, but it was unlikely that he could help without the authority of the minister himself. Burns waited in the office all afternoon, until eight o'clock that night. The receptionist tried to be helpful. She finally suggested an introduction by a suitable Argentina agent. She cautioned that the agent selected must be acceptable. There were some who were not. She declined to name them. Burns knew no agents, of course.

Dejectedly, he walked down Nuevo Julio Street all the way to Florida Street. He was still a mile from his hotel, wondering when he could get a flight back to Canada. He would have to admit to his second failure in a week, first Char Lake, and now Argentina.

Unexpectedly, he met a familiar face on the street. Neither of them could believe that it was not a case of mistaken identity. Johnny Barker was head of the export department of Pullman-Standard Car Manufacturing Company. He lived in Chicago. He was an old friend of Tom Cable's from the San Francisco days. He was making his regular tour of South American countries. He

was excluded from the national railway rehabilitation program by the Canadian financing. He was returning to Chicago the following night. He would be glad to take a message to Cable.

In a convenient bar, Burns explained his difficulties. He described the attitude of the other Canadian manufacturers. They had been unwilling to even talk to him. Barker indicated that he was on good terms with them since he was not seeking the same business. He suggested that if they were not seen together, he might be able to get some information as to where the deal stood, who to see, and what agent to select. He promised to go right back to the hotel, get the Canadians together for a nightcap, and find out what he could. He would meet with them again tomorrow morning before he left. Meanwhile, he suggested that Burns get lost and meet him about two in the morning two blocks along Florida from the hotel.

The night crowd thronged Florida Street, closed to vehicular traffic at night in favor of shoppers. A little after two, Johnny Barker appeared. He guided Burns to a little bar behind the Plaza Hotel, one not frequented by foreigners. Barker had been there alone before. He knew his way around. They ordered drinks at a small booth. Barker waved away several "B" girls who asked to join them. One or two of them kept coming back, as Barker told Burns all that he had been able to learn at his impromtu going away party. Burns planned to see him off at the airport next evening. Barker would report then on what more he could learn during the next day.

Barker was anxious to live it up a little on his last night in the city. He finally allowed one of the girls to join him. He ordered her a drink and they began to converse, she in Spanish, he in a form of English with an "O" suffix on each word. She seemed to understand. As they seemed to be enjoying themselves, and not wishing to get involved this night, Burns moved to a seat at the end of the bar. He still felt little hope for success here. He would make a reservation for Canada, perhaps on the same plane that Barker was riding, on the first lap of his return trip to Chicago. He noticed Johnny leave with the girl. He continued to contemplate his failures.

An attractive Argentine girl, in her twenties, entered the bar from the rear, with a small briefcase under her arm. With some terse orders to the bartender, who paid respectful attention, she went directly to the cash register. It was almost in front of where Burns was sitting. The bartender brought her a glass of red wine. She started to work, obviously reconciling bar checks and invoices with the cash register tapes.

"Could you ask your bartender to get me a drink?"

She did not look up, but called to the bartender in perfect English.

"Teevee, serve this man. Be quick. There's money to be made." And to Burns, still not looking up, "You want Scotch, *si*?"

"No. I'll have what you have there. I must be alert tomorrow."

"You are a wise man. It is wine from Rosario."

Teevee brought the wine quickly, spilling a little as he put it down on the bar. Still not looking up, she gave a curt order. "Teevee, you spilled it. Bring another. Be quick." Still looking down at her work, she spoke to Burns again. "Why are you not enjoying yourself with the girls, *señor*?"

"Because my first day in your beautiful Argentina has been a complete failure. I am going back to Canada tomorrow, discouraged in a day."

This was a different approach from the ones that the American tourists used. She looked him over, as she looked up for the first time. He saw that her eyes were jet black. She looked more Italian than Spanish, except for the styling of her jet black hair and the lightness of her skin.

"Yes? We have business problems here. People steal. It is very difficult."

A slight smile revealed white, regular teeth, and sensitive lips, carefully outlined. *She is the girl friend of the owner*, he thought.

"Can I help? I have nothing else to do until my plane leaves tomorrow," Burns said.

She did not object when he walked around the end of the bar.

A half hour later, a chauffeur in a uniform and hat appeared. The girl closed her briefcase on the receipts for the day. She shut the cash register. Teevee looked relieved. Burns and the girl left the club through the back door, as Johnny Barker returned through the front, a surprised look on his face.

Barker left for Chicago, next day. Alton Burns did not leave for Montreal.

In the following days, Burns still made little progress with the officials of the Argentine National Railways. When he failed, Gladys tried her best to make appointments for him, speaking in Spanish. Neither the general manager or any of his assistants would keep an appointment. The story was always the same. Call tomorrow. Junior officials dared not talk. Gladys went with him to the offices of the minister of railways and communication on three different days. The minister was not available, and his assistants failed to keep appointments.

With Gladys's help, he made enough progress in other areas to keep his hopes alive from one day to the next. She assigned her part-time chauffeur, an old employee of her family, to Burns. He canvassed all of his taxi driver friends. A list was compiled of all addresses to which drivers had been instructed to take the Canadians staying at the Plaza Hotel. While some were useless (two were whorehouses), three were multistoried buildings with many offices. The list led Burns to about twenty agents, or lobbyists, working with the minister of railways, or with the National Railways. Most were ten-percenters who claimed firm relationships with government or railway officials. Burns took notes, formed opinions, and left his calling card, with a promise to consider drawing up an agency agreement later. To those who had been promised agency agreements with other Canadians, Burns explained that while the others were interested in complete cars, he was interested only in one component from which an extra-large commission could be derived, with others being none the wiser.

It was soon established that the key man was General Alfredo Miranda, minister of railways and communications. His son was a frequent patron of the little bar behind the Plaza. José

Miranda was twenty-six, a smart, presentable young man. He had just graduated from M.I.T. in the United States. While he now worked in the Ministry of Railways, his position did not involve a great deal of responsibility. His father had plans for him, but right now he was not ready for marriage or great responsibilities. At the little bar, he met Gussie, a chubby little Uruguayan girl. She amused him.

In conversations with Burns in the little bar, José disclosed that his father had plans to make him general manager of the National Railways some day. He had the education, but little experience, which would make it easier for his father to justify his selection. Burns thought that a period of employment as a trainee in the Engineering department of the Canadian Government Railways might be best. The Canadian government sponsored a program of taking trainees from foreign railroads to broaden their experience. José took the matter up with his father. The general agreed.

Burns put in an overseas call to Jules Lamont. With a great deal of difficulty understanding each other over the noisy radio-telephone link-up from Buenos Aires to Montreal, Lamont agreed to provide a place for José in his operating department. Lamont did the usual amount of grumbling, but most of it was lost in the transmission. He undertook to employ the future general manager of the Argentine railways as soon as he could report to him in Montreal.

While José was unable to help in obtaining an interview with his father for Burns, he assured Burns that it was only because of a temporary crisis in the government which made any decisions impossible at this time. He did take all of the particulars on the product, prices, and terms to his father for action when conditions permitted. Engagement of an Argentine agent was still advisable, Burns was told. With José, Burns' list of twenty was narrowed down to three. José took these to his father, who selected one agent that he preferred. Burns drew up and executed an agreement.

Within a few days, it was obvious that Gladys' small bar was not doing well. In spite of the many affluent guests, mostly

Americans, staying at the Plaza Hotel, few found their way into the small bar right behind it. Most of the patrons were army members from the barracks nearby, or small shopkeepers. They came in at the happy hour for a sip of cheap wine and free cheese snacks. Late at night the soldiers got drunk on Argentine beer. More profitable sales of imported whiskey and gin were rare.

One night, at her suite in the Claridge, Gladys mentioned that as a seventeen-year-old girl from Rosario, she had danced in the old National Opera House. As the lush days of dictator Peron passed into memories, the opera house was closed. Gladys wanted to show it to him and see it again herself. They visited it the next day. Bribing their way past an obliging, old watchman with the memories of his own, they walked around the vacant theater. Gladys described what it was like over ten years before, filled every night in the season. Its original splendor was evident, but the velvet seats and the heavy curtains were rotting now, and the gold leaf was chipping from the lofty ceilings. On their way out, Burns stopped at the street to look at the tattered marquee. There were just enough letters left to spell out the word "Playboy."

The next morning, while Gladys was asleep, Burns found the old watchman. Not only willing, but quite ingenious, he took down the old letters and part of the frame. In a couple of hours, he erected them over the door of the little bar behind the Plaza Hotel. He rigged lights to illuminate the sign at night.

"Playboy! What is that? Playboy?" she said when she went in to collect the receipts. However, when she totalled the take for the night and found about five times the usual receipts, she was convinced. Whatever it was, it was good for business. Americans from the hotel flocked in at the familiar name. Gladys' "B" girls could be as entertaining as bunnies.

"How much did it cost?"

"About five thousand pesos. They had no use for it at the opera."

"I must pay you five thousand pesos!" She clutched her little bag of receipts for the day. "Tomorrow."

Chapter 25

He looked at his watch. It would be almost noon in Montreal. It would be about eleven in Chicago. He was not sure. It didn't matter. It was earlier in Chicago. He was concerned about the departure of the Canadian trade attaché, with this talk of a revolution. Could it be that the Canadian government was withdrawing its trade attaché and the financing? If that was possible, every day here was wasted.

On the other hand, he was sure that Buckley's call was simply to confirm that Cleveland Steel had met the test requirements. They would be asked to quote prices. It would be a week before he could expect to get an indication of them from Ives or Marra, so that Acme could quote competitively or lower. If he was not in the country, he could not be expected to quote first.

If the threat of revolution blew over, the air might be cleared. He might be able to consolidate the gains that he was led to believe had been made with Miranda. It might be possible to obtain a commitment in another week.

Rousseau had tried to be helpful in the last few days before suddenly deciding to leave. It was possible that he had been instructed to avoid revealing the attitude of the Canadian government. Burns thought over his last conversation with the attaché. Was there a hint that he had missed. He was not sure.

He decided to call Montreal before taking Buckley's call.

"Montreal, Montreal, Buenos Aires calling Montreal, person-to-person for Vivian Stuart——your party is ready, señor."

"Mr. Burns . . . "

"Miss S., I can't hear you well. I will speak slowly. You do not speak until I say 'over.' Our connection is by radio to New York. This is important. I leave for Uruguay in an hour. Things do not look good here. Do you read me, over."

"Yes, I read—Uruguay—not good . . . "

The transmission seemed to be spotty from New York, but OK from B.A.

"Please get money from Richard Jones. Take a first-class flight to Miami today. Phone the Roney Plaza Hotel, on Collins Avenue, for a reservation, and stay until you hear from me. A French-Canadian named Rousseau will be staying there with his wife, who is also French-Canadian. He is about thirty-five, dark, five foot eight. He is with the Canadian government as trade attaché in Buenos Aires. He is meeting his wife at the Roney Plaza for a holiday. Find him, but do not introduce yourself. Do not speak to him. They will speak French. Sit near them around the pool, or at the bar, or in the dining room. Take notes of every French word you hear at Roney Plaza. Do you still read me? Do you understand? over."

"Yes. I read——understand——notes——French——pool ——When——hear from. . . ."

"I will phone you at the Roney Plaza tomorrow from Montevideo. If you find out what I think you will, I will join you at the Roney Plaza as soon as I can get a flight. If Rousseau is not going back to Argentina, I will join you at the Roney Plaza by Tuesday. Did you get that? Over."

"Yes—understand—If   French—not—back—join   me— Tuesday—double bed."

"I could not hear you well, but if you think that I will need a double bed, please reserve one. over."

". . . at Roney . . . "

When Burns hung up, for a second, to signal that his call was finished, that same operator began working on the Chicago call.

"Chicago. My party is on the line, Chicago."

Burns could hear Buckley better than Vivian Stuart, but the transmission through New York was still garbled.

"—Alton—news, good news. Cleveland—failed—tension member."

"I don't understand, Buck. Do you hear me? Over."

"—Steel failed—tension member at—column guide,—strange—cracks at column guide—investigating.—need second dynamic—new samples. Ives—very tough—Horse—changed—tough on them."

"Good news, Buck. What happens now?"

"Ives—tough—no alternative—seven days—retest—six new castings—must fly— St Louis—charter transport—cost fortune—impossible—seven days—order ours."

"Cleveland Steel are smart foundry people, Buck. Over."

"Only seven days—new tests—tough deadline—Ives."

"Things are not too promising here, Buck. Revolution expected, Canadian trade attaché has gone. I expect to be back in Canada in a few days."

"Suggest—back—Canada—next week—move fast."

"Thanks, Buck. I'll call you Tuesday."

"Are you finish, Señor Burns?"

Burns' thoughts were racing as he shaved and packed. How could Cleveland Steel's castings have failed? Could it be another failure such as Abe Sinski had described that night in Chicago? Cleveland's vast experience would tell them that where a thin section joined a thicker section chiller nails must be placed in the mould. The thinner section cools faster than the thicker section. If the rate of cooling and shrinkage is not controlled by the use of a few chiller nails, hairline cracks are formed. Any good foundry engineer would know that. Nevertheless, the news was comforting. Acme's chances of getting the order without devastating competition and marginal, if any profit, looked infinitely better.

Having faced utter hopelessness since it was learned that Cleveland Steel was in a position to challenge, he comtemplated the worst that could happen now. From what could be understood of Buckley's conversation, Ives had allowed Cleveland only seven days to produce satisfactory results from a second test. He calculated twenty-four hours at least, to modify the patterns. It would take another full day or more to carefully cast new specimens. Allowing a full day around the clock to cool and clean, it would take another day to deliver six heavy castings fifteen

hundred miles to Eagle Steel's test laboratory. That left less than three days to rush through a full cycle of static and dynamic tests, setting the same specimens up with cranes on two machines. It seemed impossible.

If time permitted, he had no doubt but that Cleveland Steel would isolate and correct the cause of failure on the first test. With the time allowed, however, any small delay could cause default. There could be short power failure which could shut down the furnaces for a few hours. The charter plane could be delayed by weather this time of year. A compressor failure could delay the cleaning a few hours. There were so many little things that could cause default if Ives held firm. For the first time in three weeks, Burns felt his confidence returning. The sun was shining and there was not a cloud in the sky as he checked out of the Plaza Hotel. He had to steady himself. Cleveland Steel could still do it. They were competent and ingenious.

At the airport, the three of them waited for Gladys. Young soldiers milled about inside and outside of the terminal, machine guns dangling carelessly. Gladys entered from the parking area, closely followed by two soldiers. She walked erect, heels tapping on the terrazzo floor. She looked annoyed but haughty as ever in the presence of inferiors. José disappeared. While Burns stood, not knowing what to say, Gussie smiled and gushed over one of the soldiers in Spanish. She, evidently, knew him. Gladys disdainfully ignored the soldiers and Gussie to speak to Burns.

"Señor Ingeniero Burns, I hope that you have a nice trip to your home in Canada. I will see you soon."

She took his hand and squeezed it, while the soldier, who was not joking with Gussie, watched. "You go now. Do not wait for me. I will see you very soon. Go." She walked with him to the departure gate for the flight to Montevideo, passing him an envelope while their backs were turned to the soldiers.

Aboard the old DC3, José had chosen a double bulkhead seat for the three of them. He was comfortably seated at the window, a drink in his hand already. The attractive Portuguese stewardess had a drink for them in each hand, wrapped in a napkin. Burns gave her the tickets from the envelope that Gladys had given

him. Gussie sat by the window opposite José. The latter began talking to Burns, next to him, as soon as the hostess left.

"Don't worry, Mr. Burns. We Argentines are used to these things. Gladys knows important people. She will have things fixed and join us in a few hours. Of that, I am sure."

On the short trip across the wide mouth of the De La Plata to Montevideo, Gussie remained silent. She understood little English. Burns had questions to ask about Gladys and her background. At times, when they were alone, he had tried to question her. She had always answered very briefly, never offering any more than he asked, often remaining silent, merely nodding or shrugging her shoulders. He had found that pursuing questions with her was useless, if not dangerous. José had some information, although much of it was vague.

Gladys Gomez Aguillio came from the city of Rosario, or near it. Her grandfather and her father had been prosperous farm machinery dealers. They operated large farms and vineyards, themselves, in this fertile area on the Parana River, northwest of Buenos Aires. When Gladys was very young, both her father and her mother were killed in an accident. It could have been a traffic mishap or a drowning in a boat on the river. José had heard both stories. At any rate, Gladys had been sent to live with her maternal grandmother in Buenos Aries. She was sent to a convent until she was sixteen. She resented her strict, religious grandmother, and rebelled at the discipline of the nuns.

At the convent, she studied ballet. Her looks, her figure, and her talent made her a popular amateur performer. She often danced as a juvenile at the old National Opera House.

Her grandmother was well connected in Buenos Aires. She was on social terms with the president and his first wife. At a reception at the Casa Rosada, Gladys met a young army officer from the Dominican Republic. He was serving as ambassador to Argentina. After less than a month of chaperoned meetings, he asked her to marry him. Anxious to get away from the domination of her grandmother and the nuns, she accepted. It was a big wedding at the big cathedral across from the Plaza.

Her husband enjoyed the variety that surrounded the diplo-

matic corps. As a very young Argentine matron, she was expected to remain at home, attending only the formal affairs with her husband. She was expected to bear children, look after the house, but she was not expected to question men's affairs. Thers were no children and when her husband was ordered home upon a change in governments, she refused to leave Argentina. She was never divorced, to José's knowledge, and she did not reveal her present feelings toward her marriage. Nevertheless, a separated woman, by custom in devoutly Catholic Argentina, was considered something less then respectable.

Her grandmother disowned her, more or less, and she disowned her grandmother. She had some money from her parent's estate. Her husband, perhaps because he expected to return to her some day, deeded the beach house in Urugary to her.

She had no training of value. For Gladys, there were few alternatives. She could be the mistress of a general or a politician, she could become a prostitute, or she could operate a small business. She, obviously, although José was not sure, chose the latter. At any rate, by buying and operating the small bar, as much as she detested it, she kept all three options open. She appeared to remain aloof from most men, but if it was because she expected her husband to return, she gave no indication of it.

Some politicians and soldiers that she had known in her married days patronized the little bar, but times were bad. Sometimes the government could not pay the soldiers. They bought cheap wine, and the earnings from the bar were small. However, it seemed to be enough to enable her to retain the small suite in the Claridge, one her father had once occupied on his business trips to Buenos Aires. A part-time maid and a part-time chauffeur, both devoted to her or to the Gomez family, remained with her, at small salaries. While she answered to no one, she remained quite devout. She attended church two mornings each week and went to confession every Sunday.

They cleared Uruguayan customs and immigration quickly. Both Burns and Miranda were classed "in transito" to Canada, and Gussie was a Uruguayan national. A little Beechcraft took them to the dusty Punta del Este airstrip in a few minutes. A

wizened little man in a uniform cap met them in an old Mercedes, very shabby and very noisy. He spoke no English, but carried on a lively conversation with Gussie and José, as they rode the short distance to the house.

It was a large, square, pink, peeling structure, weathered by the ocean winds. The rooms downstairs were large. The furniture was sparse, stiff, and worn. The floors were clean, but of dull yellow terracotta, bare of rugs or carpets. Burns was shown to a bedroom on the second floor. It contained a stiff chair, a writing table, and a bed. There was an adjoining bathroom with ancient ornate fittings, no shower. There were no towels, washcloths or soap. He recalled that Gladys was always buying aromatic cakes of soap. You were expected to bring your own in South America. The bathroom also served an adjoining bedroom, furnished the same, except that it had a dressing room attached. In it was an old-fashioned boudoir, dressing table, a bench, and a mirror surrounded by six seven-watt bulbs. He switched them on. The voltage was low. The lights were dim. The vast spaces, the absence of any decorations, and the bare floors, made the rooms appear cold and, somehow, desolate.

After his brief survey of the suite, he moved to the high window. There was no air-conditioning. The window was half open. Air-conditioning was not needed as the sun was obscured by clouds and the breeze from the ocean was damp and chilly. About one hundred yards to the southeast there were high sand dunes blocking a view of the beach. Over the top of them, he could see the choppy waters of the river mouth. There were no trees or flowers. It was so unlike beautiful Argentina, only a couple of hours away across the wide river.

José arrived from somewhere on the same floor carrying two Scotches in goblets without ice. He explained that the refrigerator was not working. He suggested that Burns bring his drink downstairs. The old man had prepared some lunch, some native wine, the inevitable cheese, some cold beef, and bread. José advised that if Burns went out he should take a jacket. It could get cold, as the fall winds blew in from the ocean to the east. After lunch, José and Gussie went upstairs for a late *siesta*, or an early

mattress game. Burns, at a loss to know what else to do, strolled over the dunes toward the beach. He had a copy of the B. A. American newspaper that he had not read.

Mounting the dunes, he could see nothing for miles except sand and a few deserted beach houses. Summer was over here; it was spring in Canada. Over the dunes, on the wide beach, it could have been the Sahara desert. The wind was chilly. In the lea of a large mound of sand, Burns lay down to read. He drowsed. An hour passed, perhaps two. He was awakened by the sound of a small plane. It circled once, then landed about one quarter mile to the east, where the beach was widest, smooth, and hard. With the propeller still turning, a trim figure stepped out onto the wing and down to the sand. As she hurried away, the plane wheeled, ran down the beach with the wind, turned, and took off into the wind. It quickly disappeared over the river.

Burns stood rubbing sand from his eyes. He recognized Gladys walking toward the house. She had not seen him. A small figure in a uniform cap was struggling over the dunes to meet her, his feet slipping. He took her bag and gestured in Burns's direction.

Gladys removed her shoes and ran to meet him. She was dressed in the same knitted costume that he had seen her put on in the Claridge that morning. It seemed a long time ago. Now, she wore a knitted sweater over it, stretched tightly across her breasts. She carried a similar knitted sweater, of mottled color, on her arm. When they met and kissed, she handed it to him.

"I knitted it for you to take back to Canada, where it will be so cold for you, my darling, but as it is cold here, you need to put it on now."

"Thank you, Gladys. It is nice, so thick. But I do not find it so cold here behind the dunes and out of the wind."

She sat down wearily. He rolled the new sweater. He gently laid her back, with her head on the rolled sweater. He lay beside her, his arm across her breasts.

"Now tell me what happened in B. A."

"It was nothing. Just some problem with my visa."

"But the revolution. Was there fighting?"

"No, of course not. Argentines do not kill each other. Your Canadian embassy may say so, but they are stupid. They know nothing."

"What is happening?"

"The president and his ministers will resign. It is the custom. We will have a new president, perhaps three. Then, most of the ministers and their people will come back. Everything will be as it was before. The old president may be accused of something, but he has already left for Lima, or for Chile."

"What about José's father?"

"He resigned, too, and went to Bahia Blanca. He will be back. He was a general in the army. He knows the big generals well. I saw him. José is going to his training with the railways of Canada and after that he will come back to his position as manager of the National Railways. No problem. It is not like Canada, with your French and your English killing each other, your blacks and your Jews."

He had just read the news of the kidnap and murder of a Canadian cabinet minister by French-Canadian radicals, so there was not much that he could say in defense of his own country.

"But you have different races in Argentina. Your first name is Gladys, obviously English. There must be some English in your family."

"No! Gladys is Argentine."

"Your second name is Gomez. Your mother's people must be Spanish."

"No, Argentine."

"Your last name is Aguillio. That is Italian. There must be Italian blood on your father's side."

"No, Argentine." Her voice disclosed her irritation.

This was the way that all past attempts to penetrate her background or feelings had ended, but he tried once more.

"You have said before, Gladys, that Jews and blacks are not welcome in Argentina. You were married to a Dominican. He must have been black."

"No, not very black." She thought for a few seconds. "But not very white, either."

As they lay silent, with their own thoughts and memories, the sun was setting. In the shadow cast by the dunes, it was cold. He was first to notice it.

"They were planning some dinner at the house when I left. Perhaps we should go there. You look tired."

"What are your plans, my darling?" She had never called him by his first name. When she introduced him, it was Señor Ingeniero Burns. When they were alone, she used some endearing term. It seemed to be a custom with Argentine women, whenever they addressed men with whom they were intimate.

"I must go to the communications office in the morning. I may be needed in Canada. Anyway, it seems that I can't do much in Argentina, until there is a new government. The Canadian trade attaché has left. It may be weeks or months before the National Railways officials are confirmed and are able to proceed with the rehabilitation program. I think that I must take a flight to Miami tomorrow."

"No, no," she cried, plaintively, stamping a barefoot on the sand. "You can stay at the house here and I will come often."

"I am sorry, Gladys, but I think that I must go. I will know definitely tomorrow when I phone. Please let us forget it to-night."

"You will go with José to Montreal?"

"No, I will go to Miami. I have some business there. I will see José in Montreal, after he is settled in his position with Mr. Lamont. I have arranged for one of my staff to meet him and find accommodations for him when he arrives."

"A woman, I suppose."

"Yes a beautiful Roumanian girl. I think José will like her."

"I think yes; and you? Who do you phone tomorrow and who do you you meet in Miami? Is it your secretary. Señorita Stuart, perhaps?"

"She has looked after my business while I have been away."

"Is she pretty?"

"Yes, I think so, but not like you, Gladys."

"I do not like her. I want that you should dismiss her as soon as you see her."

With that settled, she stood up and brushed the sand from her skirt. They walked slowly over the sand dunes. In the dusk, the dimly lit house across the sand looked cold and cheerless.

Chapter 26

An early spring, after the cold and the snows, can make Montreal a very beautiful city, too. The morning sun was warm on the sunny side of Stanley Street as Burns emerged from the LaSalle Hotel. Breakfast with José Miranda had been pleasant. He was happy in his temporary position as an engineering trainee on the Canadian Government Railways.

Leaving Montevideo, he had taken a flight by way of Mexico City to Montreal. Burns had taken an earlier flight to Miami. Immediately on arrival there, Burns had phoned Sandra and asked her to meet José on arrival. She had reserved a room for him at the LaSalle. He had taken a small suite until he could locate permanent quarters. The old hotel more resembled an Argentine hotel than others in Montreal. He felt at home there and stayed on.

Crossing Dominion Square, Burns admired the new green leaves on the soft maples. Their seeds, like large, green, flying insects, fluttered down and covered the walks. Beds of crocus still bloomed, while in other beds tulips were budding out. The grass was blue-green of the first growth. A balmy breeze made a light coat comfortable. Enjoying it all, he walked down Beaver Hall Hill and across Victoria Square.

On the twentieth floor of the Empire Bank, he exchanged cheerful greetings with the receptionist and entered his office marked "Executive Vice-President—Private." He felt good. A couple of days in the Florida sun had given him a good rest. To-

morrow was the deadline for Eagle Steel to complete their tests, but Burns had a strange feeling of anticipation today.

The first thing that he noticed was the new ornament on his desk blotter. It was a little palm tree with two small figures in loin cloths embracing at its base. He was still looking at it when Vivian Stuart entered from her little adjoining office.

"That thing was on my desk when I came in. Somehow or other, someone suspects that we were together somewhere in the South."

"Well, I don't care, if you don't. What's new?"

"Mr. Buckley called about a half hour ago. He was not in his office. He had just returned to Chicago from St. Louis. He has some news for you. He asked if you had talked to Mr. Ives this morning. He does not want to talk to you before you have talked to Mr. Ives."

"Has Ives called?"

"No, he is in Char Lake. It's only seven-thirty there now. I'll put a 'hold' on for his call. I'm leaving your mail."

"I hope that you don't lose your lovely tan, Miss S."

"There have been snide remarks about it. Wait until they see yours."

He had an hour to look over his mail and financial reports before the phone rang.

"Hello Alton, Hal Ives here. I hope that you don't mind the collect call. I am not in my office."

"Glad to hear from you, Hal. How's Togo?"

"Wonderful. We made a half-mile track at the farm and my trainer has been working him out for a month. He can do two-five allright. I've entered him in a dozen or so races for this summer and fall. He'll beat any horse in Ontario. Hope you don't mind?"

"Actually, Hal, I don't have any interest in him myself. I only took him because I did not want to hurt Mike's feelings by refusing. Please do what you like with him. Just consider him your own."

"I'll talk to you about it when I see you, Alton. I had a feeling that you were not too interested in owning a horse, yourself,

even such a beast as Togo. That is not what I called about. Cleveland Steel castings failed on the final test."

"That is hard to believe. Where was the weakness this time?"

"They failed this time at the juncture of the tension member and the journal box pedestal. It was at the change in section again, but at the opposite end of the tension member. There were hairline shrinkage cracks. The thing is that they have had two chances and we can't wait a day longer. You have the order, Alton. I am sending out the letter of intent today. The formal order will be delivered to you in your office Monday morning. Either Matt or myself will bring it in for your acknowledgement, assuring us that you can meet the production schedule."

"We'll produce for you. I can't say that delivering that volume in six months will be easy, but with Cleveland Steel out of the picture, we can use their foundry facilities as well as our own at Commonwealth. We already have one complete set of patterns and one backup set. We will turn over the spare set to Cleveland Steel's licensee, Standard Steel, right away. We'll start today on two new back-up sets, one for each foundry, so that there will be no interruption in production at either foundry."

"You have an order for almost thirty million and that is only the start for this year. Not bad, eh?"

Hal Ives was enjoying his ability to make this announcement to his friend and former boss.

"Thank you for this wonderful news, Hal. I'll start production within an hour. This order will have my personal attention every day until it is completed."

"I'll see you on Monday, Alton."

"Thanks again, Hal."

Burns' hand shook as he put down the phone. He reached for Vivian Stuart's button, but before he could press it, her voice came over the intercom.

"I'm holding Mr. Buckley on the line, Mr. Burns."

He picked up the phone again, his hand still shaking.

"Hello, Buck. We have the order, all of it, thirty million. What happened?'

"Congratulations, old boy. I knew, but I wanted to give Hal Ives the chance to be first to tell you. You owe that horse a kiss in the ass. Ives really went to bat for us this time."

"How could an old reliable engineering firm like Cleveland Steel redesign a product after one failure and have it fail again?"

"They didn't. Our engineers stressed out the design. It is OK. It was OK in the first place, for the first test, too. We think that the faults arose rushing production to meet Ives' deadline."

"But how? Both failures occurred because shrink cracks formed at a change of section, but once in one place, and once in another entirely different location."

"As we see it, both areas required chiller nails in the mold. While they may melt into the molten metal, there is usually some traces left when they are used. We sawed through the sections, after the tests. On the first test there were no traces of them at the location of the failure. On the second test there was definite evidence of their use, and, failure did not occur at that spot. On the second test failure occurred in an entirely different area, where we think that chiller nails should have been used. We could find no evidence that the mold had contained any. It appears that in the rush to produce samples within the time set by Ives, the chiller nails were improperly located, or left out altogether."

"Well, Buck, it is Cleveland's problem. We have a thirty-million-dollar order to fill. I am grateful for your help. Joe and Tom did their parts. Hector Muir helped, too, and, as you say, we owe that horse's ass a kiss for helping to set that time limit."

"Which horse's ass, Togo or Hal Ives? Let's forget that. He came through in the end for you. I'm sending Abe Sinski tomorrow to help you to get into production. Meanwhile, congratulations, again. We'll see you soon. Sandra should be happier."

"She will be in seventh heaven. Thanks again, Buck."

Burns stretched back in his chair. It was still hard to believe. After looking at the ceiling for a full five minutes, he rang for Vivian Stuart.

"Is Mr. Hopkins back yet."

"I think so, but I heard Maggie say that he was not intending

to come into the office for a couple of weeks, now that you are back."

"What are you doing now, Miss S.?"

"I am typing up the notes that I made while I was eavesdropping on Mr. and Mrs. Rousseau around the pool at the Roney Plaza. I am translating them into English."

"That is not important, now, Miss S."

"It was important enough to get you back from Argentina. By the way, congratulations on getting the big order."

He attempted a serious look.

"You are listening in on my phone calls again. Remind me to fire you for that—next week."

"The French have a saying that covers the situation."

"Yes? What is that?"

"It has to do with executive vice-presidents who sleep with their secretaries."

Chapter 27

It had been snowing lightly all night but the snowflakes melted when they fell on the pavement. It had been a warm fall with a long Indian summer. The Montreal winter was now setting in.

Burns left the Cantlie House and walked along Sherbrooke Street. He looked around for a cruising taxi. He continued walking down Peel Street with his thoughts. Where had the spring gone? The hot summer in the foundries had vanished, unoticed. Fall sped by the same way. Time had passed so fast this year. One day he would be in one foundry trying to make patterns last another week. The next day, he would be in another foundry, hundreds of miles away, urging the molders to greater production, a bottle of Scotch at the end of the shift for the team putting out the most. Another day, he would be in the roller bearing plant conferring on work standards with the union stewards. Following up; then he would be in a car building plant, making sure that all of the parts supplied by Acme, from different plants, fit together. Saturdays and Sundays were the same as weekdays.

Today, it was all over for this year. The last shipment was delivered. The last check from Char Lake would be in this afternoon.

Henry Hopkins had been coming into the office less and less frequently, staying only an hour or two. They had not talked about the Char Lake order, although Hopkins was certainly aware of the tremendous volume of business. Burns assumed that attempting to record it in his notebooks was all that Hopkins did when he came in. To Burns, these records were now superfluous.

The chartered accountants were now keeping the accounts, reporting to Burns weekly.

Hector Muir was satisfied. As it had turned out, Matt Marra and Hal Ives authorized cash payments on receipt of shipping documents. Acme had little need for extraordinary financing. Now, Muir was sure of Burns being able to satisfy all of the bank's claims on him, personally. Most important to the banker, he could foresee Acme, under Burns's control, developing into a much larger account.

Burns had asked Hopkin's secretary to arrange a meeting with the old man for three P.M. that day. By that time, Burns expected to have a final check from Char Lake. He would open the meeting by tabling it.

It was getting colder. His leather-soled shoes slipped in the film of slush on Beaver Hall Hill. The snow was accumulating on the frozen grass of Victoria Square. When he reached the twentieth floor in the oak-panelled elevator, he had made up his mind. With the long Canadian winter at hand, he felt tired and the need for a change.

Vivian Stuart had arrived by taxi ahead of him. She was laying out mail on his desk. She greeted him as she always did, as though she had not seen him since the previous afternoon.

"Good morning, Miss S."

"Good morning, Mr. Burns. There is a lot of mail today. There is one letter marked 'very confidential' delivered by hand by Mr. Duggan of Canadian Industrial Corporation."

"You can open it. I know what is in it. It is confirming a conversation that I had with him yesterday. While I am going over the mail, will you please reserve a flight to Buenos Aires for the tenth of this month. You can have the travel agency make a reservation for me on arrival at the Plaza Hotel. Leave the return portion of the airline ticket open and the duration of the reservation at the hotel indefinite."

"Buenos Aires? Why are you going back there? Or should I ask?"

"A couple of good reasons, Miss S., aside from the fact that it is summer there now. José Miranda is leaving this evening to go

home. He has been appointed general manager of the Argentine National Railways. The government seems stable, now. The Canadian government has sent back its trade mission. There may be some big railway contracts given out soon. I want to be in on the ground floor when José assumes his new position. Secondly, I am just too tired to face a long Canadian winter without a break. You should see the trees and flowers that will be in bloom in that beautiful country at this time of year, Miss S."

"I would like to. And that reminds me. Mr. Miranda called. He wants to drop in to say good-bye at noon. He said that it was important that he see you before he leaves."

"OK, Miss S. I'll be here."

Vivian Stuart was out making his reservations when the receptionist announced Mr. Miranda and at the same time handed him the check, received from Char Lake. When she ushered José into the office, he was accompanied by a well-dressed, strikingly beautiful woman. She was dressed in a grey mink coat, with matching turban hat. Her high heels made her an inch taller than José. Her black hair fell to her shoulders. Long black lashes made the large, slanted eyes look even larger—those cat's eyes. Her appearance was as interesting as it had been a year ago on that station platform in the town of Mount Royal.

"Señor Alton, I want for you to meet my wife of one day and one night of delight, Señora Sandra Sandosi Miranda."

Burns did not try to hide his complete surprise. He took José's hand. and shook it warmly.

"José, my sincere congratulations to you both. When I first saw Sandra, over a year ago, I thought that she was the most fascinating woman that I had ever seen. Today, I am sure that she is the most beautiful woman in the Americas, North and South. May I?"

Sandra offered him her lips in a gentle kiss that would have thrilled any man, Burns thought. He took her by the hand and led them to the couches in the corner of the office.

"I suppose that you are leaving for Argentina with José. Montreal will never be the same."

"Yes. My papers are not in order yet, but José will take me

in as a tourist until he arranges things in his own country. We were married in the Orthodox church here yesterday. We will marry again in José's church in Buenos Aires."

"I am sure that both of you will be very happy. You will be proud of her, José, even in B. A., the city of beautiful women. Incidentally, I hope that you will give me a chance to see what kind of hostess she is. I plan to leave here on the tenth for B. A., myself. I thought that we would be a couple of lonely stags, as we were on my last visit, José. It looks as if I will be the only lonely stag now."

"You will always be welcome at our house, Alton. We will be settled by the time you arrive. My father will tell you where we are—I think that it will be the house in Los Olivas. But no, we will meet you at the airport. You might get lost in B. A. *si*? Lost in the Claridge Hotel, perhaps."

José looked at his wife proudly and continued, "We will never be able to repay you for what you have done for us—the experience that you arranged for me on the Canadian Railway enabled my father to appoint me without critics. You arranged for this lovely creature to meet me and make my stay in Montreal so happy."

Sandra took a small parcel from her handbag.

"This is a small gift from my father and me. We hope that you will understand. You have made me happy with my José. My father is happy since June, working as an inspector for Acme. Both of us wanted you to have something."

Burns went behind his desk to unwrap the package, gaily decorated with a red ribbon and bow. Inside there was a small velvet jewel box. Laid out on the satin lining, there were six, shiny, but common-looking nails. Burns took them out one by one and silently placed them in a row on his blotter. He understood now. The chiller nails missing from the Cleveland Steel castings? He would not ask.

José stood to examine the nails closely.

"Why, they are just common wire nails, my dear. What do you expect him to do with them. I thought that it was something valuable. Is it a joke?"

"No, it is no joke, dear José. You would not understand."

José still looked puzzled, as Burns went around the desk to embrace Sandra.

"I understand, Sandra. Please phone your father before you leave. He is in Hamilton today. Tell him that I do understand and that I will never part with his gift."

As they left, José was still puzzled.

"You must explain to me, Sandra, when we are in bed in Argentina. Why are nails so valuable in Canada? Perhaps we can export some from Argentina."

When Burns returned from seeing them to the elevators, Vivian Stuart was tidying up his desk.

"Why were those cheap nails on your clean blotter? I threw them in the wastebasket. Mr. Hopkins came in early. He is waiting for you."

"Miss S., please pick every one of those nails out of the wastebasket and put them back in their box. Each one was worth five million dollars."

"What? I don't understand."

"Don't you remember that some chiller nails were left out of Cleveland Steel castings? They failed under test, and we received the thirty-million order from Char Lake."

"These are the chiller nails that were left out?"

"I really don't know, but they certainly bear a close resemblance." Burns picked up some files that he had ready and departed for Hopkins' office.

In the large, dark office, Henry Hopkins looked up from his notebooks. He had been making some calculations with a short, yellow pencil. Burns noticed how the man had aged; the shock of hair in front of the bald spot was completely white. His spectacles seemed to draw his ruddy face into wrinkles at the brow. In spite of the cruise and his leisure time, he retained no tan from the summer. He looked grey, tired, and confused.

"Sit down, Alton. Y'can't trust these God-damn accountants. Wish we didn't have to have 'em, but with all these new taxes an' government reports, guess we gotta. God-damn government is killin' business. There's new tax laws every three months, it

seems. It's makin' business too complicated for me. Makes me wish we were only doin' a cupla' million a year like we usta."

"Henry, I consider myself an engineer, not an accountant. I have been too busy during the past nine months to study records. I have left the accounting to our accountants. I have been getting from them a weekly report, our bank balance, and a printout on orders delivered. When the big order came in, you were away. I felt that we needed the best of accounting, and I am sure that Byers is providing it. I have taken their figures as being reasonably accurate. Hector Muir, our banker, has been watching carefully."

"Well, Jesus, here's how I git it figgered. We will deliver and get paid for thirty-nine million, six hundred twenty-five thousand, two dollars, and twenty-five cents this year. I can't b'lieve these God-damn figgers, but I can't fault 'em either. Our business was always kinda steady. You could keep track of it." Henry Hopkins shook his head as he examined his little notebooks again, thumbing through three pages at a time. He studied some scraps of paper on his desk, accenting a decimal here and there with his stub of pencil. "Net profit, before taxes, it says here, is one million, nine hundred eight-one thousand, one hundred seventy-five dollars, and eight cents. Is that right?"

"That is what I have on my printout, and I have no reason to doubt it. Our outside auditors have done a prelimary survey and they agree."

"I suppose you want yer bonus, Alton. That was a God-damn good deal that you made with me last year, eh? Did you know about this God-damn Char Lake thing then?"

"No, Henry, honestly, I did not know much about Char Lake then. I was thinking of expanding our business about one hundred thousand a year, here and there, as in the case of the water coolers and the Precision bearings for the A. & P. Railroad. It was with these kinds of increases in mind that I asked that our contract be revised by addendum."

"Got a copy of our contract, right here." Henry Hopkins took a document from the roll-top desk behind him. "You get your basic bonus under the old contract on the first one hundred and

fifty thousand. Right? That's seven thousand, five hundred, right? To tell the God-damn truth, I didn't pay much attention, I didn't think that we would ever make over one hundred and fifty thousand in a year."

Burns had opened a binder on the other side of the desk. He was studying the accounting printout. Hopkins glanced at him and continued, "And you get twenty-five percent on everything over that—twenty-five percent, is that right? Jesus Christ, that is something like four hundred fifty-seven thousand seven hundred ninety-five dollars for a total bundle of four hundred sixty-five thousand two hundred and ninety dollars plus dividends. I didn't get a quarter of that in thirty years, and you have only been with the company for four years. An', on top, you get your salary and your God-damn big expense account, too."

"You can forget the expense account and the salary, Henry. I blew it all and twenty-five thousand more, which I borrowed from the Empire Bank on my own account while you were away on your cruise. I didn't expect to make a half million in one year, but I'll be glad to accept it. I think that I earned it, and I do appreciate the chance that you gave me to earn it."

"Well, I guess that we can afford it the way Char Lake paid up. You gotta check there? The final payment?"

"That's right, Henry. This is the check for the final payment on a hard year of work. With this, both of our accountants and our auditors advise me that you will be able to declare a dividend to yourself and Mrs. Hopkins totalling about seven hundred thousand dollars, after providing for taxes and allowing the same amount of working capital as of the first of the year to remain. I think that this is fair and I will vote my shares accordingly, when we hold our annual general meeting. In addition, of course, you have had your salary, your expense account, and the Cadillac."

"Yeah, but I have been with the company for over thirty years. I never got no bonus of half a million when I worked only four years."

"But, Henry, don't forget that you will be getting another three hundred forty-three thousand or so for your stock in the company. That's about a million in a year. There's not too much wrong with that, Henry."

"My stock? Henry pretended to look surprised. "Oh yeah! That God-damn contract again." Hopkins turned the pages of the contract to one already marked with a piece of scratch paper. Burns could see that the pertinent clause was already underlined in pencil. "Yer gonna take stock as part of yer bonus, eh? That leaves the old man out in the cold. You own the company, right?"

"Henry, I would like you to retain a qualifying share, if you wish to remain a director. We will elect you chairman of the board. You can keep this office and . . . "

Burns allowed his voice to trail off as the old man shook his head. He removed his glasses and rested his forehead in his hand for a few seconds, before replying, "Nope. No way. When I'm out, I'm out. You would be the boss. I would only be a God-damn figgerhead. No way!"

The old man fell silent again. Burns shuffled his papers to avoid looking at him, until he put on his glasses again. Hopkins gathered up his notebooks. He shook his head again and repeated what he had said before, "Nope! Two cooks spoil the broth. I don't wanna be any God-damn chairman of the board, takin' orders. My wife wants to go to Florida for the winter. My son's down there, y'know. Ill come in and clean out my desk next week. Right now, I'm goin' home and break the news. Nope! No God-damn chairman of the board for me.

"Think it over, Henry. Talk it over with Mrs. Hopkins. If you change your mind before Thursday, please phone me."

When he opened his portfolio to pack his black notebooks, he noticed the letter. He held it out to Burns.

"Read that one, Alton. Canadian Industrial Corporation are offering five hundred dollars a share for Acme stock. I suppose that you will sell to them now that you got all the God-damn shares. That'll make you a millionaire in four years, with that God-damn contract . . . "

"Yes, Henry, I knew of the offer. I have been talking to Duggan, and I have a copy of the offer. I've told him that I will meet with them after the first of the year. If we get another order next year from Char Lake, they will have to pay another two hundred a share."

"You bastard, Alton!" Hopkins was smiling now. It was evi-

dent that he had anticipated this situation. He seemed relieved now that it was over. While he had not anticipated giving up his company with pleasure, he had not enjoyed the complexities that growth brought with it. On the other hand, he had seen the company languish. In his heart, he had known that he would have to face the choices of seeing the company die or giving it up. The choice had been made for him. He did not have to change a thing.

"Congratulations, Mr. President, Alton G. Burns." Hopkins held out his hand.

"And a happy Christmas to you and Mrs. Hopkins," Burns said, taking the hand.

As he walked to his own office, Alton Burns looked at his watch. He had not relished the thought of this meeting. He was glad that it was over. It had ended better than he could have hoped. He was sure that the old man would be happier without responsibilities for events that he found it onerous to understand.

He glanced into Vivian Stuart's office as he went by the door. She was not there, but her purse was on the desk. She was waiting inside his office.

"I have your reservations for Argentina."

She was walking toward the door as Burns picked up the envelope.

"Just a moment, Miss S. There are two tickets here. One is in your name."

At the half-open door, she stopped and smiled. "Since there would be little for me to do in the office while you are away, your office manager has granted me leave of absence for as long as you are gone. I've just got to see what is so attractive about the Playboy Club behind the Plaza Hotel in Buenos Aires."